THE HUMAN SIDE
OF INFORMATION PROCESSING

Organized under the auspices of the
Danish IAG – IAG
IFIP Applied Information Processing Group

NORTH-HOLLAND PUBLISHING COMPANY
AMSTERDAM ● NEW YORK ● OXFORD

THE HUMAN SIDE
OF INFORMATION PROCESSING

Proceedings of the Copenhagen Conference on Computer Impact – 78
October 25-27, 1978

edited by

Niels BJØRN-ANDERSEN

Information Systems Research Group
Copenhagen Business School

1980

NORTH-HOLLAND PUBLISHING COMPANY
AMSTERDAM • NEW YORK • OXFORD

ISBN: 0 444 85415 0

Published by:
NORTH-HOLLAND PUBLISHING COMPANY – AMSTERDAM • NEW YORK • OXFORD

Sole distributors for the U.S.A. and Canada:
ELSEVIER NORTH-HOLLAND, INC.
52 VANDERBILT AVENUE
NEW YORK, N.Y. 10017

Library of Congress Cataloging in Publication Data

Copenhagen Conference on Computer Impact--78, 1978.
  The human side of information processing.

  "Organized under the auspices of the Danish IAG -
IAG, IFIP Applied Information Processing Group."
  1. Electronic data processing--Congresses.
2. System design--Congresses. 3. Computers and
civilization--Congresses. I. Bjørn-Andersen, Niels.
II. Title.
QA75.5.C65 1978   658'.05   79-24403
ISBN 0-444-85415-0

PRINTED IN THE NETHERLANDS

FOREWORD

For some time Danish IAG has arranged several international conferences as we find international inspiration and exchange of experience as a prime objective of IAG.

In Scandinavia we have a deep interest in the human side of the changes in our society and because of that we were very glad that professor Niels Bjørn-Andersen accepted to become Chairman of the Programme Committee for the Copenhagen Conference on Computer Impact, as Niels has a good reputation within this field.

The attendance, presentations, and discussions at the conference have proved that we had found an area of interest to many specialists and non-specialists within the computing field.

It is a pleasure for me to see these proceedings and it is my hope that we shall see further positive development over the coming years to make our individual lives better and not worse.

Johs. Frederiksen
Chairman
Danish IAG

PREFACE

This volume is the proceedings of the Copenhagen Conference on Computer Impact 1978.

The conference was arranged by the Danish IAG, the Danish part of IFIP's Applied Group.

The programme committee consisted of

> John Banbury, GB
> Jan Bendix, DK
> Niels Bjørn-Andersen, DK
> Rolf Høyer, N
> Fred Margulies, A
> Anders Petersen, DK
> Edgar H. Sibley, USA
> Tilo Steinbrinck, D
> Richard J. Sullivan, GB
> Norbert Szyperski, D
> Arnoud W. Zijlker, NL

I should like to thank DIAG and especially Th. Herborg Nielsen and Johs. Frederiksen for offering me the challenge of chairing the programme committee and for giving me a completely free hand to decide upon the professional contents of the conference.

Thanks also to all the authors and discussants for their contributions and their readiness to accept the ideosyncracies of the editor in order to provide some overall structure which hopefully will be of value of others than the editor.

Ken Eason was kind enough to offer his assistance with reading all manuscripts and correcting the most obvious violations of the English language, and Ulla Pyndt and Agnete Kitaj carried out the tedious task of typing the manuscripts in camera ready form. I owe them all my most sincere thanks.

> July 1979
> Niels Bjørn-Andersen
> Conference Chairman

CONTENTS

Computers may worry some spectators
When approaching man's role as creators
But I'll have no fear
And will shed not a tear
Unless man starts acting like computers.

INTRODUCTION

Niels Bjørn-Andersen

Information Systems Research Group,
The Copenhagen School of Economics
and Business Administration

The interests and concern expressed today
in relation to computer technology in
many ways are parallel to the anxieties
associated with the introduction and
maturing of other technologies. Therefore
we need a historical perspective in order
to evaluate the impact of computer technology on individuals, organizations and
society.

The Human Side of Information Processing
N. Bjørn-Andersen, editor
© IAG
North-Holland Publishing Company, 1980

Furthermore I think it is correct to say that technological developments have become the most dominant factor in our Western economic, political, and even cultural life. In the history of technical developments one might distinguish between
four types of technologies,

1. Material technologies (from handtools to machines)

2. Energy technologies (from muscle power to nuclear power plants)

3. Communication technologies (from horse riding to flying and
   from pigeons to telecommunication)

4. Cognitive technologies (from abacus to electronic computers)

These technologies are used in a number of areas to extend or to substitute for
human capabilities. The material and energy technologies are used to substitute
or extend the hands of man, for example, to handle larger quantities of material
more accurately. Communication technology is used to extend the capacities of the
legs for faster communication. Finally, computer technology provides us with the
opportunity to extend and perhaps in small areas even substitute for man's intellectual capacity.

Even though we might expect these technologies to develop along different lines,
certain general patterns emerge very frequently when new technologies appear. The
invention is followed by attempts to innovate the technology. The focus is on
making it more reliable.

At this stage nobody worries about the discomfort of the operator, as he is very
often identical with the innovator. Later on the technology is used in the horse-
less carriage fashion where the new technology is employed to perform the same
tasks as previous technologies.

Eventually, the action of the mechanism gets faster or more reliable. The use gets
more widespread and other problems come into focus. These are normally of two
kinds, the operator problems and the societal problems.

The problems of the operator are well illustrated by the introduction of the automobile technology. In the early days, focus was very much on getting reliable
batteries, engines, suspension, etc. It was a struggle to get the hardware working.
The manufacturers who were able to solve these problems gained a competitive advantage. At a certain time the relative benefits of technological advancements in
this area became smaller, and the focus shifted to the ergonomic problems of the
operator. E.g. safety measures, the comfort of the seats, the placing of controls,
etc. This is now where there is scope for improvements over and above the activities of competitors.

The societal problems are illustrated by the introduction of the nuclear technology. Important scientific work was carried out all over the world to understand
and possibly exploit the fusion process in order to achieve badly needed energy.
A lot of pioneering work has been carried out, resulting in many power plants.
Today the basic technological issues have been solved but the questions of pollution from accidents in power plants, the storage of radioactive wastes, fear of
sabotage which might create a need for a higher level of surveillance and police
control, the risk of centralization in society, etc. are still very much unsolved.
The level of consciousness within the population about the potential risks associated with the nuclear technology has been raised to such an extent that the
usage of the technology is threatened as we see it for example in Denmark, Sweden
and the Federal Republic of Germany.

These two examples illustrate how the emphasis in relation to new technologies is shifting from a narrow focus on technical aspects to a much wider perspective where sociological and psychological issues become the most critical ones.

Role of information systems	Poul Hansen: Perspectives in mass-communication and telecommunication. Bo Hedberg: Using computerized information systems to design better organizations and jobs.

	Administrative Systems	Decision Support Systems
Impact of information systems (Descriptive)	Andrew Pettigrew: The politics of organizational change. Ulrich Briefs: The impact of computerization on the working class and the role of trade unions.	Ken Eason: Computer Information Systems and managerial tasks. Robert Tricker: Order or freedom - the ultimate issue in information systems design.
Design of information systems (Normative)	Frank Kolf: Guidelines for the organizational implementation of information systems - concepts and experiences with the PORGI implementation handbook. Enid Mumford: Participative design of clerical information systems. Peter Docherty: User participation in and influence on systems design in Norway and Sweden in the light of union involvement, new legislation and joint agreements.	Anthony Hopwood: Towards designing management accounting systems for the support of the new concepts of enterprise accountability. Ian Mitroff: Towards a logic and methodology for 'real-world' problems.

A look into the future	Per Gröholt: Social development and accountability, professionalism and the future role of systems designers. Russel L. Ackoff: From information to control.

Figure 1. General classification of papers in the book

In order to handle these issues within the computing field, we are faced with the same problems facing all new technological developments; the problems of how to assess the impact of the technology and how to control it. The authors and speakers at the conference have been selected and invited in order to get the best possible coverage of these two main problems.

The book contains all the papers presented at the conference, and in addition two other features of the conference are included. The first is the limerick used in the introduction of each speaker. To some people this may seem to make light of a serious subject. However, it is my firm belief that the impact of technology is too important not to be joked about. That is to say humour provides the opportunity of seeing oneself in a different perspective.

The second feature included in the book is an extract of the discussion that followed each paper. In order to increase the dialectics of the conference, practitioners were asked to prepare additional comments on the paper.

The structure of the book is outlined in figure 1. The papers by Hansen and Hedberg serve the introductory purpose. In the paper by Hansen the nature of the future technologies and especially the telecommunication technologies are described and attention is drawn to the significant role of these developments, the large investments in these technologies, the potential future impact they will have on society, and the astonishing lack of interest on the part of politicians, decision makers, etc.

Hedberg presents a historic perspective on the systems design process. He provides a classification model with four stages or types of systems design strategies indicating substantial changes in the role of the systems designer. These range from the stage where he is almost solely in charge to the stage where he might disappear alltogether as the systems users get more competent and design tools more readily available.

The main contents of the book may be described by using the two by two matrix in figure 1, separating administrative systems from decision support systems and separating the descriptive aspects of how information systems change or are used to change organizations and the role of the individual.

The impact of administrative information systems are dealt with in the papers by Pettigrew and by Briefs. The former takes the view of the political scientist and presents a series of power concepts to be used in an analysis of the impact of information systems on power relations. Briefs takes these arguments further in his Marxist analysis of the impacts of information systems on the working class. He argues especially that information systems cannot be seen in isolation as these are just another tool used by the capitalists in order to increase profits with little concern for quality of working life or for the number of jobs lost.

The normative guidelines for designing information systems taking into account individual, organizational and societal aspects have for quite a while been in heavy demand. Many designers who have realized the importance of 'the human side of information systems' have to some extent been in the dark about how to cope with the 'soft values'. In the papers by Kolf, Mumford and Docherty we are presented with a number of tested and well-documented tools and methods for dealing with these aspects. The PORGI project presented by Kolf lists a number of formal methods for taking these aspects into account and Mumford specifically reports on practical experience with two methods used in a participative situation where the users themselves are carrying out the analysis and the specifications of the information needs.

In the paper by Docherty the formal rules and regulations on systems design in Norway and Sweden are described and discussed. Evidently the Scandinavian trade

unions have been pioneers in securing agreements and laws giving the unions participation and in some cases co-determination in decisions on new information systems.
To a large extent this requires knowledge and Docherty discusses trade union activities in initiating research and in educating their members. Finally he considers
the crucial choice for every trade union of whether to follow a conflict or a co-
operation strategy with management on systems design, an issue which Briefs also
discusses.

The last part of the book is primarily concerned with decision support systems.
Eason reports from a large international research project on how information systems
have changed the task content of managers, and the kind of interaction most condu-
cive to solving the managerial task.

Tricker on the other hand takes more of a top managerial view by pointing out some
of the problems confronting this group in trying to control the use of the computer
resource, and in trying to change the organization with the aid of information
systems.

As to the question about how to design decision support systems Hopwood and Mitroff
agree that the traditional ways of designing information systems are not adequate.
It is not possible to develop consistent goal structures for an organization, derive information needs from these and build integrated information systems for satisfying the needs.

Mitroff talks about the risk of committing 'type three' errors - where the most advanced computer assisted tools are used in solving the wrong problem with the greatest precision. To avoid this Hopwood suggests that alternative accounting systems
be developed and that the organization invests in furthering dialectics. This view
is supported in the paper by Mitroff who is furthermore proposing the use of as-
asumptional analysis to bring forward the underlying values and ideas held by different subgroups as a basis for the development of information systems supporting
different views.

The final part of the book is called 'a look into the future'. In this section one
of the non-academic authors - Gröholt, a systems manager - stresses the point of social accountability in future systems design. Unless social and organizational
aspects are analysed in great detail and taken properly into account there is a
high likelihood that the systems will be resisted by the users. Furthermore he
stresses how user participation is part of the normal procedures in his company,
and he supports the argument introduced by Hedberg in the start of the book that
the traditional systems designers will disappear and that design to a greater extent will be taken over by the users themselves.

Finally the last paper is contributed by Ackoff. The possibilities of computer
technology providing better control are elaborated and the importance of using
systems theory is emphasized. When dealing with systems characterized by an enormous inherent complexity which to a large extent precludes development by trial
and refinement processes, ordinary reductionistic mehtods fail. These methods fail,
since the solution to component problems seldom amount, collectively, to the solution of the overall problem. Instead, the emphasis must be based on a system theory
where the focus on every problem is enlarged to include the highest level (system)
which may possibly be influenced.

It is my hope that the richness of information in the articles will challenge the
readers to expand their problems. For too long design of information systems has
been treated as technical problems only. Some benefits have certainly been achieved,
but the major benefits with this technology lie in the broader perspective.

A Director General from Copenhagen
will make sure there is no mistake-n
about technological perspectives
and investment initiatives
even though our parliament will be shaken

PERSPECTIVES OF MASS-COMMUNICATION AND TELECOMMUNICATIONS

Poul Hansen

Danish Post and Telegraph Office
Copenhagen

Current technological developments in
telecommunication are described (viewdata, teletext etc.) together with future
developments in satellites, stored telephone exchanges and videophone. Furthermore the possibility of two-way mass-
communication is discussed. The advantages of these technological developments
from an ecological/environmental point of
view are presented and certain social
problems are raised. The key role of
technicians as advisers to politicians is
emphasized.

The Human Side of Information Processing
N. Bjørn-Andersen, editor
© IAG
North-Holland Publishing Company, 1980

INTRODUCTION

I am going to talk about "Perspectives of Mass- and Telecommunications", and my view of Mass- and Telecommunications will be influenced by my role as head of the Danish Post and Telegraph Office, and I would begin by describing our organisation. The Post and Telegraph Office is a Government service institution selling its services to customers who must all be offered identical terms. We run postal, giro, telephone, telegraph, telex, and datel services - nationally and internationally. Most of the local telephone services in Denmark are operated by semipublic telephone companies. In this connection, the Post and Telegraph Office acts as a contractor in relation to Danmarks Radio (the Danish Broadcasting Service) and the Air Authorities. As a public service we consider our activities from both commercial and social points of view.

In this paper I shall consider the telecommunication and data communication aspects of our work but omit the postal communications.

CURRENT DEVELOPMENT

Three important developments are already in progress, namely teletext, viewdata, and electronic text processing (ETP).

1. Teletext

Danmarks Radio has started a limited experiment with a teletext system in Denmark. Teletext is a form of one-way communication of text based on the free transmission capacity of the normal TV signal and is conveyed by TV transmitters. To be able to receive the special teletext signal, a TV receiver must be equipped with a special decoder.

In Great Britain where the system has been in use for well over a year, both service material, e.g. weather forecasts, football pools, TV programme schedules and foreign exchange quotations, and current news are transmitted.

2. View data

As in the case of teletext, the viewdata system uses a modified TV set with an external or built-in decoder and a control unit for the selection of information.

Unlike teletext, viewdata is a two-way service in which a connection is established between the users and a viewdata computer via the public telephone network. The system offers, in principle, an opportunity to select from an unlimited number of pages containing news and information. It is assumed that a typical computer will contain 50,000 to 100,000 pages, and the average access time will be less than two seconds.

The British Post Office has been running a viewdata pilot project for some time, and is now beginning a larger experiment with 1,000 users (both private individuals and companies in trade and industry).

3. Text Processing Systems

A third technological development is going on within computerbased text processing systems (ETP). Some of the key factors will be a continued reduction of the prices of minicomputers and electronic/magnetic stores. These systems offer definite possibilities of rationalization and saving to trade and industry and public administrations.

Initially, process-controlled text systems may be expected to find application in the secretarial, typing, and filing functions of offices, but the development of relatively low-priced screen terminals is also anticipated. Such terminals may, with advantage, be used by single office staff members, and a totally paper-free

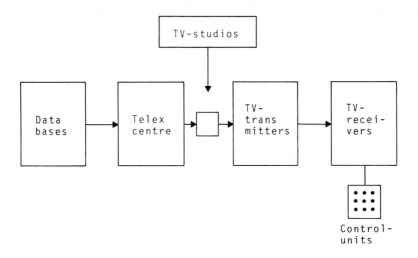

Principle lay-out of a <u>teletext</u> system

Figure 1

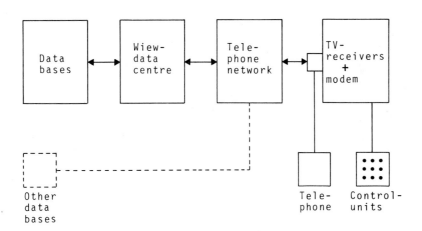

Principle lay-out of a <u>view data</u> system

Figure 2

automatic system may thus be established.

This development will have to be followed by changes in telecommunication systems if direct communication between the automatic systems of different offices is to be possible.

According to surveys carried out, almost ten per cent of all correspondence contains graphic information and pictures, etc. This information cannot be input directly into the automatic text processing systems. At the beginning, telefax (that is, electronic transfer of text, drawings, signatures, etc.) will be a more appropriate new medium.

A complete information processing system for modern offices must be based on technical equipment for both internal and external communication, i.e. terminals of various kinds, control units, computers for processing and storing of information, and communication equipment for transmission of information between the internal terminals as well as between these and external terminals and systems. The Danish Post and Telegraph Office will be involved especially in the transmission phase.

NEW PERSPECTIVES IN TELECOMMUNICATIONS

A number of general perspectives in telecommunications are important from the viewpoint of the Danish Post and Telegraph Office.

With respect to intercontinental connections the development will be characterized by the fact that ever larger band widths can be provided for the same cost, and this will apply for both submarine cables and connections via telecommunication satellites.

Development of the capacity of telecommunication satellites has been even faster than that of submarine cables. A decisive factor in this respect has been extensive and constructive co-operation between a large number of countries. The telecommunication satellites are owned and operated by an international consortium (INTELSAT) with approximately 100 member countries. The rate of development can be judged by noting that the first telecommunication satellite, TELSTAR, had ten telephone circuits. This may be compared with the INTELSAT IV with 5,000 circuits plus two TV channels and INTELSAT IV-A with 6,000 circuits plus two TV channels. The INTELSAT V series which is now being developed and produced will have a capacity of 12,000 telephone circuits and two TV channels.

Efforts are also being made on the European level to establish a satellite system for telecommunication purposes. Preparations have now progressed so far that it is almost certain that the system will be implemented.

Of great public interest is the possibility of TV programme transmission by telecommunication satellites. In this connection the Nordic Council of Ministers has decided that the question of a Nordic TV and broadcasting via satellite (NORDSAT) must be examined more closely in order that the Council of Ministers can decide on the further progress of the matter in the autumn of 1979.

With a view to reducing technological and financial risk it will be expedient to let systems develop successively, for example, in two phases, the latter of which should aim at full channel capacity for a Nordic exchange of programmes. The number of channels of the first phase will probably be limited, for example, to four covering the eastern group of Nordic countries (Denmark, Finland, Norway, Sweden), and 1 or 2 covering the western group of Nordic countries (Iceland, the Faroe Islands, and parts of Southern Greenland).

In principle, the question of implementing the NORDSAT project is a matter of introducing a completely new form of mass communication. The study is organized in expert groups dealing with the following issues:

> Technical and technical/financial issues
> Culture and programme policy issues
> Legal issues
> Financial issues.

The possibility of direct TV satellite transmission to home receivers lies 5-7 years ahead, but there may also be a possibility of TV satellite transmission being spread to specially built receivers with special aerial systems. This kind of TV service is less expensive to implement than a direct TV service to all households and will presumably be of importance, first and foremost, to the developing countries where the need for information is immense and the number of teachers is extremely limited. The number of illiterates on the earth has hardly decreased in recent decades, and it is hopeless to attempt to solve this problem within a single generation by the use of traditional teaching methods in countries like e.g. India.

The different types of satellite transmitting information to the earth about weather conditions, soil conditions, pollution, and plant diseases on the basis of satellite observations are of great furure importance and will no doubt make it possible to create a better and safer life for generations to come.

Radio astronomy has incidentally contributed considerably towards increasing our knowledge of the universe. A radio telescope can receive information over much greater distances than an optical telescope. It is, therefore, important that ITU (International Telecommunication Union) conferences have resulted in international agreement that a number of radio frequencies shall be reserved for radio astronomy.

Moving back to earth to the fields closer at hand, I can mention that the future development of the telephone will be influenced by a change-over to the use of stored programme telephone exchanges. For decades we have been accustomed to using a telephone in the way dictated by the technical conditions of the systems.

Stored programme telephone exchanges will offer a number of new possibilities, for example:
1) the possibility of simple calls to the telephone numbers called regularly by the single subscriber,
2) the possibility of transferring a telephone call to a subscriber directly to other numbers, thus making it unneccessary to wait for calls at home,
3) the possibility, if desired, of learning who has called.

We are thus moving in a direction which permits man to dictate what he wants from the telephone system, instead of the system (or its shortcomings) fixing the terms.

Incidentally, it is no doubt typical that only primitive technologies dictate terms which offer no choice. We are now in a period when technology offers us ever new possibilities in many fields. We are heading towards a highly developed technology which offers many applications.

The video telephone is one of the future prospects of telecommunication technology which is mentioned most frequently as a result of the triumphal progress of television. For some years its possibilities in everyday life have been assessed differently. Partly, it may be used by subscribers, partly it may be placed in special conference rooms in large cities to replace the need for extensive travelling to business meetings and conferences of various kinds.

NEW PERSPECTIVES IN DATA COMMUNICATION

In future, we shall no doubt have to get used to microprocessors or minicomputers being gradually added as useful elements to many of our everyday tools and components. Small computers should be regarded as only a modest beginning.

The interconnection of computers via the telecommunication network has resulted in a data transmission service, first as private networks and now to an increasing degree as public data networks. The development of data transmission has progressed faster in recent years than the development of any other kind of telecommunication, and it seems as if this development is going to continue for some time yet.

In order to meet the increasing demand for data transmission, Norway, Sweden, Finland, and Denmark have decided to establish a Nordic public data network which is expected to open for Danish subscribers in 1979.

Efforts to rationalize the total process of trade and industry can be made in the service field with the greatest advantage because this field absorbs an ever larger proportion of expenditure. Hence it may appear that the interaction between computers and sources/centres of information through data transmission can constitute the most important single factor in the rationalization of trade and industry.

Already to-day data transmission is used for remote control under conditions where risks unpleasant and very difficult working conditions exist.

The importance of being able to utilize electronic control systems grows gradually as human activities exceed their more traditional limits. Compared to electronic systems, man has many handicaps. Sleep is a must, his speed of reaction is slow, and the reliability of his reactions hardly stands comparison with the reliability of electronic systems.

We know that the effectiveness and reliability of the electronic systems are improving all the time, but there is no prospect of human qualities undergoing a similar development. So there is every indication that electronics and data transmission will gradually reduce the necessity of human presence in the more dangerous places of work on land, in the air, and in space.

In order to facilitate the exchange and processing of data, which is a prerequisite to the functioning of modern society, a large proportion of the population have to make daily trips. Children must be sent to school, and their parents must go to work by car or train. Busy businessmen go from town to town by plane. These forms of transport have no utility in themselves, and they all contribute to the depletion of the earth's resources in a relatively short time although they were created by nature through thousands of years.

Extensive use of data transmission and other forms of telecommunication will result in a higher degree of liberty to select the locations of administrative centres and enterprises. Besides, it will create the basis of a cheque- and cash-free society, with the resultant possibilities of extensive simplifications of monetary transactions.

Centralized or decentralized solutions can be chosen depending on the general interests of society.

But we must face the fact that developments within computer technology will create a number of problems of a human nature. In itself, it can hardly be called an unfortunate development that actual routine work is reduced in size because most people want to have an area of work involving some sort of challenge. However, the development involves a risk of unemployment, which is serious already to-day, growing considerably. A quite subjective consideration on my part is that I think computer technology can also be developed for use in areas of work which are to-day regarded as quite qualified jobs, though of a routine nature.

In the long term, it is, therefore, my opinion that problems may occur in finding subjects suitable for takeover by people displaced from responsible administrative functions. There is a risk of a vacuum being formed between some levels of staff.

However, it is possible that these difficulties can be counteracted to some degree by the possibilities created by recent trends to involve larger groups of staff in decision-making processes. I think that it is important to ensure a co-ordinated and concurrent development in the two fields - data control on the one hand and staff co-operation on the other hand. Human contact which is lost by the use of the impersonal data technology must be re-established in some other way.

DEVELOPMENTS IN THE MASS MEDIA

Developments in the mass media, (broadcasting, TV, and the daily press), will also be influenced by the new technological possibilities for sending ever increasing amounts of information to the population. It will presumably be done in the form of technically ever more advanced information systems. For example, electronic newspapers may be transferred to the home on a screen terminal or on printed paper. To en even higher extent than to-day it will be possible to revel in current news, information, and entertainment, all of it presented by means of the most perfect techniques.

Another field with exciting possibilities is cable TV which, compared to broadcastings, permits a considerably higher number of programme channels. Technically, fifty or more different TV channels can be transferred without difficulty. The channels can be used, for example, in connection with local or regional radio and TV transmissions which may become useful contributions to the strengthening of local contacts.

The danger of developments in the direction of ever more extensive and technically perfect mass communication is that an increased one-way communication is thus created. We passively receive centrally drafted information, entertainment, TV education, and news, without being offered any effective possibility of active involvement. TV will provide a few fixed "menus", but it will not satisfy the need for dialogue.

I think that in reality everybody will agree that, in principle, it will be a development which may have a number of adverse effects. Among other things, we will, to too great an extent, become regimented spectators in the debates about society, and most people will no doubt feel that their share in the responsibility is not very large.

In an effective democratic society there ought to be some possibility of a dialogue with the Government, and some possibility for the individual citizen to select his own sources of information.

We have seen in other areas that a valuable tendency towards increased two-way communication has been created. At school the teacher does not just speak from his desk to the pupil but there is a dialogue. Within trade and industry the increased communication between managers and employees or workers is now becoming a fact in most places, and its value is largely accepted.

Through radio and TV telecommunication technology has created effective methods of communication "from the few to the many". But we need an effective means of communication "from the many to the few". It is, of course, a much more difficult problem since, among other things, registration and classification of the many individual communications are difficult.

The development of digital systems operated by fast computers with effective data reduction must be an important step towards solution of these problems.

If the technical problems are solved, it will, for example, be possible, in centrally placed computers, to register the opinions and wishes of the citizens in connection with given situations which are transmitted locally or nationally over a TV channel. It will thus be possible for the participants in a Town Council debate to receive guidance on a data screen, for example, about the attitudes of viewers to the questions debated. It might also be possible to imagine a more differentiated response from viewers. However, it will no doubt have to be realized that it will be a question of choosing between a number of standardized answers in order that they may be sorted electronically. I hope that in this way it will be possible to experience an increase in the active interest in and joint responsibility for the administration of society.

The possibility of a two-way communication in this way can, of course, be utilized in many other ways, for example, for two-way teaching, market analyses or in the replacement of functions which are conducted by manual methods to-day (for example the reading of electricity meters or similar equipment).

In the long term a number of advantages may be obtained from cable TV integrated with other telecommunication services in cables with large band widths and by the use of digital systems. If it is assumed that "The Wired City" will have broad band cables to homes, it will be possible to transmit video telephone, telex, data between home and office as well as electronic newspapers and electronic mail which can reach the receivers every day of the week. The electronic systems never need a day off on Saturdays or Sundays. Furthermore, there will be special two-way circuits to all districts of towns for the collection and spreading of information about traffic conditions, pollution, and many other things. "The Wired City" may soon become a reality, and"The Wired Nation" where single cable systems may be interconnected via telecommunication satellites,is anticipated in the U.S.A. where long distances are to be covered.

It will be for telecommunication technicians to show in the years to come how all these new facilities can be best used for creating the most satisfactory ways of life under different conditions. It will also be important to ensure that the solutions chosen are financially appropriate and that they will not use more of the limited resources of nature, especially radio frequencies, than strictly necessary. For this reason cable TV should, in the long term, be given some preference over normal broadcasting. Since broadcasting and TV transmission can in some cases be faster and cheaper than cable TV, we shall, however, no doubt find both cable TV and broadcasting of local programmes for many years yet.

The assessment of cable TV as an alternative to broadcasting also involves strictly political aspects. As compared to broadcasting, the geographical spread of cable TV can be effectively controlled.

CONCLUSIONS

It is important to ensure in the years to come that the development of telecommunication is given a high priority, and that it will not be stopped unnecessarily for reasons of economy or as a result of a more or less pronounced aversion to technical development. The fact that telecommunication may take over more and more tasks in society in a way which is favourable to ecological development means that it should be possible to anticipate an ever larger share of the national product for investments in telecommunication systems. But it is also important that telecommunication technicians should understand the importance of making it clear to the responsible leaders of our society what favourable possibilities the development of the telecommunication technology offers us.It will be necessary for telecommunication technicians to take the initiative and point to specific fields in which development can take place with the best results. The goals must be fixed by the politicians after the technicians have stated the possibilities and have offered solutions based on the optimum of the available technology.

Electronics still show new methods for collecting, storing, processing, and transmitting information and knowledge. Since technological development also has the
effect that a considerable part of the electronic equipment used in this connection
becomes better and cheaper by a factor of 10 to 100 every few years, it must be
proper to expect that any welldefined problem which involves the exchange of information and the collection of concrete data can gradually be solved, and in most
cases it will be possible to do so by the use of telecommunication equipment which
is realtively safe and cheap.

Those who will be responsible for controlling the technical development work within telecommunication in the decades to come will, therefore, face a broad spectrum
of possibilities.

In contrast to most other technologists, the telecommunication technician will be
in the favourable position that his work will hardly contribute to increasing the
problems of society as regards pollution and environmental destruction in any essential field. On the contrary, there are good possibilities that a number of technical improvements may be placed at the disposal of society; improvements which
will reform communicattions between people and in society in general and which will
have no unfortunate ecological side effects. These improvements can increase the
effectiveness of administration and of trade and industry and they may even serve
to change the pattern of our lives towards whatever goals might be formulated.

Finally, I wish to mention that many people also see risks in connection with the
development in the area of electronics, among other risks the possible technological unemployment mentioned previously.

The International Labour Organization (ILO) has pointed out in a report that new
data processing techniques give rise to enormous problems and has, among others,
formulated the question about: Where is the dividing line between, on one hand, the
regard to be paid to the safety and to a rational organization of the work and, on
the other hand, a constant supervision of the workers at the assembly line or the
employees in their offices?

Another point of view is that there is hardly any technological limit to the amount
and kind of communication and transfer of information that is possible. But there
will no doubt be certain biological and psychological limits to what we can con-
sume; limits which it might be useful to explore.

It is the intention of the Danish Post and Telegraph Office and the Danish Academy
of Technical Sciences to establish a study group in the near future, the object of
which shall be to examine the perspectives of mass- and telecommunications. The objective of such a study group shall be to initiate discussion of the applications
and make explicit their side-effects on society, organisation, family, and individual. I hope that the study group may contribute to a drafting of the mass- and
telecommunication policy of society which I consider necessary, but which is a matter reaching far beyond the domain of the Danish Post and Telegraph Office.

REFERENCES

Sekretariatet for Nordisk Kulturelt Samarbejde (1977). Nordisk Radio och Televi-
    sion via Satellit. Vol. 7, Copenhagen.

Sekretariatet for Nordisk Kulturelt Samarbejde (1977). Nordisk Radio och Televi-
    sion via Satellit. Remissammenstälning, Vol. 36, Copenhagen.

DISCUSSION AND COMMENTS ON PAPER PRESENTED BY POUL HANSEN

HAROLD SACKMAN

What kind of long range social planning is going on? The only thing mentioned by
Poul Hansen was a recent study just being initiated. Does such a planning involve
prototype social experimentation? E.g. is there some kind of a plan to set aside
a community, give them advanced communication technology, and observe the consequences that take place?

Dr. Prewitt, a political scientist looking at the computer communications break-.
through, used the analogy of the automobile. Supposing back in 1900 we took aside
a small city, gave every one a car, and then did some social experimentation. We
would at that time have found out about traffic jams, pollution, automobile
accidents, and perhaps we would have been able to plan a little more intelligently
In this way we would have a better idea in advance based on actual empirical evidence, as to what the real social consequences are, instead of doing it from the
seat of our pants, which we are mostly doing at this particular point.

Finally, I should like to ask about the status with regard to politizing computer
communication services in Denmark. How aware is the public of the political impact? Are the politicians concerned about the vast socio-economic and political
impacts related to having a terminal in every home? For example, have they thought
about a better deal for electronic transfer systems for the ordinary consumer?

I am concerned about this area because the consequences are being defined and formulated by industry on their terms, on their grounds, and by their ground rules.
And I am not sure that this is necessarily in the best interest of society as a
whole.

POUL HANSEN

I believe very much in social experiments. But to be quite honest, we have ideas,
but have taken no steps towards practical implementation of major experiments up
to now. We hope to be able to carry out some experiments on the teletext system
and presently we have started an experiment with terminals for deaf people.

Furthermore, we have also had a Nordic group looking into the consequences of
sending up a Nordic satellite for spreading broadcasting and TV in the Nordic
countries.

A debate in society is difficult to achieve, and the politicians are not interested
We have written about it, we have talked about it, but no one cares. Danish politicians do not allow themselves to become involved in long range planning.

I have recently had a chance to visit the Tama New Town project and got some inspiration which I feel we might benefit from, if there was a political will to
launch such projects.

PETER SØRENSEN

I agree with most of Poul Hansen's presentation, and one of the important issues
is that transportation of information is far cheaper than transportation of people
and physical matters. It is interesting to note that due to this basic fact, in my
opinion, the entire postal service will become obsolete. Perhaps you have some
comments on that.

The technology we are concerned about has a number of advantages from an ecological point of view. With a widespread use of this technology, pollution is reduced and the energy saving far exceeds the energy consumption.

When we talk about technological advancements, economics have a major part to play. For instance, the cashless society is still far away because it is so expensive to process transactions that for a long time we shall need coins and small bills for small daily expenses.

I found the comments on two-way mass-communication systems very interesting. However, there is a risk that only those very interested will be at home to watch television and thus be able to push buttons. In this way we get perhaps too large an influence by those who are interested and all the passive people are not even asked. You may argue that this is really what we want, perhaps it is.

Furthermore, we might mention that we are talking about very large sums of money compared with other investments in society. Few politicians are aware of this. I doubt that we will get the priorities right as there are major pitfalls and obstacles ahead. We are not so perfect in introducing technology and the introduction may take longer than we expect.

POUL HANSEN

I represent an organization applying the technology, and we try to formulate problems for discussion. We do not want to provide the solutions. I do not know what will happen if we provide television with twenty channels. There is a risk that we make the citizens more passive. Perhaps we even make them more frustrated and aggressive if we deliver an enormous volume of one-way communication. We certainly need investigations and more debate. The man in the street is not involved, and there is a risk that a small group from industry and/or government will take the decisions without any public commitment.

I do not think that the postal service we know today will stop. Our investigations show that it will continue to grow for the next ten years. From then on the growth in information exchange will take place via telecommunication and the volume of transactions to be handled by the postal service will stagnate but not disappear.

The investments in telecommunications are certainly very large. The total investments in Denmark in telecommunications for the next ten years will be between 18 and 22 billion Danish kroner.

A.W. Zijlker

I am not worried about the apparent lack of awareness in society today. In Holland public opinion is becoming more aware since the beginning of 1978, as is reflected in the amount of attention being paid to this subject by the newspapers; and if they become aware the politicians will become aware.

My second point is that everybody up till now has been 'concerned' with the 'risks' and 'dangers' of communication. I should claim that open communication in itself is a guarantee for greater stability in society. All our activities with new technology are in a sense experiments. They are not called so but they are, and the results are publicly available and publicly debated. Everybody can see where things are going wrong. The more we open up the information channels the better the chance that we will react properly.

A good example is the multitude of activities embarked upon all over the world to counteract the 'energy crisis'. The danger lies not in this crisis having occured

but in the possibility that a potential crisis of this kind might stay undetected
for too long through lack of free information!

POUL HANSEN

I too have great hopes for an enlightened public debate. I might mention that
unions seem to be aware of risks from the new technology, especially unemployment.

NIELS BJØRN-ANDERSEN

We foresee large investments in the new communication technology, and many of us
have an intuitive feeling that there will be very important repercussions for
Society. It was also clear from the lecture that there is a whole range of different options but as Sackman pointed out, who are to evaluate these options, who
are the watchdogs, do they have enough resources to carry out proper evaluations,
and how may these evaluations be channelled back into influencing the technology?
It seems to me that this area is far too important to let market mechanisms and
self-control on ethical grounds be the only constraints on technological developments.

A Swede by the name of Hedberg
Brings data on computers and work
His research is quite clear
The designers disappear
Shall we raise them a stone in Gothenburg?

USING COMPUTERIZED INFORMATION SYSTEMS
TO DESIGN
BETTER ORGANIZATIONS AND JOBS

Bo Hedberg

Swedish Center for Working Life,
Stockholm, Sweden

Participative design of computer systems
in two companies is described. The author
concludes that socio-technical designing,
on its own, is a dead end. It does not
break the vicious circle in which people
replaced by computers, jobs are degraded,
and powers are centralized.
Organizational and individual needs must
be the starting point for systems development. The problems must be defined from
both managers' and workers' perspectives.
Participative designing must replace designing by specialists. Socio-technical
designs must be supported by changing values and rewards, and by changes in the
power structures. Computer technology can
then be used to create better organizations and jobs. The long-term perspective:
organizations are self-designing and systems designers are gone.

The Human Side of Information Processing
N. Bjørn-Andersen, editor
© IAG
North Holland Publishing Company, 1980

INTRODUCTION

Struggling to find a way to start this paper my eyes fell on the CCI-78 brochure
and on the three themes which provide the platform of this conference. The first
theme spells out the need to understand how information systems and related technologies affect people and organizations. The second theme concerns how such understanding can be put to work to control changes in social systems and to support
organizational learning and decision making. The third theme has to do with the
future roles of systems designers and computer departments. How will these roles
change?

The first theme implies that too little is known about how information technologies
shape people, jobs, and structures. The second theme implies that designers who understand these relationships will be able to control design outcomes. The third
theme implies, I assume, that systems designers should be promoted to organization
designers and that computer departments ought to move on to the O & D trade.

At first glance one is willing to support all these themes and implications. We do
need more knowledge about interactions between man-technology-task-structure variables. We ought to plan changes of jobs and work organizations. The day when such
issues were lumped together in conferences like this under the label of 'social
implications' should be gone. People and human needs must be the starting point for
designing, and they should have implications for the technologies, not vice versa.
This would turn designers' world upside down and that would most likely also affect
systems designers and their departments.

On second thought these themes and implications are far from self-evident. Is it
lack of knowledge that leads designers to produce information systems which make
good use of computers and bad use of people? Can knowledgeable designers really
ever control the development of complex social systems? Should systems designers
and computer departments really have roles to play in the future? Are they needed,
and are they desirable?

I shall attempt to present both the pro case and the con case with respect to the
three conference themes. The pro case will no doubt have most supporters among the
conference participants. The themes express what many concerned computer specialists believe today: Human factors must be recognized; Socio-technical designs
should be strived for; New demands will be laid on designers' shoulders; The con
case will have fewer listeners. It brings up the concept of power and the issue of
values. It questions the designers' mission and their ability to design. It argues
that socio-technical designing, on its own, is a dead end.

I wish I could show you nice examples of good, human, considerate designs-- facts --
and then use my fantasy to project these developments into a rosy future -- fiction.
But instead I shall argue that these good, human, considerate designs are mostly
fictions, and that the facts call for radical changes with respect to how we view
information systems and set out to design them.

HOW KNOWLEDGE LEADS TO BETTER DESIGNS AND NEW DESIGN ROLES - THE PRO CASE

The history of technology development shows how those who exploit new technologies
move from naive applications to more sophisticated ones as they learn and as their
technologies mature. The industrial revolution started as one of machine-making
and factory-building. Gradually designers discovered that machines were manned by
people, and that these people had arms, legs, and even souls. Safety concerns, er-
gonomics/socio-technical designs, and self-realization were stations along the
road. What started with Spinning Jennies and steam engines now proceeds with job
enrichment and semi-autonomous work groups. Knowledge about how technology affects
people (cuts off arms, destroys lungs, causes stresses and strains, leads to bore-
dom and lack of control) enriched the model of man and led to improved designs.

Computers, and information technology as a whole, is going through a similar cycle. In fact, one can identify and label some maturity phases of information systems design (Figure 1).

	MISSION:	PURPOSE:	ORG.DESIGN:	DESIGNERS:
PHASE I	Design IS	.. to exploit new techno-logy	by surprise	pioneers
PHASE II	Design IS carefully	.. to minimize social impli-cations	by mistake (not intended to change)	taylors
PHASE III	Design IS delibera-tely	.. to change organizations	by purpose	change agents

Figure 1.

Maturity phases of information systems design

Computer specialists were initially mainly concerned with exploiting the new pos-sibilities that information technology brought. First generation, second genera-tion, third generation computers. Time sharing, virtual memories, microprogramming, terminals - the technology variable set the pace. Designers were pioneers and had a share of the marvel. Organizations were designed by surprise. 'Social implica-tions' began to appear.

Learning from implementation difficulties and design surprises designers began to reconsider their accomplishments and to develop the role of the informed and considerate taylor. The phase II designers study the organization they design for, describe its goals and decision procedures, interview people,and select terminals, reports, chairs, and workplaces that fit human fingers, eyes, minds, spines, and buttocks. They attempt to taylor information systems to existing social organiza-tions. Project teams -- representing both technical and organizational expertise -- and user participation in designing represent attemtps to widen the knowledge base and to come to grips with systems implementation.

When system taylors found that 'organizational bodies' often changed as a result of getting new 'computer suits' and started to comprehend the complexity of the full design task,the more humble role of change agent began to emerge. Also, sy-stems designing was increasingly seen as a means to set organizations in motion. Change processes, organization development, and learning organizations became catchwords for the new movement.

These three maturity phases, if they describe reality, demonstrate that increasing knowledge about technological impacts can lead to more responsible designs, widened perspectives and new roles for systems designers and computer departments.

Lacking thorough empirical support for my statement, I would claim that the pro-fession of systems design currently is in the middle of the transfer from phase I to phase II on the presented scale. The debate has often moved into phase III, though, but practise lags behind, as always.

What comes next in the maturity cycle? One can only speculate. My phase IV candi-
date looks as follows (Figure 2).

	MISSION:	PURPOSE:	ORG.DESIGN:	DESIGNERS:
PHASE IV	Design IS partici-patively	.. to create learning or-ganizations	self-designing, evolutionary	gone

Figure 2.

...... and then ?

A FEW ENCOURAGING EXAMPLES (STILL THE PRO CASE)

The Volvo automobile assembly plant in Kalmar, Sweden, is often taken as an example
of good, considerate socio-technical design. Self-suppporing work groups with some
autonomy rotate jobs between group members. The physical working conditions are excellent. Each group has its own coffee room, sauna, and factory entrance. Union
representatives, managers, and various experts have participated in a joint effort
to design the factory.

The Volvo-Kalmar plant is interesting also from an information systems design point
of view. The removal of the assembly line and the relative autonomy of the production groups demanded advanced computerized information systems so that each group
could plan, monitor, and evaluate its production. Computer terminals are placed in
each team area for this purpose.

The loosely coupled assembly stream requires a significant increase of information
processing for coordination and control. An overall picture of the production systems has to be compiled at the same time as required information is fed back for
performance, evaluation, and correction.

Three computerized information systems serve and support the working groups (Figure
3).

(1)   A process control system which controls and directs the transportation
      vehicles in the production system. Information from the process control
      system is fed forward to working groups so that they can get a picture
      of their potential work load via their computer terminal.

(2)   A production control system which gives each work group written spe-
      cifications for each car that is to be assembled.

(3)   A quality control system which feeds back quality control results to
      the work group. Quality control is normally carried out on a spe-
      cified sample of the production. When errors are detected, the sample
      size of the quality control is increased by 100%. The responsible
      group receives a message on their terminal and are requested to correct
      the errors. When the error rate is back to normal, the alerted quality
      control is set back to standard sample size after a time delay. The
      quality control system monitors some 3000 control points in each car
      and uses its stored information to build up experience based on ob-
      served correlations and regressions.

Like all computer technology the set of new computer systems introduces possibilities for centralization as well as for decentralization. The apparent decentralization of responsibility to the work group is matched by a corresponding centralization of the ultimate control. But managers merely receive hard-copy summary reports. Only workers, supervisors, and quality control engineers have easy access to on-line terminals.

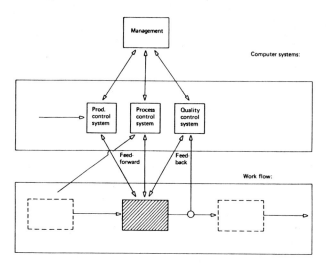

Figure 3.
Information systems for increased self-management at Volvo-Kalmar (Hedberg, 1975)

The new technology offers a potential for increased autonomy in each work group. Each team area can be made into an intimate workshop with its own discretion and responsibilities. The computer technology offers a potential for improving workers' influence in one of the most criticized areas of modern production.

The Volvo-Kalmar plant shows that concerned designers who understand technology impacts and who develop social systems purposively and in cooperation with workers and managers can greatly improve the functioning of modern organizations.

Let us move on to another success story where the author played the role of change agent.

The Housing Loan Agency (HLA) had existed as a separate subsidiary of a large bank for about ten years. Its staff had grown from a handful to about sixty in that period. In 1976 the data processing volumes called for new computing facilities and a new on-line information system. Consultants were called in and reference groups were formed in due democratic order. Union representatives, managers, and external computer experts soon came up with a feasibility study and a consultants report which suggested that an on-line information system should be installed. Of its around one hundred pages, the consultants' report spent almost ten discussing human needs, terminal requirmments, and a summary of some initial interviews. The organization chart was also included. The remaining ninety pages were devoted to the issues of data-base organization and file conversion. The consultants represented a solid, early phase II design tradition.

Some union representatives who found these apparent priorities somewhat remarkable requested that the present author should be called in to talk about his own re-

search on computers in banking and to challenge the consultants' report. The managers agreed, and a one-day seminar with the project group, the consultants, the
HLA managers, and representatives from all HLA units was scheduled. The seminar
raised the question of what organization the managers and employees wanted to create and what kind of work roles would be desirable in the future HLA. A discussion about ideal organizations, models of man, and good and bad jobs in the pre
sent HLA started. These issues had not been raised in the consultants' report or
during the feasibility study. At that end of the seminar day managers and members
of the project group concluded that further systems development should be preceede
by discussion of alternative scenarios and job requirements for the HLA of the futu

The project group used the summer of 1977 to formulate different and detailed scenarios for alternative future HLAs. The present organization was heavily specialized. The task of handling housing loans had been broken down into subtasks of
accepting loans, computing interests, negotiating loans, and terminating loans.
Accounting, financing, document filing, and security handling were other subfunc-
tions. All these tasks were handled by separate units, and tasks inside each unit
were further decomposed into specialities. To an outside observer the HLA appeared
as a 'mental assembly plant' where loans were produced, repaired, and discarded.
To country banks and house owners who HLA served the organization appeared as an
impersonal loan machinery where ecah phone call was answered by a different specialist.

The three scenarios that the project group developed tried to come to grips with
HLA's specialization and lack of continuity in customer contacts. All loan handling
should be dealt with inside a working team. And each team should have one geographical region to serve. Groups could rotate tasks between members, if they wanted.
Customers should learn to know the HLA staff which served their region. Enriched
work roles, a total view of the housing-loan cycle, and break-down of special staff
units were central themes in the presented organization charts. The scenarios varied only with respect to how radical the departure from the present organization
would be.

In the early fall of 1977 the project group invited all employees of the organization to a three-day conference on the scenarios. The purpose was to formulate an
organizational platform and specified human and organizational objectives for the
new computer systems. One half of the HLA staff worked with this problem during
the first day. The other half of the organization attended the second day. Elected
representatives from ad hoc working groups that were formed during the first two
days met on the third conference day to synthesize the conclusions and to formulate a programme for the further development.

The first two days followed the same format. After an introductory presentation by
the present author on socio-technical designing and strategies for systems development, the ad hoc working groups sat down to formulate the 'model of man' they
wanted to see incorporated in the new system and in future work roles in 'the
good HLA'. A simple model-of-man scale -- theory X vs. theory Y dimension, (Hedberg and Mumford 1975) -- was used to initiate the discussion. The model-of-man
formulations were then used to identify good and bad jobs in the current organization and to formulate job demands for the new system. The group reports were
summarized at noon.

In summary, the groups unanimously expressed theory Y ideals and asked for wider
tasks, more responsibility, less monotony, more opportunities for learning,
and personal growth in their jobs. Both staff and managers who participated in
the group work agreed on this matter. The afternoon was spent presenting and discussing 'the good HLA' scenarios. The morning discussions on job demands fore-
closed that the afternoon group work would call for organizational changes. And
it did! Instead of advocating a slightly modified version of the present organization -- as the inventors of scenarios had guessed -- the working groups spoke
in favour of the most radical HLA scenario. They wanted the information system to

support a work organization with total loan handling and regional responsibility in each administrative unit. The groups also demanded more time to develop their proposals and substantiate their claims and objectives.

The same development took place during the second day, when the rest of the employees worked on the same problems. Also they wanted more time to follow-up their one-day involvement in the future organization. The HLA management decided to halt the consultants and the scheduled systems development for a period, pending the results of continued working group discussions. Two months later a full organization proposal together with job demands and a development plan were laid on the project leader's desk. Everybody in the organization had participated in developing this action programme,and they demanded that it would form the basis for further systems development 'providing that no overriding technical or financial constraints were detected'. The document also called for introductory EDP courses for all employees. A task force would study experiences from similar computer systems in other industries. The ad hoc working groups wanted to go on to develop and prepare the new work organization. The computer specialists (consultants) declared that they could work from the new platform. The narrower computer systems development had been delayed by about three months as a result of the widened staff involvement. On the other hand, there was now strong and solid backing for the action programme. The project leader felt that the 'interruption' had improved the system and greatly increased the likelihood of its assimilation in the organization. Many problems that traditionally are labelled as 'informing', 'educating', implementing', and 'motivating' future systems users appeared to have been solved through the ad hoc working groups.

The HLA case illustrates that it is possible to bring in both technical, organizational, and individual considerations in one single design process and to design purposively and with considerable staff involvement to create better jobs and organizations. And -- as the third theme of this conference proposes -- it suggests changing roles for systems designers and computer departments as collaborators with managers and users in planned work improvement and organizational change.

So much for the pro case. Let us now turn the coin and look at the other arguments and the other facts of the presented examples.

WHEN GOOD AMBITIONS FACE UNCHANGED POWER, VALUES, AND REWARD SYSTEMS - THE CON CASE

Better understanding of the impact of information systems on individuals and organizations .... Is knowledge really what the computer world is lacking? Would knowledge about computer impacts, per se, improve tomorrow's information systems?

Well, current developments do not support this assumption. There is very much information available about how computerized information systems affect people and their decision making, attitudes, work roles and organizations. The references to good and solid research in this area are so many that I refrain from the job of listing a fair sample. If only a fraction of this knowledge was used in practical systems development, new information systems would be quite different. But that has not happened. Knowledge about computer impacts appears to rest in research reports and in the hearts and minds of those who are affected. And neither source is well connected to the mainstreams where new systems develop (Hedberg,1978).

Rather than escaping into the search for more knowledge, we should perhaps look around to see why existing knowledge has not improved developing systems. What are the possible obstacles? Let me suggest three:

Our educational systems are effective barriers between the understanding of human and organizational impacts and the systems design trade. The dominance of technology issues in the various curricula that are used to teach information systems, computer science, programming, and systems design to students at high schools and universities, night classes, and in-house training programmes is striking. There is little room for behavioural and social sciences to change the scene. There is even less room for real people to give witness about real impacts.

The Teichroew committee on information systems curriculum (Teichroew,1971), the ACM curriculum proposal (Aschenhurst,1972), and Couger's undergraduate programme (Couger,1973) have been put forward as good, balanced teaching programmes, but all these proposals treat human and organizational impacts as 'social implications'.

The Swedish Office of the Chancellor of the Universities drew up a programme and policy statement in 1977 for a three-year university education in information systems design. The programme attempted to integrate the human, technical, organizational, and societal sides of information systems and computerization. The 1978 version of this curriculum at Stockholm university shows that 40 credits out of a total of 120 shall be devoted to 'relevant social sciences'. The curriculum designers have not even bothered to think through these needs. The students can select economics, sociology, psychology, education, business administration or any other introductory course in the social science faculty. The degree of integration is nil. Students who intend to become advanced programmers are advised to select another 10 credits of mathematics and statistics within the free 40-credit lot. The introductory course of the programme sets the tone, and it speaks for itself (Figure 4).

Two credits of forty are devoted to people, organizations, and society at large. No wonder that knowledge about computer impacts does not reach the future designers.

1st semester	Introduction to systems science - definition of systems, systems analysis	3 cr.
	Computers and programming	5 cr.
	Statistics and mathematics - statistical measurements, algebra, exp. and log. functions	5 cr.
	Group work (statistics)	7 cr.
2nd semester	Mathematics and statistics - sums, integrals, elementary logic, linear algebra, statistical inference, prohability theory	8 cr.
	ORIENTATION ON SOCIAL SCIENCE	2 cr.
	Systems analysis, systems development	6 cr.
	Applications	4 cr.

Figure 4.

Introductory course to information systems at Stockholm university 1978

Another force that shapes systems designers and their systems is the professional journals. The topic they deal with and the systems that are put forward as pace-setting examples direct designers' attention and influence their priorities.

A count performed at the Library of the University of Wisconsin-Milwaukee (St. Pierre 1975) classified articles appearing in 48 computer and information systems journals during 1972-75. While 721 articles on hardware equipment were recorded, 218 on time-sharing, and 150 on programming, there were in the same journals only 55 articles concerning computer impacts on people and organizations. With these priorities in professional journals, would more knowledge about computer impacts really help to create better systems? Maybe a first priority should be to redesign the journals.

A third obstacle that intimately relates to the two above, but that most likely remains for quite some while even if education and journals are changed, is the values and reward systems within which designers operate. Our previous research (Hedberg and Mumford,1975) has pointed to considerable discrepancies between the values-at-large the designers confess to and the values that they feel they can work towards in their jobs. Designers design to please those who control the rewards (Churchman,1971). They live in a world where technical constraints, cost budgets, and deadlines are real and demanding, but where human needs, democratic organization structures, and user participation are little but window dressing (Bjørn-Andersen and Hedberg,1977). Should we moralize over that they first attend to problems of costs, timing, and technical functioning and that their private models of man differ from those which they build into their designs? No, they act according to the rules of the game they are in! It is these rules that must be changed!

My conclusion is that the road to better information systems initially must go through educational reforms, substantially changed contents in professional journals and at professional meetings. In this way we might hope to see gradual changes in professional values. But these changes are not likely to come about easily. Those who advocate technology are more resourceful than those who advocate man. Moreover,user participation in systems development rests on shaky grounds in most countries. Changes in the distribution of power are needed to give voice to human needs and desires and also to revise reward systems so that designers are able to work towards their values. Thus, power changes and consequent changes of priorities, attentions, and values are needed before improved understanding of the impact of information systems on humans and organizations will improve information systems, as seen from the latter's point of view. Widening designers' perspectives and changing their reward systems so that they can design with people, tasks, technology, and structure in mind is a first step towards better computerized systems.

But this first step has limited possibilities. Let us proceed to the second theme of this conference:

"We want to control and plan for change in the social system instead of being taken by surprise.." So far the second theme. Who are "we",and who is usually taken by surprise? Well, "we" are seemingly the designers. The surprise is theirs too, I assume, although the worst surprises usually hit the users.

Is it likely that even very knowledgeable designers can change social systems - - such as industrial firms and government bureaucracies - - in a planned fashion? I do not think so. The complexity of design tasks, even in simple organizations, is likely to exceed designers' comprehension in almost any case. Designers can at best be facilitators of change - - stumbling blocks which make organizations trip. This is not to say that designers should not try to move social systems towards more desirable states. They should only realize that their rationality is limited and that their control is weak.

Designers should furthermore be reluctant to provide organizations with goals and to assist them in problem solving. Many, maybe most, organizations invent their goals after the fact to explain what they have been doing (Weick,1969; March and Olsen,1976),and modal organizations are action takers that dissolve problems rather than problem solvers that take actions (Starbuck,1977). Designers who want organizations to behave more rationally - - as they do in the textbooks -- can cause serious problems by providing problem solving systems for action taking organizations, and by overstating the directive role of organizational goals.

The discussion above indicates my firm belief that the short-term prescriptions above (educate the designers, etc.) hardly are any long-term solutions. Narrow-minded designers can do much harm,but broad-minded computer specialists can do only a limited amount of good. There are simply other things than designers' understanding that affect systems designs. Designers must realize this and adjust their roles. So, this precludes my reaction to the third theme of the conference; System designers should only rarely design information systems in the days to come. Designing should be turned over to the people who use and need information systems. Computer specialists can act as translators and facilitators, and information analysts can help people in organizations to structure and grasp their information flow. But systems designs should evolve from within organizations.

If there is another role for tomorrow's designers that role should be to design and manage organizational metasystems. Systems for systems design are needed. Governance systems as well (Hedberg et.al. 1976). Organizations ideologies -- or myths -- need improved carrying systems so that organizational beliefs and attention foci can be changed effectively (Hedberg and Jönsson 1978). These are tasks which will require talented designers in the future. Whether today's designers will move into that role remains to be seen.

So much for the con advocacy. Now, let us return to the empirical examples.

HOW ENCOURAGING EXAMPLES GROW LESS ENCOURAGING (NOW THE CON CASE REMEMBER!)

Early in 1974 the bright, colourful Volvo-Kalmar plant stood ready for automobile production. Insight from ergonomics and industrial psychology, together with safety and health concerns, had led to a production layout that looked as a considerable improvement to everybody involved. The assembly line was gone. Heavy lifts, and awkward working positions were taken away. Work teams began to take production responsibility for their work areas.

The Volvo workers soon discovered that the assembly line was still there, although no longer visible to the eye. Weekly production plans arrived from the Volvo headquarters in Gothenburg. The buffer zones of each team area were too small to allow much variation in work pace. The visionary plans said that workers should be able to vary their work pace and to take breaks at their own discretion. The small buffer zones and the production demands from related team areas made this discretion fictitious. The unions decided to negotiate a fixed working schedule with predetermined pauses and production stops.

Also the job rotation prospects turned out to be less intriguing. Not all teams rotated jobs. The door assembly area was broken down into sub-assemblies. Workers who were trained as generalists - - and able to move in wherever required -- were better paid and became a factory overclass.

New models and varieties were introduced and intermediate work stations had to be set up between some team areas. This consumed already scarce buffer space, and allowed work teams even less variation in work pace. The hidden assembly line began to emerge.

The quality control system -- that was intended as a feedback learning loop to the work teams -- was terminated. It was judged to be too complicated. And besides, there was not much to learn. Quality control remained in the hands of control engineers and foremen.

The degeneration of the Kalmar solution has several partial explanations. First, the new factory design resulted from a management initiative to come to grips with high absenteeism and personnel turnover. Those were the symptoms one wanted to remove. Job rotation and a nice work environment were supposed to motivate the workers and to increase their identification with the company. Second, neither the power structure nor the reward systems were changed so as to fit the new work organization. The work groups elected their spokesmen, but the power resided with the foremen who were appointed from above. The piece-rate wage system from conventional assembly lines remained unchanged. Third, the assembly line was never really taken away. Tight production plans from the headquarters gave the narrow frames within which variations could occur. Small buffer zones and gradual crowding made the discretion span even narrower. Each work group was closely dependent on its surrounding peer groups.

The degeneration of the Volvo-Kalmar plant illustrates that good ambitions and knowledge about how technology affects people may be insufficient as a basis for lasting solutions. If the power structure remains unchanged and the controls and rewards are the same it is predictable that new systems for administration and production will degenerate to a point where they fit the previously established meta-structure.

What happened at the HLA? Well, the employees' action programme was handed over to the managers and to the design team. The computer specialists declared that the new computer system could be built to meet the new requirements, and management decided that the new directives should influence the design solutions given that cost and time constraints were not violated.

Then the consultants went on with their file conversion work. Both management and the computer specialists grumbled that the employees' action plan and organization model were vague and unspecific. In December 1977 the consultants were asked to study the feasibility of the new plans. The employees had not received any answer by September 1978. Systems development went on in the meantime.

'There is too much work to do with the system. Organizational changes must be postponed'. 'Widened task-handling is possible, but full loan-handling by one person requires too much skill'. 'We are building the system for the present organization. It can probably be used for one of the proposed reorganizations, but then it will not be optimal at all'. These are direct quotes from people responsible for the HLA system during the fall of 1978.

The employee mobilization at the HLA had shown that ordinary clerks and computer laymen could formulate rather precise requirements for systems development. The HLA process went wrong thereafter. The management, the consultants, and the leadership of the systems project were unchanged. The rewards and punishments for the project leader had no provision for organizational changes and job design. Management gave little support. The consultants kept on working on their technical solutions. The cost budget and the time schedule remained virtually unchanged.

The HLA systems project had initiated a staff movement, but there appeared to be little readiness for change in the executive systems. Both members of the project group and active employees who had formulated the action programme were deeply frustrated by the end of the summer of 1978. Detailed design objectives, concrete work role descriptions, knowledge about computer impacts, and massive personnel backing were not enough. The rules of the game had not been changed.

The dismal endings of the two stories that started so well indicate that sociotechnical and participative designing are dead ends unless they are matched by simultaneous changes of values, rewards, and powers in the systems that control the development.

The pro and con cases are presented. Some conclusions can be drawn.

CONCLUSIONS

Computerization has hitherto mainly been a naive response to vaguely formulated problems of efficiency and motivation in organizations. Symptoms -- such as personnel turnover, absenteeism, and wage demands -- have been 'cured' by rationalization. Instead of taking away the causes of social problems, one has attempted to take away people. Degradation of work has continued. The new work organizations and job contents have been equal to, or worse, than the ones that initially caused problems, so further computerization has been called for. A management perspective and specialist designs have characterized this negative development cycle (Figure 5).

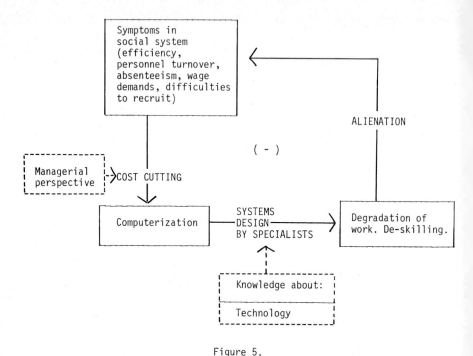

Figure 5.

Systems design - naive managerial perspective

Current forces now attempt to change this negative cycle by entering more knowledge about man and organizations into the design process. The managerial perspective remains (Figure 6).

Neither of these approaches creates positive cycles where people in organizations learn and develop as their organizations grow increasingly democratic and efficient. Both these approaches diminish man and, eventually, replace people by technology. Both these approaches are based on managerial problem definitions and designs by experts.

Systems design in the tomorrow's world cannot remain unaffected by changing values and power balances in society at large. Unless new computer systems manage to improve organizations also from the employees' point of view and to redistribute power in accordance with democratic values these negative cycles will remain. This requires that managerial perspectives are matched with workers' perspectives and that systems are designed in joint efforts between workers and management. Consciousness about power, values, and reward systems has to be added to knowledge about technology, people and organizations (Figure 7).

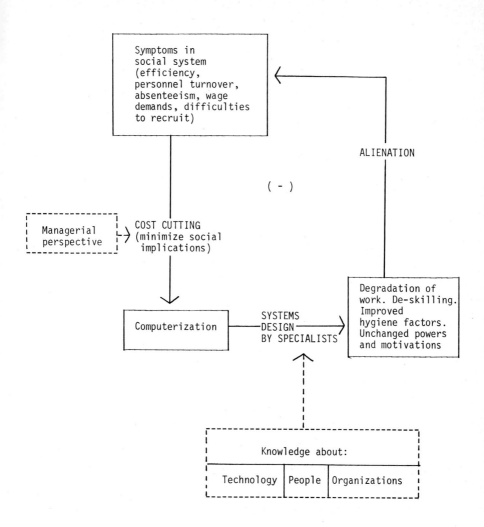

Figure 6.

Systems design - widened managerial perspective

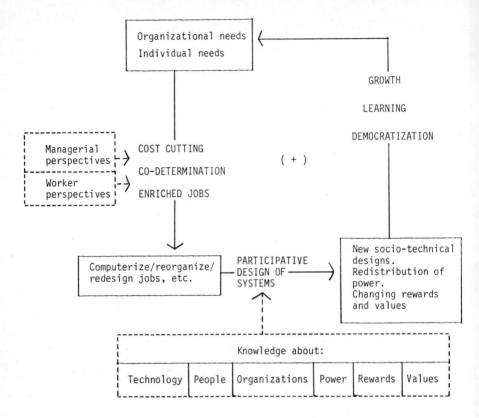

Figure 7.

Systems design - participatively and based on
managerial and worker perspectives

The thesis of this paper can be summarized as follows:

(1) Computerized systems can be used to design better organizations and jobs.

(2) Knowledge about how computers affect people, jobs, and organizations is
a necessary -- but not sufficient -- basis for better designs.

(3) As long as managerial perspectives dominate problem formulations, design
tasks, and reward systems, resulting systems will at best improve organizations from a managerial point of view.

(4) Managerial perspectives must therefore be confronted with worker perspectives, and systems must be designed participatively.

(5) Participative designing will raise questions of power, rewards, and
values, in addition to traditionally recognized needs.

(6) Socio-technical designs are not enough. Lasting improvements must also
involve changing values, rewards, and power structures.

(7) Systems designers are, fortunately, not able to control changes in social systems. The future will not make them more able to do so. But

they will -- hopefully -- be more aware of their inability and help organizations to learn and develop from within.

(8)   If there is a role for systems designers and computer departments in the future, that role is as a catalyst, facilitator, and collaborator for change.

REFERENCES

Ashenhust, R.L. (1972). A Report of the ACM Curriculum Committee on Computer Education for Management. Communications of the ACM, May, pp. 363-398.

Bjørn-Andersen, N. and B. Hedberg (1977). Designing Information Systems in an Organizational Perspective. In P.C. Nystrom and W.H. Starbuck (eds.), Prescriptive Models of Organizations. TIMS Studies in the Management Sciences, No. 5, pp. 125-142.

Churchman, C.W. (1971). The Design of Inquiring Systems. Basic Books, New York.

Couger, D. (1973). Curriculum Recommendations for Undergraduate Programs on Information Systems. Communication of the ACM, December.

Hedberg B. (1975). Computer Systems to Support Industrial Democracy. In E. Mumford and H. Sackman (eds.), Human Choice and Computers. North-Holland, pp. 211-230.

Hedberg, B. (1978). The Design and Impact of a Real-Time Computer System. In N. Bjørn-Andersen, B. Hedberg, D. Mercer, E. Mumford and A. Solé (eds.), Systems Design, Work Structure, and Job Satisfaction. Forthcoming.

Hedberg, B. and S. Jönsson (1978). Designing Semi-Confusing Information Systems for Organizations in Changing Environments. Accounting, Organizations, and Society, Vol. 3, No. 1, pp. 47-64.

Hedberg, B. and E. Mumford (1975). The Design of Computer Systems: Man's Vision of Man as an Integral Part of the Systems Design Process. In E. Mumford and H. Sackman (eds.), Human Choice and Computers. North-Holland, pp. 31-59.

Hedberg, B., P.C. Nystrom and W.H. Starbuck (1976). Camping on Seesaws:Prescriptions for a Self-Designing Organization. Administrative Science Quarterly, Vol. 21, No. 1, pp. 41-65.

Hedberg, B., S. Sjöberg and A. Targama (1971). Styrsystem och företagsdemokrati. BAS, Gothenburg, Sweden.

March, J.A. and J.P. Olsen (1976). Ambiguity and Choice in Organizations. Universitetsforlaget, Bergen.

St. Pierre, W. (1975). Classification of Computer Periodicals. Working paper, University of Wisconsin-Milwaukee.

Starbuck, W.H. (1977). Designing Information Systems which are not Supposed to Help Organizations Solve Problems. Working paper, University of Wisconsin-Milwaukee.

Teichroew, D. (1971). Education Related to the Use of Computers in Organizations. Communications of the ACM, September, pp. 573-588.

Weick, K.E. (1969). The Social Psychology of Organizing. Addison-Wesley, Reading, Mass.

DISCUSSION AND COMMENTS ON PAPER PRESENTED BY BO HEDBERG

TILO STEINBRINCK

I should like to take the role of a very conservative manager. That is necessary because the ideas presented by Hedberg are quite interesting, but practical life is different.

My first point is that computerized information systems are not permitted to change existing social structures. Computers are auxiliary equipment, and they are not permitted to change the social life of mankind.

Secondly, computer systems are only communication systems comparable with railway systems, telex systems etc. These did not really change social systems, they only changed the way people communicate.

Thirdly, faults in existing organizations will not be remedied through the introduction of automated systems.

Fourthly, social change will not be made by means of computerization. If the experiment at Volvo has some negative aspects, it cannot be due to computerization.

Fifthly, I have considerable doubt/whether alienation from this new technology by different groups may be prevented by means of socio-technical information systems. Every progress we step in technology brings more alienation. That is inevitable. Therefore, human social systems should be made more easy, more transparent and better understandable. Perhaps that is possible by means of information systems.

However, even in the role of a very conservative dp-manager, I would say that something may be done to improve the situation. We must work in project groups with all parties involved, we must design alternative systems, we must have users to follow the optimizing plan of the system, we must carry out design so as to fit exactly the social structure, and finally we must make sure that we only aim for evolutions and not revolutions.

BO HEDBERG

I appreciate that Steinbrinck makes these remarks as a pretended conservative manager. If many managers hold these views they will invite revolutions rather than evolution in their companies. If we do not see what is happening and keep persuading ourselves that things are in good order and that we can maintain social structure as suggested, we are in for big problems, as norms and values in society are changing and employees' consciousness rises.

We have already a situation where the power balance decided upon by parliament in many industrialized countries is not really reflected inside firms. That represents a risk, and I feel we ought to use computer technology to change the social structure in firms in response to those challenges. Those who control the use of information technology have power, and people begin to understand that. But unions have in my opinion been late in discovering that and developing strategies to share this power. Some unions are now developing their policies and are taking initiatives in that area, however. It is very important that this work continues. The more the managerial attitude presented by Steinbrinck is prevalent, the faster this process is going to develop.

ANDERS PETERSEN

We should not use any kind of technology without from time to time re-evaluating our needs, wishes and way of life. We must learn from our experiences and utilize the new possibilities that technological innovations give in a reasonable way. Hedberg has been through this process and his conclusion is "Sociological and participative designing are dead ends unless they are met by simultaneous changes in values, rewards and powers in the systems that control the development". As I see it, this is a political statement. I should go as far as to say that maybe the statement is right. Maybe life would be easier and better if changes of the power structure were accomplished. But on the other hand, I am very sure that this would also mean new limitations which we would like to change. So, in my opinion we have to live with the fact that there are possibilities and limitations in whatever political system we have. Within the existing framework of our society there are a whole range of unused possibilities for designing better organizations and better jobs. That is the challenge of our work, and that is why most of us like it.

The design model presented by Hedberg in the 'pro-part' of the HLA-case has many good elements. It forces the users to concentrate on their own work situation. It forces them to focus on what they think is a good system. They work almost as professional planners but without taking the limitations into account. But after that they have to look at the limitations and define the resulting system. If the difference between the ideal solution and the modified one is too big we have an excellent basis for discussing the possibilities of taking away some of the limitations because the good arguments have been formulated. However, in this process of defining what constitutes a good job and a good organization, we often get into trouble, because the users disagree among themselves and frequently their view differs from that of the sociological designer.

Therefore, I should like to pose three questions to Hedberg:

1. How do you define a good system and how do you evaluate the characteristics of it?

2. How in your opinion do users define good systems?

3. If user requirements are different from yours, then what?

BO HEDBERG

Those questions are quite tricky. I cannot alone define what is a good system for others. They themselves must participate in defining what is good from their experience and standpoint. However, that does not mean that I do not believe in leadership and expertise. In my perspective, we still need experts and people who take initiatives. But there must be more of a balance. Computer systems of the future should result from design dialogues or negotiations between users and professional designers. This requires that development resources are more equally distributed so that employees can take initiatives and present their own alternatives.

Having said that, I might add as my own opinion that a good system is one that does not last very long. The designer's /job is not to erect systems palaces which will be around for a long time to commemorate the particular design team. Instead designers should facilitate the abandoning of systems. They should encourage processes and self-reliance rather than stability and dependence.

I do not believe that users yet demand these properties of new systems. They are scared by uncontrolled changes and react positively if status quo is preserved. But these demands are going to come as employees consciousness increases and they begin developments of their own.

HAROLD SACKMAN

The underlying philosophy in Hedberg's stimulating paper seems to me to be how to create more humanistic systems. I know that Robert Jungk, who was originally invited to be here, would also have emphasized this key philosophical value of humanistic design. One of the most precious values of democracy for the individual is the right, and the ability, to design and shape one's own future. This is democracy.

Democratic values are very deeply rooted. Hedberg mentioned that the educational establishments in Western democracies have very severe limitations. That is well taken. The main thrust of the philosopher John Dewey is that educational reforms are essentially cultural reforms. The whole culture has to change before significant changes in the educational system are accomplished. So there is a major task ahead in the interplay between this new technology and the social values we hold dearest.

However, the participative techniques we have discussed today are very limited and primitive. Steinbrinck made the very constructive and helpful criticism that participation should not be restricted to the design phase but should be extended to the entire life cycle of a system.

We used to crack a joke back in the late 1950's about the earliest systems that were developed (especially the SAGE command control system). What the systems designer said was, "Stick the system together with glue and rubberbands, whistles and bells, wrap it up in a pretty way, run up to the wall, and heave it over the wall. The users catch it on the other side - and then the system designers run like hell in the other direction. The poor user is stuck with it." All of us have thousands of stories to illustrate this. The important improvement in participation is that we change from design to participation throughout the entire life cycle of a system.

I will go a little farther than Hedberg in emphasizing values, rewards and power that need to be changed in order to achieve successful participative design. I think that leadership is also very important. Knowledge, competence, good organization, intelligent planning, and division of labour are other necessary prerequisites.

It is essential that one does not see the participative approach as a panacea. It has many limitations. Let me be the devil's advocate and indicate some of the problems that plague participative design:

- It takes longer elapsed time

- It is more inefficient to have more people and more groups

- It invites systematic manipulation of individuals and groups

- It increases opportunities for polarization and obstructionism

- It invites mediocrity and superficiality

- It limits creativity, as a vast amount of the social science literature has shown that the committee approach is more likely to be unimaginative

- It politicises the design process which can be dangerously counter-productive

- It represent a higher risk for not arriving at best solutions as we all know that majority opinion can often be wrong

- It particularly needs professionally trained group facilitators that know how to run groups effectively and how to conduct group sensitivity training. You cannot just get people together and have them work smoothly without getting to know each other

This criticism is offered in a positive and constructive way, because I believe, with Winston Churchill, that democracy is the least worst form of government. It is our job to improve democracy as best we can.

There is a keen fellow Pettigrew
Whose apples blossom each day anew
When the question is power
He descends from the tower
And joins in the systems stew.

THE POLITICS OF ORGANISATIONAL CHANGE

Andrew M. Pettigrew

School of Industrial & Business Studies
University of Warwick
Coventry

Starting from the assumption that organisations can profitably be understood as political systems, this paper argues that a key requirement for systems designers in the future will be their capacity to understand and influence the political processes surrounding their attempts to create change. The point is made that changes in the size and cost of computers will reduce the dependency of users on large central systems departments and lead systems designers to take a more active stance in generating and maintaining their power base and managing their boundaries with users and other groups.

The Human Side of Information Processing
N. Bjørn-Andersen, editor
© IAG
North-Holland Publishing Company, 1980

INTRODUCTION

Systems designers are in the business of trying to make changes happen. Like other technical experts such as operational researchers, planners, and organisation development consultants, systems designers are required not only to have a mastery of the technological skills which surround their work but also the social and influencing skills which can translate this technological mastery into economic and socially useful outcomes. This translation process cannot be taken for granted. The history of many systems departments is replete with examples of rationally conceived technical solutions to problems which were never accepted either as solutions or problems outside the walls of the computer department. The research work of Whisler (1970), Powers (1972), Mumford and Pettigrew (1975) and others indicate the gap which often exists between the design of a system and its implementation.

In this paper I shall take a brief look at some of the causes of resistance to technical changes and highlight some of the factors at the individual systems designer level and the computer department level which can facilitate change. A key theme in the analysis will be the recognition by the designer of organisations, not just as systems for processing information, but also as political systems where many of the transactions occuring within the organisation are bounded by and concerned with the acquisition and maintenance of power and status. Given that internal consultants such as computer experts rarely have the formal authority on which they can create the climate for and the reality of change how are they to exert the leverage required to implement technical solutions? The suggestion in this paper is that systems designers need to be sensitive of and active in the political and organisational cultural settings of their work. In short, they need a power base.

In what follows I shall outline what is meant by organisations as political systems, define political behaviour as an individual and group phenomenon and demonstrate how political energy is released in organisations in times of change. The final section of the paper will trace out some of the implications of this analysis for the systems designer both in terms of how individual computer experts generate and maintain their power base and how in more general terms computer departments manage the boundaries with other parts of their organisation.

ORGANISATIONS AS POLITICAL SYSTEMS

An organisation can survive only to the extent it creates and maintains the coalition of support necessary for operation. The same may also be said of sub-systems within an organisation such as a computer department. Survival and most certainly growth in an interdependent world is a function of success in managing boundaries with related systems. In the language of Political Science such related systems are often described as interest groups. Identifying interest groups and the patterns of attitude and relationship between them is the starting point for the analysis of organisations from the political viewpoint.

Interest groups form in organisations around a variety of axes and for a variety of reasons. The most common base from which individuals develop a sense of group identity and interest is from the way functions and activities are divided. Thus in universities individuals will cohere around disciplinary departments and in business groups of production people, salesmen and researchers will see that they have interests to project and protect in their relationships with others. Political consciousness and action, however, does not just emanate from the division of labour in a firm. Depending on the issues of the day groupings of people may form around newcomers and oldtimers, progressives and conservatives, those in favour of growth and those against growth or those in large departments and those in small departments. While in any particular organisation it may be possible to identify the structure of interest group formation that structure is rarely immovable.

Interest groups are continuously evolving in response to intraorganisational and environmental changes. As we shall see one of the key factors likely to disturb any structure of interest group formation is the prospect of technology led change and the appearance on the organisation horizon of a new group of experts pushing those changes.

The major things which separate out interest groups are their preferences and objectives. Interest groups may also acquire a distinctiveness because of their dress and behave differently, (Pettigrew and Bumstead 1976) or because they have the short term time orientation of the production man or the longer term time orientation of the basic researcher (Lawrence and Lorsch 1967). Groups may also have different cognitive styles (Doktor and Hamilton 1973), may make certain assumptions about preferred and even legitimate styles of problem solving (Keen 1977) and may use different languages and attach differential meanings to the same language (Pondy 1976, Pettigrew 1977a). One often hears the person whose advice is spurned remarking if only the users, or the production people or the management or some other grouping had been less 'irrational'. An analytically sounder and more neutral starting point for looking at organisations is not to think of the irrational ones (usually those out there) and the rational ones (us) but to see organisations composed of interest groups each with its own form of rationality and each competing for space in the problem solving and strategy formulation processes of the organisation.

The competition between the carriers of different forms of rationality is of course bounded by certain rules and norms of behaviour. Such competition is also constrained by the existence in most organisations of a dominant interest group and the vocabulary, values, patterns of behaviour, priorities, and preferred styles of problem solving that dominant interest group has embedded into the organisations culture. There are often good commercial reasons why in some organisations the Board is dominated by the star people from the marketing, production or technical functions, or in times of financial stress by accountants. But this means that the representatives of other forms of rationality will have a lesser role in formulating the dominant idea and in influencing the language and content of problem solving in the organisation.

The preceding analysis has indicated that a starting point for analysing organisations as political systems is to identify interest groups within the firm and the patterns of attitudes and relationships between them. This significance of group behaviour should not blind us, however, to the role of individuals in organisational politics. Political processes evolve at the group level from the division of work in the organisation and at the individual level from associated career, reward and status systems. Groups develop interests based on specialized functions and responsibilities; individual careers are bound up with the maintenance and dissolution of certain types of organisational activity and with the distribution of organisational resources. The scarce resources over which groups and individuals may compete include salaries, promotion opportunities, capital expenditure, new equipment, and control over tasks, technologies, people, information, or new areas of a business. At various times claims are made by interest groups and individuals on scarce organisational resources. The scope of the claims is likely to be a reflection of the group or individuals' perception of the criticalness of the resources to its survival and development. The success of any claimant in furthering his interest will be a consequence of his ability to mobilise power around the demands he is making. It is the involvement of interest groups in such demand and support generating processes, which constitutes the political dimension. Political behaviour is defined as behaviour by individuals or, in collective terms, interest groups within an organisation, which makes a claim against the resource sharing system of the organisation.

One crucial and little understood aspect of this process of power mobilisation around interest based demands is the way individuals and groups construct and manage the meanings around the demands they are making for organisational resources. In presenting a demand that resources be allocated in a particular way, perhaps to

buy a new type of computer or to spend project time in a potential user area, the
claimant usually encounters a question about that demands' legitimacy in its particular institutional context. There is clearly a point at which any particular
demand may be unsupportable, and the issue becomes not one of trying to force a
preexisting demand through but determining how the existing demand can be modified
so that its power requirement can be assembled.

In considering what demand for resources is presented and how it is presented and
later modified, issues of legitimacy are likely to be crucial. The degree of legitimacy possessed by an activity in an organisation such as the application of computer technology and the credibility of its individual practitioners is likely to
be a highly diffuse and moveable resource, but one whose significance and unequal
distribution can structure the outcomes of competition for resources. Politics
concerns the creation of legitimacy for certain ideas, values, and demands - not
just action performed as a result of previously acquired legitimacy. The management of meaning refers to a process of symbol construction and value use designed
both to create legitimacy for one's own demands and to 'delegitimize' the demands
of opponents in a resource allocation process. Therefore a fundamental factor in
the life history of a demand will be what does it symbolize, what does it mean, not
only to the party making the demand but to the other interest groups in the process

Key concepts for analysing this process of the management of meaning are symbolism,
language, belief and myth (see Pettigrew 1977a and 1977b for an extended discussion on these concepts). These concepts provide the conceptual link necessary to
understand the relationship between political processes and the organisational
cultural setting in which those political activities occur. Those systems designers who understand the dominant forms of symbolism, language, belief, values and
myths of the organisation which surrounds their work will be in a much more informed position to connect their preferences, technologies, values and styles of
problem solving to that organisation than those designers who do not include political and cultural variables in their framework of diagnosis and action.

ORGANISATIONAL CHANGE AND THE RELEASE OF POLITICAL ENERGY

The previous section has emphasized some of the language of political analysis
and has indicated how divisions form and political processes develop in organisations around the distribution of system relevant scarce resources. Here the
writer will explore some of the reasons why the release of political action is
often associated with change.

Political activity in organisations was found to be particularly associated with
change by Burns & Stalker (1961) and Pettigrew (1973). Since internal consultants
such as systems designers are the initiators of many organisational changes their
activities and plans are inextricably bound up with the politics of change.
Major structural and technical changes, or even the possibilities of them, have
political consequences. Innovations are likely to threaten existing parts of the
working community both by the way they may unscramble current distributions of
resources and by the sheer operational difficulties of absorbing the new skills
and procedures associated with novel patterns of working. Mumford & Pettigrew (1975)
in studies of the purchase and implementation of computer equipment demonstrate
how the innovation process may be used to achieve group or individual objectives
or safeguard group interests, with both computer specialists and users seeking to
use the change situation to promote their own interests and secure more influence
and control in the organisation.

During the planning and implementation of change additional resources may be
created and appear to fall within the jurisdiction of a department or individual
who had previously not been a claimant in a particular area. This department or
its principal representative may see this as an opportunity to increase his power,
status and rewards in the organisation. Others, often the users, may see their

interests threatened by the change, and needs for security or the maintenance of power may provide the impetus for the release of political energy. In all these ways new political energy is released and ultimately the existing distribution of power endangered.

These processes are likely to receive their most volatile expression not, as is often imagined, just at the implementation of changes but during the decision to go ahead with the change (Pettigrew 1973). Constraints may be set during the decision stage which can make resistance and manoeuvre at later stages of the change much less effective. The issue, therefore, is less one of where and when political energy is likely to be released than one of to what extent will it be released within the change process.

It is to be expected that the concern with the existing and future distribution of resources in the firm and the systems of power, status and careers based on those resources will be highly correlated with the extent of the envisaged change. Large scale changes in structure involving the evolution of new departmental groups and the demise of others or the appearance of new technologies may threaten quite fundamentally existing lines of activity and interest. The area of the firm affected by the change may also be a significant independent variable when determining the level of concern with the change and the amount of interest group based energy which is released in stopping or slowing down the change. One indicator of the amount of political energy released might be the amount of time taken in making the decision to go ahead with the change. In a study of a series of computer purchase decisions in a single organisation there was tentative evidence in support of this hypothesis. With each new computer installation the computer technologists gained more influence over the critical as distinct from the peripheral areas of the business. As the technologists moved from peripheral areas to core so they encountered more secure, powerful and vested interests. As they re-defined business activities more within the rationality of computing so the dependency of others upon them increased and their potential power as an interest group became more visible. Thus the level of political energy within the computer department's sphere of activities increased, both from those in the core areas of the business who wished to slow the computer peoples progress, and also from within the computer unit itself as different sub-groups attempted to influence the design of each new installation in such a way that their existing control over it was either maintained or enhanced. (Pettigrew 1973).

Additional momentum is likely to be given to these political processes by the amount of slack in the organisation at any point in time. It is important to know, for example, whether the changes are being made in conditions of growth or zero-growth. The zero-growth situation resembles rather closely some of the conditions of the zero-sum game. If changes are made at the point in time when organisational participants perceive the organisational resource cake to be either fixed or reducing in size, such perceptions are likely to raise people's awareness of the current distribution of resources and therefore what the proposed change can do to that distribution. Conversely the degree of threat created by a change may be less in conditions perceived to be a non zero-sum game or in times of organisational growth when the future might contain the possibilities for increased resources or the same proportion of resources as in the past.

SOURCES OF UNCERTAINTY DURING ORGANISATIONAL CHANGES

In a recent book Zaltman and Duncean (1977 p. 88-89) have summarised much of the research on the sources of resistance to change. Zaltman and Duncan express their arguments in terms of proponents of change (systems designers in our case) and the target system of change (the users). Amongst their general conclusions they indicate that resistance to change occurs when:

1. The change is not compatible with the cultural values of the change target.

2. The change threatens the self esteem and cohesiveness of the target system.

3. The change alters the balance of interdependency between groups and the distribution of power between individuals and groups in the target system.

4. The change involves users acquiring new technical skills and the users do not perceive they have those necessary skills to implement the change.

5. The change target is not clear of the objectives and rationale behind the change and therefore perceives there is not a good chance of successfully achieving their objectives.

6. The change target is not involved in creating the climate surrounding the change, does not feel there is a potential for change in the system, and has little control or influence over the change process.

The above factors, and the others which Zaltman and Duncan mention, all point to various sources of uncertainty, and the management of that uncertainty as being a crucial aspect of the management of organisational change. These uncertainties have been pinpointed in the research on the more specific topic of the implementation of computer technology. Bjørn-Andersen et al. (1979) in reporting the results of an international study of computer systems and work design in banks note how the use of computers in banks has been controlled by the dominant power groups. The banks were careful to control the level of intra organisational uncertainty by protecting both their technical core, the procedures and practices used to carry out the business of banking, and their organisational culture whilst at the same time attempting to reduce a source of uncertainty in their external environment which was affecting their efficiency and increasing their costs, namely, the difficulty of recruiting high calibre staff. One significant consequence of this control strategy, which in some cases meant that the computer experts in the banks were not allowed to introduce advanced systems in which technical objectives predominated, was that the bank clerks were highly approving of the new computer systems.

Earlier research by Mumford and Pettigrew (1975) pinpointed sources of uncertainty and cycles of response and counter response to uncertainty which produced much less approval of technological change than the above studies in banks. The design phase of technologically led change frequently takes place in an environment which is technologically dynamic with new and better methods for solving the problem continually appearing as a consequence of developments in hardware, software and peripheral equipment. Planning and implementation have to embrace a large variety of technical, social and economic factors, many of which may be overlooked until they are forced to management's attention by a danger signal of some kind. In addition the dynamics of this form of innovation and its non-programmed nature lead to political behaviour as groups and individuals seek to use the fluidity of the change situation to promote or protect their own interests. User departments, in particular, experience great uncertainty when faced with new computer systems; frequently they have little experience of either computer technology or large scale change. Coping with it may bring interpersonal stresses which arise from the need to interact with new groups or groups which they normally prefer to keep at a distance. They will have to establish relationships with the computer specialists and are likely to be subject to considerable pressure from top management for fast and successful results. These sources of uncertainty, technical, operational, political and interpersonal lead to actions which may heighten the tensions between the individuals and groups in the change process.

The analysis so far in this paper has defined what we mean by organisations as political systems, discussed political behaviour as an individual and group phenomenon, highlighted why and how political energy is often released in organisations in times of change and indicated the kinds of uncertainties and consequent resistances which have been associated with attempts to introduce computer systems. The remainder of the paper will discuss some of the implications of this analysis for the behaviour of the system designer and the way the computer department links itself with the rest of the organisation.

IMPLICATIONS FOR THE SYSTEMS DESIGNER AND HIS DEPARTMENT

The above analysis has suggested that the systems designer-user relationship takes place in the context of organisational life where political actitivy is pervasive and real. Furthermore, the activities of systems designers, especially in so far as they demand changes in organisations, will affect the distribution of actitivities, status and power and thereby involve both designer and user in those political processes. If that involvement is not proactive, then it will be reactive, as the political behaviour of others acts as a constraint on the range of behaviour possible for both user and designer. A key implication on this line of reasoning is that the effective systems designer requires a knowledge of the political processes in his own organisation and as a minimal condition an <u>awareness</u> of how the particular projects he is working on relate to, and by implication, alter, those processes.

There is, of course, a considerable difference between a systems designer being aware of the political context and consequences of his work and being able to translate that heightened awareness into effective action. Consciousness of the systems repercussions of a change has to be tied to a power base that can facilitate change. But what do we mean by power and in what sense is it realistic for systems designers to accumulate the resources which may make up a power base?

Power is defined here not as an attribute or substance possessed by someone in isolation but as a relational phenomenon. Power is generated, maintained and lost in the context of relationships with others. Power involves the ability of a person or persons to produce outcomes in line with their perceived interests. For the systems designer the capacity to produce those outcomes will be a function of his awareness of, possession and control of and tactical adroitness in utilising certain power resources. Previous research by Pettigrew (1972 and 1975a) on the potential power bases of systems designers and programmers indicates that system relevant expertise, control over information, political access and sensitivity, credibility and the power derived from a cohesive group can be of significance in making and preventing changes from happening. More recent work (Pettigrew & Bumstead 1976 and Pettigrew & Reason 1978) is exploring the extent to which the power bases of internal consultants can be attributed to cultural identification, the capacity of the person initiating changes to understand and use the various beliefs, myths, codes of practice and language systems of the organisation to which he belongs. This aspect of power, developing the right kind of legitimacy, has been attended to earlier on in this paper in the discussion of politics as the management of meaning. Paradoxically in certain organisational cultures it may be that one of the characteristics of an effective initiator of change is that he symbolises to others continuity rather than change.

But it is also crucial to recognise that the power and image of individual systems designers is wrapped up with the power base and legitimacy of the department from which they come. One of the characteristics of many change projects in organisations is they invariably start off with tremendous drive and energy and then falter and peter out on the way. If the change is being pushed by a small group of internal consultants either from a project team or specialist department, the specialists are likely to take on some of the characteristic values of an innovative sub-system. The specialists will exhibit and experience high involvement in the task and unit goals, high energy given to the solution of novel and consequential problems, a strong sense of group identity leading to extensive ingroup social contact in and out of the work place, the development of group rituals often as a way of socialising new members, and unconventional styles of language and dress (Pettigrew 1975b). The effect of these rituals and values is to increase the group: level of awareness of itself and its commitment to its task, and at the same time to separate out the group from its environment. Therein lies one of the central dilemmas of specialist-based attempts to create organisational change. The very mechanisms and processes which give initial erngy to the changes also create countervailing sources of organisational energy to slow **down the process** of change.

This dilemma of activities designed to create commitment within a specialist department, cutting that department off from sectors of its environment, suggests that a further practical implication of this analysis is that specialist units such as computer departments require a policy for boundary management. Boundary management refers to the system of exchanges a department, an activity or a role has with its environment. These exchanges include how the department:

- acquires its inputs (resources) and disposes of its outputs (services)

- how it exercises influence

- how it builds a network of relationships and activates its image

- how it protects its integrity, territory and technological core from environmental pressure and threat

- and how it co-ordinates its activities with other departments, roles or organisations.

Boundary management is an important consideration for all systems but it is particularly crucial for service activities within organisations. Advisory functions do not by definition command line authority, neither can they assume that their advice will always be listened to or their services needed. In this situation the legitimacy of the activity and the credibility of individual practitioners has to be developed and maintained over time if the actitivy is to flourish. The development of the resources which form the power base for carrying out the advisory activity, together with the stance any particular department adopts about where its project activity and client systems ought to be, indeed whether that department actually monitors its environment and formulates policy on such issues, all represent areas of choice and action in this key activity of boundary management. There is some evidence that the advent of smaller, less expensive computers is leading to a decentralisation of control of computer hardware and a lessening of dependency of users and potential users on a central core of computing expertise. If this trend continues, systems designers will have to be ever conscious of their power base and of formulating a strategy for boundary management.

REFERENCES

Bjørn-Andersen, N., B. Hedberg, D. Mercer, E. Mumford and A. Solé (1979). The Impact of Systems Change in Organisations. Sijthoff & Noordhoff International Publishers BV. (Forthcoming).

Burns, T. & G.M. Stalker (1961). The Management of Innovation. Tavistock, London.

Doktor, R. & W.F. Hamilton (1973). Cognitive Style and the Acceptance of Management Science Recommendations. Management Science. Vol. 19, pp. 884-895.

Keen, P.G.W. (1977). Cognitive Style and Career Specialization. Chapter 4 in Van Maanen, J. (ed.), Organizational Careers: Some New Perspectives, Wiley, New York.

Lawrence, P.R. & J.W. Lorsch (1967). Organisation and Environment. Harvard University Press, Cambridge, Mass.

Mumford, Enid & A.M. Pettigrew (1975). Implementing Strategic Decisions. Longman, London.

Pettigrew, A.M. (1972). Information Control as a Power Resource. Sociology, Vol. 6. No. 2 pp. 187-204.

Pettigrew, A.M. (1973). The Politics of Organisational Decision Making. Tavistock, London.

Pettigrew, A.M. (1975a). Towards a Political Theory of Organisational Intervention. Human Relations, Vol. 28. No. 3 pp. 191-208.

Pettigrew, A.M. (1975b). Strategic Aspects of the Management of Specialist Activity. Personnel Review, Vol. 4 pp. 5-13.

Pettigrew, A.M. & D.C. Bumstead (1976). Strategies of Organisation Development in Differing Organisational Contexts. Working Paper. University of Warwick School of Industrial & Business Studies.

Pettigrew, A.M. (1977a). The Creation of Organisational Cultures. Working Paper pp. 77-11. March 1977. European Institute for Advanced Studies in Management, Brussels.

Pettigrew, A.M. (1977b). Strategy Formulation as a Political Process. International Studies of Management and Organization, Vol. VII. No. 2. pp. 78-87.

Pettigrew, A.M. & P.W. Reason (1978). Alternative Interpretations of the Training Officer Role. A Research Study in the Chemical Industry. Working Paper, University of Warwick, School of Industrial & Business Studies.

Pondy, L. (1976). Leadership is a Language Game. Working Paper. College of Commerce & Business, University of Illinois at Champaigne Urbana.

Powers, R. (1972). An Empirical Investigation of Selected Hypotheses related to the Success of Management Information System Projects. Ph.D. Dissertation, University of Minnesota, 1972.

Whisler, Thomas L. (1970). Information Technology and Organisational Change. Wadsworth Publishing Co.,Belmont California.

Zaltman, G. & R. Duncan (1977). Strategies for Planned Change. Wiley, New York.

DISCUSSION AND COMMENTS ON PAPER PRESENTED BY ANDREW PETTIGREW

MAX ELDEN

I should like to point out that I am speaking from experience in the Scandinavian
countries. I would characterize the paper by appending in a management context to
the title. What we have heard about is the politics of organizational change for
systems designers from a management perspective. It has been useful, especially
the ideas of different rationalities and different kinds of languages through whic
interests are articulated. It almost sounds, however, as if the designers have a
relatively apolitical task.

The designers I have talked to are very clear about the power structure in which
they operate and what it is possible for them to do. They are interested in discussing things in technical and economic terms, because for them dealing with the
issue in that context is one way of maintaining their power. So I am seriously
concerned about the extent to which we should help systems designers understand
their power base even better. My guess is that they know it already fairly well
and that we should help others (e.g. users) develop comparable power bases to articulate their own interests. We have some experience with this form of action
research approach in Scandinavia.

However, in the Scandinavian scene one must realize that we have

- labour-management national contracts in which trade unions have
  the right to participate in the design of computer systems,
- shop-stewards that have company paid release of time to become
  experts in data processing,
- a law which gives all employees the right to participate in the
  development of new systems,
- trade unions which command public funds to carry out action
  research about the consequences of automation.

So we are in a situation where trade unions are very strongly involved.

This leads to what could be called the politicalization of organizational change
and the possibility of trade union guided systems development, e.g. in Norway one
leading trade unionist has already begun to talk about the need for licensing the
development of new technologies.

With this in mind I should like to put three brief questions to Pettigrew:

1. What do you see as the relationship between power bases and participation.
   I think it makes sense for people, as we are seeing in Norway, to say 'I
   do not want to participate in systems design. I have too little power in
   relation to the experts and management. If I participate I am likely to
   come out worse'. (I.e. by being a hostage to sanction decisions that they
   cannot influence). We have research showing that this is in fact what u-
   sually happens.

   What do we do in this situation? Incidentally this is a case of what the
   political scientist calls 'symbolic politics'; where one is given symbolic
   rewards but has no real power (e.g. 'hostage effect')

2. We can define politics in many different ways. Pettigrew defined it in
   terms of resource allocation and in terms of the possession of political
   resources that can influence the behaviour of others. But one might also
   talk about politics in terms of vision and values. What is a good society

and what is a good organization, and that would lead us to alternative
ways of designing good social structures? Is action research necessary
here? We have a lot of policy analysis in general. Could we have a policy analysis of systems design? In that case I would require systems analysts to stay with their designs - to follow up for real. Designers should
be kept around to pick up the pieces after the introduction of their system
instead of rushing on to designing the next new system and perpetuating
their same shortcomings on a new group of users.

3. One of the key things which has emerged in American political science in
   the last fifteen years is the importance of "non-decision making" as a
   power strategy. People who have the most power stay in power by defining
   what the public debate is going to be about, e.g. in the United States
   for many years there was no debate about race issues and no debate about
   women. That was defined as irrelevant. There is much power in defining
   what is relevant. Non-decision-making is going to be an increasing problem for systems designers because workers and trade unions have previously been defined as non-relevant in systems design. This has changed fundamentally in Scandinavia but what does this really imply for politics
   of organizational decision-making? To what extent are productive organisations equivalent to civic policies, for example we do not have majority
   votes on systems design, not yet anyway.

ROLF HØYER

A realist self-conception, or self understanding, is generally very important and
valuable. It is generally regarded as a main characteristic of a mentally sound
person. A criterion of a confused, or mentally ill person is a massive unrealistic
conception of self in the interrelationships with others. This is very important
to realize if one wants to succeed in a business enterprise, as a line executive
or as a systems designer. The American psychologist, Goffman, among others, has
illuminated these issues, using the role concept, particularly in the book "Life
as a Stage". Later Berne emphasizes this, notably in his book "Games People Play".

Realistic role conception and understanding of the games within the role systems
are important knowledge for any ambitious systems desinger. The 'power game' is
here a subset of the more general role game people play.

In his paper Pettigrew has given a valuable contribution to the process of self
understanding of system designers, as he has illuminated the power system and the
power game within a business organization, and has even suggested normative rules
on behalf of the system designer for how to survive in the power jungle. We learn
from his lecture not only that "if you can't beat'em, join them", but "if you can't
beat'em, join those with the best proper power base, and identify and avoid those
with power bases who are aiming their weapons at you", which indeed sounds as a
reasonable guidance.

However, I feel uncertain whether this is specific for the systems designers. I
think it is valid for most kinds of change agents. They may regard this as a necessary strategy for survival and success within a business environment.

To go even further, could it be valid knowledge for every business executive?
Knowing and mastering the power game within an organization is often claimed to be
the best way for successful implementation of your ideas, and even for your progress and success. The Italian 'organization researcher', Machiavelli, explored
these issues in the 16th century.

However, I am not at all interested in enhancing the power base of the systems designers. On the contrary, in my work, I am frequently, as an organizational consultant, confronted with the task of reducing and fighting the immense power position

of the system designers.

Actually, I think that quite frequently they succeed too easily with very dubious
innovations. In practice, we observe that new computer systems deteriorate existi
power bases, and that the possibilities of self control and autonomy in work grou
are severely reduced.

As a result of the implementation of extensive computer systems, the amount of in
formal control in the hands of the individual employees or work groups is signifi
cantly diminished. Unfortunately, the loosers in this power game have very poor
weapons with which to defend their power bases and their autonomy against the far
more influential and powerful change agent, the systems designer.

Therefore, instead of being solely interested in building kingdoms of formalized
computer systems, designers should also be interested in the frequent deteriorati
in the quality of working life of the users. In this connection one should rather
discuss how to reduce the power base of the system designer, and how to build up
a stronger power base among employees as a weapon against the carriers of the tec
nology.

Power to the people - instead of more power to the powerful!

However, much power will always remain in the hands of the systems designers, and
we must ask in the interests of whom the power of the systems designers is used?
In other words: To whom does the loyalty of the systems designer belong? To top
management and to its demands (or rather to their perception of the objectives of
top management), or to the benefit of his own particular profession or ego? Or is
he concerned with justice within the organization, e.g. with power equalization
issues as we see in other activities in the strive for industrial democracy?

Accordingly, the power issue is not just a game, it is rather a question of moral
and values.

ANDREW PETTIGREW

Elden suggested that the frame of analysis presented necessarily represents a managerial view of the situation. I do not think that is true. The whole point of
looking at interest groups, of looking at the distribution of power and looking
at the way power is developed and used, is to identify alternative interest groups
both within the organization and outside the organization. In fact, an important
part of my talk was to show how interest groups in society influence the stances
that were adopted by interest groups within the firm. So I think that any analysi
which starts off by analysing interest groups is likely to uncover the very existence of multiple interest groups and would help one trying to understand their
value positions and their power bases.

This kind of thinking would lead one on to describe the relationship between political resources and participation. This relationship is not clear-cut, but there
is no doubt that the moment trade unions start participating in systems design,
they weaken their bargaining position as an interest group.

I should like to address more directly the question about whether political resources are related to participation. I think if one looks at what is going on in
British society at the moment one can see precisely how this fight for power bases
is taking place.

I think you are much farther ahead in Norway, Sweden and Denmark as you are actua
ly implementing different types of participation. We are still in the decision-to-
go-ahead stage in the UK and are debating what exactly should be the mechanisms
through which participation and democracy may actually be carried out. The solutic

chosen is obviously crucial for the different interest groups in terms of their actual capacity to influence.

In fact, most of the debate in UK is precisely about the nature of participation and the specific form it might take, because people know that once they get trapped into some kinds of mechanisms and processes this will have a very significant impact on the actual distribution of power later on in the participation process.

The third point that Elden made concerned whether the analysis could support attempts to expose non-decision making. One way to look at that is by looking at politics as the management of meaning. Especially this relates to how dominant interest groups try to define the core values, the priorities, the language, the symbols, and the myths which other people in sense are expected to accept. Of course this is a much more subtle view of the power process than the approach which only views power in terms of the possession, control and tactical use of various power resources.

As regards the comment made by Høyer, I am surprised by the catagorical statement that systems designers have immense power. I do not think that is true in the UK. In fact, if one looks at the history of many mangement services departments one finds a whole catalogue of attempts to introduce changes, which got off with tremendous drive, energy and momentum and yet were thoroughly and inevitably shunted off into the sidings.

Finally, I should like to comment upon whose pocket the systems designers are in. That is important to ask for any individual designer. Again I think there is great variability in how people interpret their position. E.g. one will find organizational development groups which deliberately adopt the values of top management and develop and build very close relationships with the top power system of the organization. This has of course very significant consequences both in ethical terms and in more strategic terms. Often those groups, one finds, do not survive for such a long time as the groups which adopt the stance that organizational development ought to be available to a variety of interest groups in the firm and accordingly build relationships across interest groups and across the hierarchy and in doing that build into their own work multiple value positions.

Ulrich Briefs is very far seeing
Soon realized where computers were leading
Pull together brothers jolly
Let's avoid computer folly
For the work of man must be fulfilling.

THE IMPACT OF COMPUTERIZATION ON THE WORKING CLASS
AND THE ROLE OF TRADE UNIONS

Ulrich Briefs

Wirtschafts und Sozialwissenschaftliches
Institut des Deutschen Gewerkschaftsbundes
Düsseldorf, Germany

Computerization has to be considered as a
process intimately linked to the conditions
of economic stagnation and crisis. It is
a strategy management uses to react to un-
favorable conditions in the environment
of business organizations.
In a social system which is based on the
exploitation of living human labor this
strategy produces overwhelming negative
consequences for the working class.
Trade unions will have to defend the interests of the working class by an enlargement of collective bargaining and by a policy to promote full employment. Furthermore they will have to develop new concepts of human work and qualifications. A
further prerequisite is a thorough democratization of production and control in
the economy as well as a substantial modification of the internal structures of the
unions.

The Human Side of Information Processing
N. Bjørn Andersen, editor
© IAG
North-Holland Publishing Company, 1980

COMPUTERIZATION, ECONOMIC STAGNATION AND CRISES

Computerization is one of the most dynamic, universal and far-reaching socio-technical processes the industrial world has ever known. It is about to transform the working and living conditions of large parts, if not the majority, of the populations of developed countries and increasingly of large parts in the less developed countries.

Computerization as a global process can be looked at from two points of view: The first is computerization as a global process, embedded in the more general process of technological development, correlated to industrial and economic growth and crises etc. The second is computerization as a typical strategy, as a system of objectives, actions, and perspectives of definite social agents to cope with specific conditions in their economic, social, political, and natural environment.

The first aspect (computerization as a global national and even international process) links it to the general economic mechanism of the capitalist countries. The basic fact of this mechanism in its present state is that a conjunction of conditions has been established which consists of economic crises and long-term stagnation on one side and of a high level rate of technological innovation (and computerization is one of the main moments, if not the dominating moment of this global innovative process) on the other side. To cite the example of the FRG (which o̶ the international level is nevertheless not the country which is worst off) we had an 8% real growth rate througout the 50s, a 5% growth in the 60s and we are down to 3% in the 70s.

At the same time we have an annual productivity increase of about 4 to 5%, but this macro-economic figure does not tell the full truth. More detailed information tells a story of rapidly increasing numbers of annual patent applications and of a shortening in the time-lag between the basic invention in the laboratory and its application as marketable goods.

If we look at the global process of computerization the basic fact is that computerization has attained its full momentum in a time, when real growth on a national level has markedly dropped below productivity increase. The essential implication of this fact is, of course, that computerization is going on in a society in which insufficient growth and accelerated innovative advances add to existing unemployment. This creates very gloomy perspectives for the working class and probably confronts trade unions and the progressive political forces with problems not witnessed until a few years ago.

To cite again the example of the FRG, we had to witness the transition from a long-established state of full-employment to a state of mass unemployment within only two years. We fear that the present unemployment, about 1 million out of a working force of some 20 millions, (the labour market statistics as in all capitalist countries, however, somewhat underrate the real loss of productive and working facilities) will have doubled by the mid-80s and possibly trebled by the beginning of the 90s.

By the way, corresponding rates of unemployment already exist in the US and in Canada, countries which are still somewhat in advance technologically.

So a few questions have to be raised:

1. Can we consider it a pure coincidence that computerization became a global mass process a few years before the present global process of economic deterioration started?

2. Is it accidental that in the FRG in the economic crisis from 1975 to now, for the first time in the after-war history, large scale unemployment among white collar workers has arisen?

3. In the FRG clerical workers are at present the professional group most af-
    fected by unemployment; has that nothing to do with the acceleration of com-
    puterization in recent years?

4. The years of economic crisis and stagnation have been particularly successful
    years for the producers of computer equipment, software etc.; is this a pro-
    cess entirely separated from the arrival and perseverance of adverse economic
    conditions?[1)]

However, we have to admit that a coincidence of computerization with the conditions
of economic crisis and stagnation may not a-priori indicate a causal relationship,
but it nevertheless at least suggests a very intimate penetration of the global process of computerization and of economic deterioration.

The further analysis of this complex relationship therefore leads us to the constituent and active parts of the capitalist social and economic system; the structure
of different and largely autonomous business organizations (and the state bodies,
how ever active their role may be) and their action rules. Computerization reveals
itself in this context as a strategy which is a deliberately adopted,planned, co-
ordinated way of acting under conditions of uncertainty, adopted by business organizations to cope with the adverse conditions in their economic, social, political
environment.

Stagnation and economic crises on the level of the national economic systems and,
hence necessarily on the international level, are identical to the prevalence of
similar conditions in a great number of individual markets, pushing firms and organizations to specific "strategies".- Accelerated computerization is one of them.

The main strategy of most firms in such a situation has to be a policy of cutting
costs and especially of cutting overhead costs and/or increasing efficiency of the
different sub-units. Computerization is principally a means to cut costs (perhaps
not immediately because of a flat learning curve of a management which nevertheless
considers itself as sophisticated) then at least in the medium-term. Even though
it adds to the share of overhead costs it is a means to reduce specific overhead
costs by introducing more standardization, uniformity, coordination into organizational structures. It is also a means by which to exert more control, closer
inspection, and more disciplinary pressure on the workers and especially on the
white collar workers who traditionally were not so deeply affected by these strategies.[2)]

Computerization thus reveals itself as a management strategy to cope with adverse
economic conditions according to what Marx called the "relative surplus" concept,
i.e. in the absence of market potentials for further growth, firms have to look inside themselves for further growth (or a stabilization) of their profits or better,
of their profit rates. This is the rationale of increased rationalization and accelerated innovative processes, as it is also the major rationale of other restructuring strategies, e.g. concentration, centralization and bureaucratization.

Some further points may be added to this view of the economic aspects of computerization:

1. Computerization at the level of a business firm's strategies is linked to con-
    centration and, of course, bureaucratization.

---

1) 1977 brought for computer sales a growth of far more than 30%. From the early
   70s onward the share of rationalization investment in total investment has more
   than doubled. - in the first after-war crisis in 1966/7 white collar workers
   were not at all affected; in 1976 more than 40% of all unemployed workers were
   white collar workers.

2) Productivity during the last centure is estimated to have increased by 1500% in
   the productive sphere and by 150% in the administrative sphere.

Computerization probably furnishes the necessary material basis for the maintenance and viability of control of the large-scale enterprises or monopolies
dominating all western economic systems.

Computerization creates possibilities for centralized control and supervision
undreamt-of until the present day. Computerization facilitates the spread of
bureaucratic structures and systems, and more detailed monitoring and control
of productive activities. (Bjørn-Andersen + Eason 1979).

2. Computerization absorbs profits which increasingly do not find more productive
    outlets. If a 25 billion DM corporation spends 4% of its turnover on computer
    equipment, this constitutes an investment of about 1 billion DM.[3] Even if we
    account for a personnel expenditure's share of 80% we still get an annual in-
    vestment sum of about 200 million DM. And in terms of working process dimen-
    sions, the process of increasing capital absorption by computerization means
    the accelerated substitution of living human work by dead work with all its
    consequences for the working-class.

3. Computerization has become a field for major government activities in quite
    different forms. These cover the range from more indirect promotion of compute
    rization by subsidies within the defense budgets as in the US to deliberate
    governmental programmes aimed at nursing national computer industries as in
    France (plan calcul) and the FRG (three "Dataverarbeitungsprogramme", a public
    expenditure of more than 3 billion DM) and to global all-embracing national
    schemes of computerization as in Japan. Computerization reveals itself thus as
    one of the major technological fields in which increasingly governmental acti-
    vities and business industries are merging. If the concept of the "state mono-
    polist capitalism" describes an existing or emerging reality, computerization
    may be one of its strongest sources of factual evidence.

But before we examine the consequences for the working-class and the response of
trade unions, we have to look briefly at the intimate link which connects the conditions of economic stagnation and crises, and the "strategies" (and among them:
the computerization strategy) of the decisive actors of the capitalist system.
These "strategies" respond to the environmental conditions but at the same time the
environmental conditions are largely generated and reproduced by these strategies.

Every worker made redundant, every percentage by which an individual firm's total
wages' sum is reduced, with or without computers, is a drop in effective demand
and this clearly tends to reinforce market stagnation. Of greater importance, every
worker thrown out of his job is a drop with regard to the production of goods and
services which thereby depresses the overall volume of "use values" which serve
to "realize" themselves in the market transactions. But the most important fact in
this context is that the worker is necessarily a loss with regard to the overall
mass of profits, at least as far as he had before been adding, how ever, indirectly,
at least, to the value of production.

Thus by adopting the enumerated strategies (and among them we have to see the computerization strategy as part of enforced rationalization) in order to get along
under adverse economic conditions the firms in their totality create and reproduce
these adverse conditions.

By fighting against the pressure on their profit rates, by computerization and othe
strategies, they create and enforce this pressure. The more successful these strategies for the individual firm, the more gloomy are the perspectives for the economic system, consequently also for its political supra-structure and the working-
class.

---

3) The final share of expenditure for "Management-Information-Systems" and organizational restructuration was estimated towards the end of the 60s by a German
   IBM management board member in the range of 4 to 5% of turnover.

The processes of computerization are thus subject to contradictions internal to the capitalist mode of production. By processes marked by the same contradictions they will contribute to a universal infrastructure of the vast majority of activities in a society which is increasingly subject to conditions of economic stagnation and crises.

In this context it will transform the working and living conditions of large parts of the population. Not only will the effects be seen on the white collar workers, where the influence of computerization has been obvious for some years, but also, as micro-processor developments show, for a substantial part of the population of blue collar workers.

This process will, to summarize results of former analyses (Briefs 1976), create a universal computerized infrastructure which will

- penetrate deeply into the processes of individual and collective work
- provide a basis for large scale integration of other technologies and contribute to the formation of more and more complex technological systems
- furnish the basis for the bureaucratic control and the monitoring of complex productive and social systems by and in the interest of the owners and management of these systems.

Furthermore, computerization will efficiently contribute to the spreading of systems of public control which intrude deeply into the personal rights of the citizens and give anonymous governmental bodies a power of repression which is hardly controllable under the given conditions.

Quite a few tendencies indicate that there will be a spread of similar systems in privately controlled economic units. Probably, there will be an increasing mutual penetration of public and private control systems.

As "employed" persons, workers are particularly subject to control by these bureaucracies, because they have to furnish information and data the use of which they cannot control in view of the "structures" (e.g. power relations) in business organizations.

These perspectives indicate the major areas of consequences for the working-class and should therefore indicate major areas of concern for trade unions.

CONSEQUENCES OF COMPUTERIZATION FOR THE WORKING CLASS

The West-German trade-union movement has not been one of those inclined to resort rapidly to strike action, but this year it has had to fight the consequences of technological change in two strike movements:

- The first was the fight of the Printers' Union against the abolition of jobs in the printing industry due to the introduction of automatic type setting systems.
- The second was the fight of the Metalworkers' Union against large-scale downgrading of workers induced by the introduction of microprocessors and of electronic systems of production control.

These two strikes have been of a prototype character, They indicate the two main directions in which problems will increasingly arise for the working class and the trade unions,

- the employment issue or as we prefer to call it: "the right to work" issue
- the total or partial destruction of qualifications and of possibilities to contribute to production in a reasonable and human way.

These problems, however, are not new ones. They are in principal as old as the capitalist mode of production. In the FRG especially the after-war period of re-construction and of rapid growth possibly obscured consciousness of these facts for some time.

The particular problem generated by computerization is caused by the two movement dealt with earlier. These are the historical coincidence of computerization with a phase of economic stagnation (a coincidence which was demonstrated not to be en tirely accidental) and the particular "use value" of computer equipment to substi tute intelligent human work.

With regard to the employment issue we have to express far-reaching apprehensions:

- If out of 5 million workers employed in correspondance activities (2 million of them being female typists) only 20% are made redundant, this alone will double the present (statistical) volume of umemployment. Some experts talk about a "defeminization" of office work.

- Though it is altogether unpredictable how many jobs will be abolished by complex data base systems, production control and information systems, computer aided design, inventory control systems, point of sales systems, electronic funds transfer systems etc., there will necessarily be a heavy reduction of the number of jobs in many of the activities affected by these and similar systems.

It is of course unsatisfactory to express apprehensions without being in a positio to give at least a rough but reliable quantitative framework. I think, however, that we have quite simply to learn a lesson from the grotesque inefficiency of the economic "sciences" to produce any reliable forecast on economic developments, an inefficiency which apparently is not all reduced by computerization.[4]

On the other hand, even if we cannot, just in the short-term, predict the future within the capitalist mode of production, we have the experience on the shopfloor of the workers themselves which is not denied by any reasonable computer manager that computer systems do abolish jobs. Individual reports indicate a range from 20 to 50% in white collar fields concerned and from virtually nothing to 40% in some blue collar fields. And we have to consider computers as a technology which is far from having reached its peak in application or efficiency.

The strongest evidence, however, comes in my view out of personal experience as a systems designer: computer systems quite simply replace human activities by machine activities. The large majority of computer applications are of this character and do not introduce additional activities.[5]

So I think there is sufficient evidence to conclude that computers will continue to substantially reduce the number of jobs in the future if the present conditions prevail.

---

4) In the FRG we presently have more than 30,000 computers and an accumulated investment in computers of certainly more than 60 billion DM. Nevertheless it is apparently impossible to predict next year's g.n.p. growth rate with a sufficient reliability. The federal government in January 1973 published a projection up to 1977 forecasting an annual average g.n.p. growth rate between 4.2 and 4.8 and an unemployment rate between 1.0 and 1.2 (growth rate attained at about 2.5% and from 1975 unemployment rate between 4 and 5%).

5) One of the basic wrong assumptions with regard to computerization was that the labour-saving effects could be compensated by the production of "more information" in the "information society". This assumption neglects the basic fact that "information" has to be relevant, has to be connected to actions, to real processes, it probably neglects the other fact, too, that in quite a few realms we have not too little but too much information.

The picture is perhaps even more opaque with regard to the qualifications issue. We know that computerization has created a vast range of stimulating jobs requiring new qualifications. We observe that in the implementation phase of quite a few computer systems groups of workers have to be ready to substitute machine functions by human work in cases of breakdown. We witness management complain of a certain misuse of computer systems, mainly routine work and repetitive transactions being assumed by computers. Do these movements indicate that computerization, instead of abolishing qualified jobs, relieves workers from boring work and gives quite a few of them more highly qualified jobs?

We have to state that computerization has effects in both directions. It creates new challenging jobs and demands more scientific qualifications, and it dequalifies workers, destroys existing qualifications, and creates a large number of marginal, boring activities with low specific qualification requirements.

Sometimes we even find that tendencies towards dequalification are confronted with tendencies towards more qualification even for the same persons.

So the overall picture with regard to the qualification issue is quite complex and presently full of contradictions. But if we try to sum up the experience to date and to extrapolate from the logic of computer systems design we have to state that the overall consequence of computerization in the qualification field leads to a tripolarization of the labour force:

1. A minority of highly qualified specialists, most of them probably college-trained, will have to meet higher qualification standards. These qualification standards will undergo a more rapid change than in the past and these workers will be put under a certain qualification pressure. The concept of life-long-learning comes in here as kind of a permanent threat and pressure.

2. A large majority of workers will be subject to working conditions which require much less specific and professional qualification than in the past. They will be performing more or less marginal and boring activities in complex man-machine-systems, where the process of work is dominated by the logic of the electronic system. These workers will be exposed to "qualification" requirements related to such "extrafunctional" qualifications as more regularity, discipline, adaptability and of course tolerance of frustration. There will be no need for them to understand the internal mechanism and structures of systems because these will be mainly maintained and developed by the specialist elite mentioned before. Life-long-learning for them means a permanent process of learning more or less trivial operations without continuity and logic.

3. An increasing number of unemployed workers who will come mainly but not exclusively from those who have been in the majority of semi-skilled workers mentioned above.

Computerization thus seems to mean the end of prefessionalism especially in clerical work. The typical white collar worker embodying a definite set of functional and extrafunctional qualifications and having accumulated a sound material knowledge in his line of profession will cede his place to the semi-skilled office worker. This worker will have a broad, but rather shallow training in school and will have no chance of acquiring any substantial functional knowledge in any line of activity.

A new but not so well integrated professional group of computer specialists will emerge. However, with increasing maturity of computers and increasing standardization and uniformity of business organizations, their numbers, too, will be reduced, and they too will increasingly be split into a privileged few and a large majority who are increasingly under social pressure.

But this process, too, is not new. One of the fathers of computers, Charles Bab-
bage, described it in the 19th century. From the work of Harry Braverman we now
have long-term evidence from the most developed capitalist country, the USA.

And we have, of course, the work of Karl Marx, who described this process as a
necessary consequence of the development of the capitalist mode of production
against the background of the technology of his days.

Computerization makes the process of degradation of human work more universal and
more powerful and it affects realms of human work hitherto not affected. It affects intelligent human work. In its principles, however, it is not new. Every
comparable technology has the same repercussions if it is developed and applied
under the conditions of the capitalist mode of production which is based on the
exploitation of human beings.

The employment and the qualification issues, however, are not the only areas in
which computerization will deeply affect the working class.

Three other kinds of consequences may be added;

1.   the impacts which are exerted to speed up work processes, making them more
     efficient, more regular and sometimes more flexible. The systems define
     work pace especially for the vast majority of marginal workers in man-ma-
     chine-systems;

2.   computer systems with their capital intensity will demand around the clock
     work to a much higher degree than in the traditional office thus introducing
     night work and shift work in offices;

3.   the impacts of complex systems of planning and control which enable a much mo
     subtle monitoring of efficiency factors and of organization of activities
     than was possible hitherto.

The latter impact will not be limited to immediate aspects of work performance but
will expand to cover personal attributes and behaviour.

It will be possible to get personality profiles and other data relevant to the
worker or jobholder. This data can be obtained by constant monitoring of his activities and behaviour and by the information furnished by medical inspection on
the shop floor, by sociological and psychological experts. Some still rather crude
but nevertheless efficient steps in this direction have been taken already.

In this context it will be possible not only to control his activities as a worker
but also his political behaviour, e.g. by a more efficient processing and transmission of all sorts of "black lists". One of the most threatening features within
the context of this aspect of computer use is thus the possibility to transport
data on workers quickly and cheaply from one firm to the other. George Orwell's
"Big Brother" thus seems to be not too far away, at least with regard to the normal workers' situation.

Thus we see that computerization offers the basis for a firmer grip on the worker
and especially on the office workers in two ways:

- the transformation of the mass of workers, especially of office workers into
  marginal workers performing highly 'Taylorized' activities

- an increase of the degree of control exerted on all workers.

Both effects have to be considered jointly. Tendencies towards increased splitting
and stratification (by concentration, centralization and bureaucratization of decision-making) at the same time will enforce the atomization of work-force and

hence foster attitudes of desolidarization and isolation. It depends on trade-union organization strategies whether this atomization can be replaced by class consciousness.

COMPUTERIZATION WILL BRING NEW DANGERS AND CHALLENGES FOR TRADE UNIONS

Computerization will necessarily bring new conditions for trade unions' activities, too, and it will by this means also affect the internal structures of unions.

Towards a new understanding of "work"

One already marked impact will be a further influx of white collar workers to trade-union organizations. The mass of these workers will be semi-skilled office workers or qualified office workers threatened by dequalification due to the increased spreading of complex computer systems.

One of the main impacts of computerization on the trade unions thus will be an enforced re-orientation towards un- and semiskilled work and a loss of some well-established and valuable traditions of professional unionism.

In this context one of the primary tasks of trade unions will be to conserve as much as possible of the consciousness and pride as producers of skilled workers. This will probably only be possible by introducing the social dimension of work in this notion of "producers' pride": the fantastic achievements of modern technology are not produced by individual workers but by the working-class as an organic body, of which the individual worker is a part.

Furthermore, they will have to transfer as much as possible of this "producers' pride" into new ideas and conception of work, of the division of labour and these new conceptions of qualifications will have to be elaborated by the workers themselves.

The Trade Union's task will be to organize the process of elaboration of these concepts by the workers themselves. This shift towards the organization of discussion processes will push trade unions towards new relations between their bases (rank-and-file membership) and their bureaucratic apparatus.

In view of the increasing 'Taylorization' of work, a rather new process in the office realms, wholistic conceptions of tasks will have to be developed, wholistic with regard to the range of functions to be performed in a job and wholistic with regard to the personality profile of workers. And this is, as Marx put it, a personality which is "rich of relations and rich of qualities".

Computers again come in here as a technology which in principle can be a facility for these wholistic tasks if conditions allow for the use of a larger share of social surplus-value for these purposes. So a further task for the trade unions will be to press for a sufficient direct or indirect allocation of surplus for these purposes.

The fight against frustration and resignation

A further kind of necessary reaction will be protective measures with regard to jobs, with respect to the intensification of work, to stress and other threats to the physical and psychical health of workers. Probably the psychological dimensions of this problem will become a central concern of Trade Unions. They will be concerned with frustration and tolerance of frustration, the internal stability of workers who have to work without knowing what is going on in the man-machine system of which they are parts, who have been exposed to boring tasks for years and decades, and to feelings of being without power and influence to gear their own work and life. One of the trade unions' most difficult but also challenging tasks will therefore be to develop a new understanding of the meaning of work.

In addition to this there will be a spread of fear, anxiety, and resignation in th mass of workers. In the FRG for instance 1 out of 4 workers has been without a job within the last 4 years. Unemployment and being out of a job will be an experience of the majority of workers and this will deeply affect not only the workers themselves but also their wives and children who are even more helpless. So trade union roles will partially be changed into something in the direction of social therapy, i.e. backing and helping their members and their members' families.

Consequently, one of the further reactions of trade unions will have to be to push for more social protection by public bodies and the organization of trade unions' own facilities for these tasks.

New contents in collective bargaining

With regard to the classical system of activities of trade unions in collective bargaining they will have to envisage

1.   a hard policy on manning agreements, a policy which has already been adopted in its basic lines by the trade unions in West-Germany

2.   a spreading policy of fixing maximum norms with regard to stress variables and of minimum norms with regard to variables such as the length of work cycles etc.

3.   a policy of prescribing minimum job requirements, a more equal distribution of tasks, more variety in work, and a certain right to intervene in the organization of systems and jobs.

One further probable strategy could be that adopted already by the Italian unions: to demand the maintenance and enlargement of qualifications by securing equal and substantial qualification opportunities for all workers; some Italian unions for example have got 150 hours/year for every worker, to be used for re-qualification measures. Trade unions will have to ask themselves whether a policy of emancipation of training from direct work requirements will have to be envisaged.

The emancipation effect will of course only really be effective if it is not the business organization alone which determines the contents of the programmes tending to re-qualification. One of the new tasks for trade unions will therefore be to negotiate agreements relating to this requirement, to look after the execution of these agreements, to provide for a "co-determination" of workers, and to contribute to these programmes in a very substantial way.

In relation to computer development, this will mean that trade-unions will have to provide for a permanent exchange of views and information between the different fractions of the "work body": the computer specialists, the organizational specialists and the workers.

The need for a full-employment policy

One indispensable prerequisite for these changes is a policy guaranteeing the "right to work" for everyone.

It is not the place here to discuss the different recipees for full-employment proposed by trade unions. The West-German trade union movement in order "to re-establish full-employment" presently demands

- a policy of stimulation of "qualitative growth" (essentially by public investment)

- reduction of work-hours

- a policy for a social domination of productivity development

The latter point is still of a rather sketchy character.

The dilemma within trade unions' militancy versus co-operation

In my view, with regard to the "right-to-work" issue there will be a polarization within trade unions into those which follow a more or less Keynesian way and those who push towards a radical alteration of the basic structures of the economic system, e.g. by a policy of socialization. Within the first group we will have a strong tendency towards active cooperation in the promotion of new technologies and especially of computerization.

To the degree in which this co-operation will be effective, there will be an increasing dilemma for unions which on one hand have to defend their members' interests by militant action as for example by strikes and on the other hand are inclined to co-operation.

This span of activities and the dilemma embedded in it will be a main characteristic of trade union policies:

- on one hand the need to protect workers from the dramatic consequences of computerization: unemployment, degradation of work, intensification of work pressure, and the erosion of rights to participate. This protection will increasingly demand direct mass strike action and other forms of overt social fights (occupation of shops, work-to-rule, sabotage, partial strikes etc.)
- on the other hand the need and the pressure of large parts of the membership for participation within the framework of a capitalist society in systems design, investment decision-making processes and training activities. Consequently this is a pressure to be positive, to be constructive and to be co-operative with regard to computerization.

The dilemma of trade unions will be that capital and state (the latter pressed by the national industrial groups concerned and deeply involved in the promotion of computerization) will offer many opportunities to co-operate. This will intrigue trade unions into the policy of the monopolies which largely dominate and set the pace in computerization. (Briefs 1976)

According to these two main directions of trade unions development we shall probably see a gap deeper than it is at present. This will be between those trade union movements adopting a militant policy of workers' protection against the consequences of computerization and those trade unions heading for more co-operation and joint management of the consequences of technological change. Probably only a small fraction of the first group of trade unions will be capable of designing a perspective for the workers and human work.

Trade union approaches to control computerization

To sum up, two main challenges for trade unions in capitalist countries will arise,

- workers' protection against the consequences of computerization
- the transformation of the economic and political structures generating and determining the definite patterns of computer development

Autonomous action of trade unions, mobilization of the workers, an emancipation of trade unions' ideologies from bourgeois thinking and a policy of distance to state action in this context will be of much more importance than in the past.

With regard to computerization the following basic lines of trade union policy may emerge in view of the far-reaching problems created by computerization:

1.   protection against the heavy loss of jobs by manning agreements, interference
     with investment decisions in computers etc.

2.   protection against the erosion of qualifications by emancipation of re-quali-
     fication measures heading somewhat towards a broader spread of understanding
     of the internal mechanisms of computer systems as well as of their organiza-
     tional consequences. Collective agreements on a national level and agree-
     ments on a medium-range plan for re-qualification measures could be particu-
     larly helpful

3.   control of the systems' design process and of the production of computer de-
     vices; one of the West-German unions has proposed the installation of public
     "supervision councils" with regard to computerization. One of the prerequi-
     sites of this is a large scale policy of creating insight into the shopfloor
     consequences of computerization

4.   the demand for a state policy which at least equilizes the expenditure on
     computer development and upon the mastering of its social consequences.

5.   socialization of the important parts of computer production and application
     units (the latter if they are operating in an isolated way, e.g. major soft-
     ware firms)

6.   the creation of a permanent discussion process and of adequate institutions
     for this process between workers producing computers and related devices and
     the users and other workers concerned in the different activity lines in
     which computer systems are applied

7.   a national planning scheme with regard to priorities of computerization, in-
     vestment to be made in computerization and the avoidance of negative social
     consequences.

These different elements would have to be combined in a truly "socio-technical
system" in which the producers in all branches themselves discuss and determine
the directions, the speed and the consequences of computerization in a frank and
democratic way. This, too, will be a necessary prerequisite for the full utilization of the positive and productive potential of computerization and it will contribute to the avoidance of computer systems which are a means of greater repression.

CONCLUSION

The process depicted - with its consequences for the working class and the trade
unions - is not so much caused by computer systems or by computerization as technological phenomena, though some of the impacts described have intimately to do
with the very material properties of the systems.

The essential fact is that computerization is going on under the conditions of an
economic system hit by economic crises and stagnation and relying on the exploitation of living human labour.

Nevertheless there are - in a nucleus form but visible - indications with respect
to positive perspectives at least for some groups of workers, e.g. by computer use

- the existing division of labour is questioned

- more and deeper training is obviously added

- decentralization of operations is to some degree promoted

- facilities for control, planning and self-management activities in the workplace are provided

- more experimentation and search for new "use values" appears possible
- the production of a greater variety of goods and services may be attainable.

So, computerization could lead to materially quite different results, different from the results described.

If, however, computer systems development is going on as it is, at the growth rates of these last years, it will mean unemployment and more restrictive working conditions for increasing numbers of workers.

So, what is needed, is a deliberate social action and a deliberate policy of production and use of computers, controlled essentially by the masses of the workers. Trade unions will have to become associations contributing to this social action by mobilizing and concentrating the productive and creative forces of the workers.

REFERENCES

Bjørn-Andersen, N. and K.D. Eason (1979). Myths and Realities of Information Systems Contributing to Organisational Rationality. Paper for the 2nd Conference on Human Choice and Computers.

Borum, F. (1977). Edb, arbejdsmiljø og virksomhedsdemokrati. New Social Science Monographs, Copenhagen.

Braverman, H. (1974). Labor and Monopoly Capital - The Degradation of Work in the Twentieth Century. Monthly Review Press, New York.

Briefs, U. (1976). Systems and Workers. Data Exchange - Periodical of the Diebold Research Program. Sept./Oct. pp. 4-12.

Briefs, U. (1976). Technologie - und Modernisierungspolitik im Spannungsfeld zwischen den Interessen der abhängig Beschäftigten und der Unternehmenspolitik. WSI-Mitteilungen, Dec., pp. 747-753.

Briefs, U. (1977). Entwicklungstendenzen in der Wirtschaft - Anmerkungen zur Notwendigkeit der Kontrolle wirtschaftlicher Macht. WSI-Mitteilungen, Dec., pp. 2-12.

Briefs, U. (1978). Vom qualifizierten Sachbearbeiter zum Bürohilfsarbeiter? - Zu den Auswirkungen der EDV auf die Arbeitsbedingungen der Büroangestellten. WSI-Mitteilungen, February, pp. 84-91.

Briefs, U. (1978). Technologie und Gewerkschaften. Die Neue Gesellschaft, July, pp. 526-532.

Briefs, U. (1978). Neue Technologien als Herausforderung für die Gewerkschaften. Blätter für deutsche und internationale Politik, Oct., pp. 1179-1197.

CFDT (1977). Les dégâts du progrès. Seuil, Paris.

Cooly, M. (1972). Computer Aided Design - Its Nature and Implication. AUEW, Richmond.

Manacorda, P. (1976). Il calcolatore del capitale - un' analisi marxista dell' informatica. Feltrinelli, Milano.

Marx, K. (1871-1883). Das Kapital. In Marx-Engels-Werke, Vol 23-25, Dietz-Verlag, Berlin, 1976.

Marx, K. et.al. (1871). Adresse des Generalrats (der internationalen Arbeiter-Association) über den Bürgerkrieg in Frankreich 1871. In Marx-Engels-Werke, Vol. 17, pp. 313-362, Dietz-Verlag, Berlin, 1976.

Nora, S. and A. Minc (1978). L'informatisation de la societé. La documentation française, Paris.

DISCUSSION AND COMMENTS ON PAPER PRESENTED BY ULRICH BRIEFS

PETER ANKER FRIIS

We must see computer technology in a historical perspective. There has been a lot of technological inventions which all require careful adoption by management staff functions and workers. What we are talking about is the general problem of change, the problem of transition.

One of the main problems in this respect is uncertainty. A lot of things are related to the difficulty of telling people about the complexity and the nature of any new technology, and its consequences upon man.

The second problem is one of re-allocation. People who used to do one task have to be re-allocated either geografically or mentally to new tasks. There is a need for retraining. New industries arise and old ones die. That is the cycle of life, and there is nothing strange about that. It is a question of productivity. If we do not take that into account, we shall see competition from nations who have got the new resources overrun the nations who have not got them.

Briefs points out the number of boring jobs. But is it not so that in industry in general we have been relieved of all physical hazards, and instead we are experiencing stress? We have to learn how to cope with stress, and among other things we shall do that via legislation.

Briefs talks on behalf of the workers. I feel that we are all affected of computer technology one way or the other. But we must not forget that the advancement of technology has led to a new level of materialistic welfare.

Furthermore, in the article Briefs 'proves' that computerization has added to the current recession and the loss of jobs. It is a very complicated issue which cannot be proved by the use of statistics.

Briefs points out that computers have had a lot of negative consequences. One is job-abolishment. It is true with regard to some jobs, but it also has a positive side which I shall come back to.

Briefs also mentions the problem of computerized systems furthering control, inspection and pressure on the worker. I do not think it is due to computers alone. It may be management philosophy, competition and other things as well. Briefs talks about de-qualification. Yes, if one measures the same job, but often other jobs are created which are more demanding. I see this as a temporary problem which will be solved by the new generation of school graduates who will be far more confident with the new technology thanks to pocket calculators, basic programming and the like.

Finally, I should like to point out some of the positive aspects of computerization. I think that a lot of workers have been relieved from boring jobs. Note for example how computers are able to control remote jobs, where there are potential hazards to life and health.

I work in a declining industry, the manufacturing industry. But as time goes by new industries and job prospects will appear due to computerization (communication, teaching, pollution control, etc.). Many of these will grow due to the properties of micros and computers.

What we see today is that the industrial society as we know it is coming to an end. We are leaving the age of industrialization and are in for an epoke dominated by service industries and maybe even for an era of self-service.

But we must also get used to an age of leisure. After all there is a limit to the consumption of materialistic goods.

In ending I should like to point out that certain computer manufacturers have taken steps to analyse these matters. This means hope for a dialogue, and maybe a way of solving many of the problems of the transition period.

H.C. PRICE

I might mention that in my hospital in certain clinics we interrogate with the use of a microcomputer. We interviewed all the patients over the last two years. As a final question they were asked whether they would prefer to be interrogated by the computer or whether they preferred to see a live specimen. All patients said they would prefer to be interrogated by the computer doctor.

ULRICH BRIEFS

I must admit that in the Federal Republic we have become quite disillusioned. We have seen the transition from a fifteen year period of full employment to mass unemployment within only two years. Especially this has taken place in the manufacturing sector which has lost one and a half million working places.

In the Federal Republic we saw a continous growth of the tertiary sector up to some years ago, but only to a very limited extent could this apparently compensate for the heavy losses of working places in manufacturing. And even though this transition might be achieved, I am deeply concerned about the prospect of living in a society where 80% of the population are employed in the so-called information industries. Especially I am worried about who is to swallow all this information.

We might ask whether computers are not just another piece of technology. I think it is not. Former technologies created a mass of new use values. We have got new products for housing, clothes to wear, means of travel etc. But computerization cannot be <u>supposed</u> to contribute very much towards new use values. Additionally, is it not <u>so that</u> computers are favouring a particular organization of our social system with mass consumerism and large scale administrative and industrial units which inevitably leads to uniformity of industrial work? That is one of the basic problems about computers and their use which has to be very carefully thought through, too.

CLAUDIO CIBORRA

Briefs mentioned the Italian experiences with the 'qualification courses' of 150 hours for workers. The experiences have taken place over the last seven years. At the moment a course is run at the Polytechnic of Milan about informatics and work organization together with the trade unions. The point is that this type of course is not a requalification course, i.e. it does not qualify the worker for any promotion in the firm. The 150 hours courses are held by the trade unions for pursuing their own objectives.

As far as the basic education is concerned such courses have been quite successful. But the so-called monographic courses at university level have been more difficult to manage. This is because the knowledge produced and the education provided does not relate closely to the working situation of the participants. In actual fact they often remain largely academic courses. And in this sense I see great hope in the developments within trade unions of guided user eduction and research which are taking place in Scandinavia.

ULRICH BRIEFS

That was essentially my point about the emancipation of education from direct qualification requirements in the job. Furthermore, knowledge to workers must always be transferred in a very close and intimate relation to the things the worker has to do.

Frank Kolf is coming from Cologne
With a handbook as heavy as a stone
About implementation,
Try PORGI organization,
He'll assure you you will not be blown.

GUIDELINES FOR THE ORGANIZATIONAL IMPLEMENTATION OF INFORMATION SYSTEMS -- CONCEPTS AND EXPERIENCES WITH THE PORGI IMPLEMENTATION HANDBOOK

Frank Kolf and Hans Jürgen Oppelland

Betriebswirtschaftliches Institut für
Organisation und Automation
and der Universität zu Köln,
Cologne, West-Germany

The last decade has confronted system designers with the problem that they have to
consider the requirements and restrictions
of human and organizational context in
system development processes. There are
many tools for supporting the technical
design activities but until now project
management is lacking effective and efficient tools for handling the human and
organizational problems in system design.
This paper describes some tools and instruments which were developed in the research
project PORGI (Planning model for the Organizational Implementation) and reports
preliminary empirical experiences from
their application in two German companies.

The Human Side of Information Processing
N. Bjørn-Andersen, editor
© IAG
North-Holland Publishing Company, 1980

1. STATEMENT OF THE PROBLEM

Literature on the development of computer-based information systems (CBIS) as well as activities of system analysts and system designers have been and still are dominated by many attempts to solve technological questions (concerning computers, programmes, data bases, methods, models etc.). There exists a continuously growing number of tools to support these activities (e.g. techniques for programme design, interactive programming support systems, documentations methods and systems etc.).

Since about 1970 some large organizations have tried to implement computer-based management information systems especially to support managerial planning and control processes. These systems perform frequently multiple functions and/or serve users in many parts of the organization. They provide users with access to data and analytical capabilities which were not previously available to them. In trying to develop such systems, special kind of 'implementation' problems were met, which system designers used to attribute to the fact that 'users' have insufficient technological knowledge and therefore are not able to make optimal use of CBIS.

More and more it became clear that the introduction and use of CBIS in existing organizational environments was confronted by large difficulties comparable to those which originate when artificial organs are implanted in the human body. In many cases potential user departments boycotted the new systems. As a consequence diligent system analysts invented an additional phase in the development process, the core of which was 'user-training'. In parallel they tried to identify the modifications of user behaviour and of the organizational structures necessary to operate the system to convince management to perform those modifications. But then new difficulties arose in the form of feed-back effects to the technological solutions arrived at in earlier phases of the development process. In many cases 'trained users' were no longer satisfied with the system, they themselves had defined earlier. As a result of the learning processes, they changed their demands and needs. New incompatibilities between the future system and its environment arose. The date of system delivery to the user had to be postponed and planned budgets could not be met; these were only a few of a large number of frustrations which hit users and system analysts participating in these situations.

Some conclusions can be drawn from these experiences. The traditional understanding of 'organizational implementation' and of its role in the process of system development has to be modified:

- the objects of system development are not only the technological components, but simultaneously and equally important are the organizational and personal components of an information system (as a socio-technical system),

- the core of system development is to produce a fit between technological, organizational and personal system components. System development can only be successful, if activities to produce this fit (to integrate system components) begin in the very first of the design phases. Organizational implementation is understood here as this central process of integrating, mutually adjusting system components (Kolf and Oppelland 1977).

We think that implementation research in the field of CBIS is a special form of technological research which should produce tools to support the activities of organizational implementation and therefore help to improve the effectiveness of system development activities. Besides that it should generate empirically founded statements of how to use these tools in the specific context. It should stress important attributes of organizational implementation in different situations. The management of system development is context-dependent. General rules and general statements must be substituted by specialized combinations of methods and techniques, taking into account the unique conditions of each case.

These objectives are pursued in the research project PORGI, which is sponsored by the German Federal Ministry for Research and Technology. Within this project we try to generate instruments for CBIS development;

- which help to measure the fit (or mis-fit) between technological, or- ganizational and personal system components (i.e. specialized methods for analysis/diagnosis)

- which help to produce a better fit between system components by concentrating on these fit problems.

This paper gives an overview of these tools and reports some preliminary empirical experiences from actual CBIS-projects in German companies in which the PORGI- tools have been applied.

2. PORGI IMPLEMENTATION HANDBOOK - THE CONCEPT

The PORGI Implementation Handbook (IHB) is a collection of tools to support prac- titioners in handling human and organizational problems in CBIS development and consists basically of five elements which will be briefly portrayed.

a. The Descriptional Framework (DF) serves as a common terminological basis for all the tools and guidelines of the IHB but not as an explanatory model. The DF contains all the principal elements potentially of relevance to specific imple- mentational situations. According to the underlying implementation philosophy we have to differentiate two areas of analysis:

- analysis of the fit between the system components 'Man', 'Organiza- tional Structure', 'Information Technology' and 'Task' to be supported (System Fit) in analogy to Leavitt (1965).

- analysis of the design process (the project organization, project management etc.) (Process-Fit).

b. The Procedural Scheme (PROC) consists of a sequence of well-known design ac- tivities. Associated with the different design activities there are implementatio- nal aspects and specific tools to support the analysis of these aspects. The con- ception of this procedural scheme has been guided by the following principles:

- Based on our definition of the organizational implementation as a process of securing the well-tuned design of the system compo- nents 'Man', 'Structure', 'Information Technology' and 'Task' specific activities have to be planned which enable us to verify the tuning from the start-up-phase of the project.

- The design activities have to be supplemented by specific analytical steps. By performing repeated status analyses of all the system com- ponents we get information about the design status of the different components and FIT of these components. The evaluation of actual and planned status indicates specific (potential) problem areas early in the design process which have to be counteracted.

- Those who are affected by system design and system use have to be involved according to the degree to which they are affected and according to their own wishes. Therefore we have to plan activities which ensure that the organization of the design process becomes a design variable too.

Figure 1. is an abstract from the PORGI-Procedural-Scheme and shows the realiza- tion of these principles.

Design Activities	Organizational Implementation (OI) Aspects	Analytical Tools
(1) Problem Definition	Identification of the 'interested' people	
- Identification and description of the problem	- Who has the problem?	PORGI-Checklist PROB
- Information about the problem	- Who articulates the problem?	PORGI-Descriptional Framework
- Evaluation of the problem	- Who participates in the evaluation of the problem? (sets priorities etc.)	PORGI-Checklist BTR-1.1 Group-evaluation methods (e.g. BASYC)
- Decision about the realization of problem analysis	- Who decides upon the realization of the Problem Analysis?	PORGI-Questionnaire BEW
(2) Problem Analysis		

- Analysis of the different elements of the problem and its context	- Analysis of problematic areas in/between the system components
	  . Man
	  . Task
	  . Structure
	  . Information Technology
		PORGI-Questionnaire 1-69
		PORGI-Checklist ZIE
		PORGI-Checklist INN

- Analysis of possible causes	- Identification of the interests of the people concerned	PORGI-Criteria-List EIG-1; AUS-1 Group-evaluation-methods
- Specification of the requirements for the system components	- Group consensus about the required characteristics of the different system components	PORGI-Checklist PROB

Figure 1.

Abstract from the PORGI-Procedural-Scheme (PROC)

c. The Pool of Methods (METH) consists of instruments, tools and methods for Analyzing and Diagnosing implementational situations. Problem-oriented questionnaires, checklists, lists of criteria etc. support the diagnosis and analysis of combinations of variables (in the terminology of the DF), which are relevant to organizational implementation activities in the specific situation.

In section 3 we will discuss some of these tools and the results of their application in actual CBIS-projects.

To analyze issues relevant to the process fit available methods are for example:-

A checklist for the identification of those members of the organization who are affected by the development process and/or will be system users;

A questionnaire for the identification of actual and required participation in system development activities.

To analyze issues relevant to the system fit available methods are for example:-

A checklist for the identification and definition of the problems in the user organization to be solved by designing a new CBIS;

A checklist and a questionnaire for the definition of project and system objectives;

A questionnaire and a checklist for the identification and analysis of the required/planned innovatorial step and its importance regarding the system components: 'Personal System', 'Organization Structure', 'Information Technology' and 'Task' e.g. task content, procedures, communication.

d. The Pool of Implementation Problems (PROB) for the contextual analysis and diagnosis consists of specific implementation problems which can be identified by a situational profile. These profiles describe those empirical situations in which that specific implementation problem has occured repeatedly, e.g. results or consequences of specific actions in the design process which deteriorate the intended implementation success. These problems lead to economically and/or socially substandard results from the system design process or system usage. Descriptions of these implementation problems use the categories of the descriptional framework and are based on those problems which have been identified in our expert interviews as typical of specific situations (Oppelland et.al. 1977). Additionally it contains theoretically or empirically based implementation problems found in the literature, case studies and the design experiences of the members of the PORGI-team. The objective of the diagnosis is the comparison of the characteristics of the individual situation and the situation of profile of the implementation problems of PROB in order to identify possible problem areas in the actual situation. Follow-up activities focus on the analysis of possible causes for that problem and possible solutions.

e. The Pool of Design Concepts (CON) supports the solution of the problems identified by the use of METH and PROB in offering appropriated implementational actions. The choice of appropriate implementational actions is supported by offering:

. general design principles and
. situational design proposals,

which can be seen as sufficiently tested and confirmed by system development practice. The description of these design concepts is also oriented to the categories of these design concepts is also oriented to the categories of the descriptional framework. In this way the situational applicability can be better evaluated in

Figure 2.
Schematic Description of the Application of PORGI-Instruments

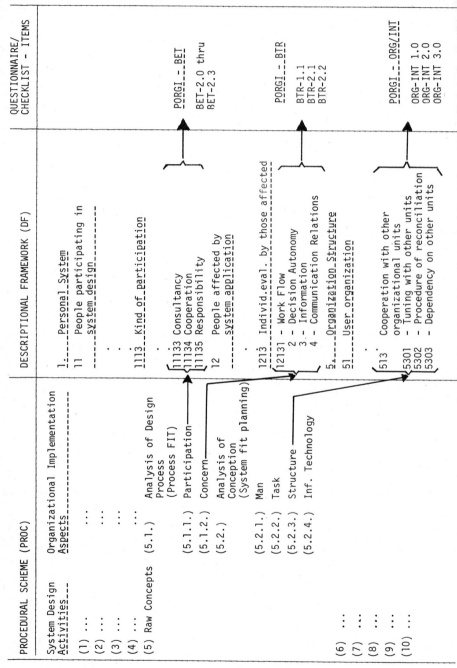

actual situations by the project manager, implementor or other people responsible for the system development.

The design concepts contain as possible implementational actions, proposals to correct (or confirm) social and organizational behaviour.

The procedural interactions of these instrumenst during a CBIS-project are as given in fig. 2. - The procedural scheme (PROC) works as a directory which tells us what steps to be taken next and what kind of implementational aspects to be considered. The details of such an organizational implementation aspect (e.g. (5.1.1.) Participation) are compiled in the Descriptional Framework, in the example the elements of the group 1113: Kind of Participation.

The Pool of Methods (METH) offers specific analytical tools for the analysis of these organizational implementation aspects, in the example the PORGI-Questionnaire BET. After having gathered facts about the specific situation by use of the PORGI-tools the problem-oriented analysis of that situation is being performed by searching the pool of implementation problems (PROB). The objective of this search is to find out whether the situational profile just gathered is similar to one of the situational profiles in the problem pool in which specific implementation problems have repeatedly occured.

If a match is found, the pool of Design concepts (CON) is searched to check whether it contains a possible solution with a similar situational profile; this would mean a solution which has proven to be useful in similar situations.

3. SOME PRELIMINARY EMPIRICAL EXPERIENCE WITH THE HANDBOOK (IHB)

We will discuss some of our instruments and tools and preliminary empirical experiences with their practical application in two CBIS-projects which were performed in two German companies. The discussion will touch on the following aspects:

- A short description of the respective CBIS-project covering the objectives, the number of people involved, and the involvement time of the PORGI-team.

- The PORGI-tools applied considering the objectives and content of the tools.

- The results of the application of the PORGI-tools.

This section will be closed by some critical conclusions regarding the methodical aspects of applying such tools and instruments.

3.1. EXPERIENCES WITH PORGI-INSTRUMENTS FOR PLANNING THE PROCESS-FIT

We started practical tests of PORGI-instruments in a well-known large-scale enterprise of the German electro industry. Their department for data processing was willing to cooperate with us in the application of methodical instruments within the system development process. This department had started the development of a new cost accounting and evaluation system (CAES) for their own hardware and software development projects, which would replace the different existing sub-systems. Therefore system development implied little technological innovation but much standardization of procedures. Directly concerned with system application were about 200 project leaders (the users) with approximately 2000 subordinates which could be seen as indirectly concerned, and a project-group of six members concerned with system design (the designers). The user project-groups belong to different sub-departments for hardware and software research and development, organisational development, maintenance tasks, and others. They are a hetereogeneous group of users with different demands and interests. The designers are members of the sub-department for organization and data processing and were partly supplemented by members of the sub-departments for accounting and software development. We joined this project (CAES) in a phase called 'planning phase I', which ends when a coarse version of the system design concept has been formulated.

This first description of the CBIS-project CAES is a result of our diagnosis of the implementation situation at the time when PORGI joined CAES. For this diagnosis we used a special checklist PORGI-SIT, which enables us to review the project history up to the actual situation. The information and answers for SIT were given by members of the CAES-project group. Some main topics of this checklist, e.g. those concerned with system development, their role in system use, the degree to which they might be affected, and the kind of participation experienced until now, can be represented in the PORGI-table BTR-BET. This table may be used in all diagnoses performed during the design process, starting with rough information about the initiating phase (as in our case), continuing with proposals or demands for adequate participation, and all together demonstrating the changes in design process organization and possible changes in process fit. Diagnosis with SIT in this case led us to the conclusion that we should concentrate the application of PORGI-instruments mainly on aspects of design process organization, on some aspects of tuning system components, and on consideration of organizational consequences. We decided to apply a special questionnaire composed of different sets of questions for each aspect, which should supply the information we need to organize the design process so that the interests and needs of those affected could be met adequately and mutual adjusting of system elements could be achieved (i.e. process fit). The questionnaire focuses on the following aspects:

. function and competence of those affected by system usage, e.g.

   .. supplying input
   .. preparing alternatives
   .. operating the system
   .. ratificating the results
   .. receiving output

. expected or known changes for task-oriented aspects of work resulting from system development and their importance for those concerned, e.g.

   .. task assignment
   .. work flow
   .. decision autonomy
   .. responsibility
   .. information
   .. quality of own work
   .. work loads/stress
   .. control by others

Additional questions on aspects of work normally belonging to this context had been removed because of the restriction to ask only not the potential users themselves but their representatives. These questions refer to, e.g.

. expected or known changes for person-oriented aspects of work resulting from system development and their importance for those concerned, e.g.

   .. personal image
   .. influence
   .. chances for promotion
   .. salary
   .. job satisfaction
   .. work load/stress
   .. self-esteem

PARTICIPATION	authorize	assume responsi-bility	cooperation consultancy	receiving information	not involved
1. What kind of participation have you experienced in the previous phase of system development?					
2. What kind of participation would you have found appropriate?					
3. What kind of participation do you desire for the future phases of system development?					

Please note reasons, when experienced kind of participation differs from the appropriate/desired participation:

ELECTION OF REPRESENTATIVES	hierarchy	qualifi-cation	available time	co-worker proposal	other
4. On which criteria are representatives for system design participation elected?					
5. On what kind of criteria do you think that elections should be based?					

Please note the reason for your desire, if it differs from your experience:

PORGI	IMPLEMENTATION HANDBOOK METH	CAES - Q

Figure 3.

Part of Questionnaire CAES-Q

In analyzing participation the questionnaire CAES-Q is used. A selected part of this questionnaire is shown in fig. 3. In the full questionnaire the first aspects covered identify those involved and the degree of their involvement. The subsequent aspects concentrate on the kind of participation experienced and its evaluation for phases, the experienced and design, already completed. Finally follows the desired participation in future phases, the experienced and desired rules for the election of representatives of a user group, the experienced and desired kind of information exchange, and the basic values in the group of representatives.

In order to support the use of system components and the interpretation of questionnaire results, we added some questions which refer to the evaluation of the system concept, personal and organizational consequences of system implementation, proposals for preparing and managing the system introduction, and personal data (age, sex, education, professional experience).

The questionnaire CAES-Q was answered by the representatives of the involved sub-departments during a session at the end of the planning phase I where the coarse version of the CAES concept was presented and modified.

We would like to point to some of the most interesting results from the use of this questionnaire:

. In no case was the experienced kind of participation evaluated as too intensive.

. Only 25% of those affected classified their participation as un-conditionally satisfactory, 75% desired a more intensive kind of participation.

. Active cooperation in system design by giving suggestions, consul-tancy etc. and participation in decision responsibility was evaluated to be positive or ideal rather than any more passive kind of partici-pation, for example receiving information about system design activities or results.

. The higher the expected importance the higher the desire for an inten-sive and active participation in system design.

. Intensive kinds of participation by those affected clearly corresponded with their ability;
  .. to realize the extent and importance of personal and organi-zational consequences of system implementation,
  .. to consider possible problem solutions and to create constructive proposals for organizational changes,
  and corresponded with their level of aspiration to obtain qualified support for system introduction.

. The attitude towards system development of those affected was rather positive. The evaluation was more critical but also more differentiated, if they had experienced a more intensive participation. Too little participation tended to result in an emotionally influenced distance from system development or a neglect of its impact.

These results confirm the importance of the consideration of system design process organization. They led to the following proposals:

. to increase the openess and transparency of the system design process by more intensive information about it, beginning for example with the feedback of questionnaire results,

. to document an individual's participation in system design activities in writing invitations, protocols, circulars etc., in order to allow for self-assessment and self-confidence, and to achieve clear responsibility,

. to consider the competence of user department's reprensentatives by paying special attention to their hierarchical status and the experienced criteria of representatives' election,

. to ask those concerned (or their representatives) about the kind of participation they desire in the next phase of system design.

The CAES-project group accepted these proposals and realized the underlying ideas. Feedback of questionnaire results were given together with a protocol explaining the critical aspects and a short additional questionnaire regarding the demands for participation. All questionnaires were filled out completely and returned to the CAES-group. Organization of participation in the planning phase II of CAES has been altered due to the results of this questionnaire.

3.2. EXPERIENCES WITH PORGI-INSTRUMENTS FOR PLANNING THE SYSTEM FIT

The application of tools and instruments for planning the System Fit was tested in another CBIS-project in a medium-sized pharmaceutical company. The company is organized in functional divisions (finance, marketing, production etc.) and operates a rather small DP-department which reports to the vice-president of finance. It is a company policy if possible,to buy software rather to make it. The PORGI-Team became involved after the company had decided to implement a specific standard-software-package of a large software supplier. The objective to the CBIS-project was to implement a corporate financial planning model for a five-year planning horizon. Some of the requirements initially stated were:

- to simulate different alternatives (regarding e.g. sales volume, prices, costs etc.);

- to state the consequences of these alternatives for the profit and loss statements and balances of the next five years;

- to set up a five-year-financial plan;

- to deduce a procurement plan for raw materials

- to perform sensitivity analyses for specific groups of costs

- to deduce a capacity and investment plan

The company's major expectations regarding the involvement of the PORGI-Team were:

- in general, to get support in dealing with organizational and human aspects of that particular CBIS-project,

- specifically to get support in

    . reaching a problem analysis and definition based upon the common consensus of all persons and departments affected by the CBIS-project and potential future use of the system;

    . reaching a project specification (including user requirements and organizational requirements) which was systematically based and took into consideration the interests of the different persons and departments involved as well as necessary organizational changes and changes in the technical design of the system;

    . identifying needs for organizational changes early in the project and developing organizational solutions.

The company and the PORGI-Team agreed to proceed along the Procedural Scheme developed by the PORGI-Team (see section 2).

| No. (1) | Div: Division / Dp: Department / Bd: Board (2) | name of organizational member/unit (3) | function in system use (4) | number of organizational members (5) | KIND OF CONCERN: 0/1/2 (+/-) | | | | | | | | KIND OF PARTICIPATION: G/D/M/I | | | | | | | | | |
					task assignment (6)	work flow (7)	decision autonomy (8)	responsibility (9)	information (10)	work quality (11)	work load (12)	control (13)	problem analysis (14)	goal definition (15)	feasibility study (16)	coarse design (17)	detailed design (18)	realization (19)	introduction (20)	evaluation (21)	project management (22)	project control (23)
1	Div.		5	2-3	1	1	1+	1	1+	0	1+	0										
2	Dp		5	1	2	2	2+	2	2+	2+	2+	0										
3	Div.		5	2-3	0	1	0	0	1+	0	1+	0										
4	Div.		5	3-5	1	1	2+	1	1+	0	1+	1+										
5	Dp		1235	1	2	2	2+	2	2+	2+	2+	0										
6	Dp		125	1	2	2	2+	2	2+	2+	2+	0										
7	Div.		245	2	2	2	2+	2	2+	2+	2+	0										
8	Bd.		45	5	1	2	2+	1	2+	1+	2+	0										
9	Dp		3	1-2	2	2	0	1	0	1+	0	0										
10			5	60	0	0	0	0	1+	0	0	0										
		External: Softw.Suppl.																				
		External: PORGI-Team																				

Figure 4.

BTR-BET I : Results of Case 2

Our first activity was to carry out the initial situational diagnosis by the use
of our checklist SIT. The main results describing the situation are shown in the
table BTR-BET I (see fig. 4) where the organizational units are made anonymous
(Col. 3). Abbreviations in col. 2 mean, Divisions (Div), Departments (Dp), Board
of Directors (BD) or Vice-Presidents (VP).

From that initial situational diagnosis we were able to identify those members of
the organization who are strongly affected by the new system and should therefore
be participants in the phases 'Problem analysis/definition' and 'Project specification'. The 'Problem analysis/definition' was performed by the use of the PORGI-
Checklist PROB. This described the unsatisfactory situation in a way which gave
a picture acceptable to all members affected by the situation.

By checking the items and associated problem causes, PROB serve as a guide for
discussion and interview with all those people who have been identified in the
table BTR-BET I (fig. 4).

As an example, the items regarding the systems component 'task' to be supported by
the new system are shown on page 3.0 of the Checklist PROB (see fig. 5). Additionally the system components 'Man', 'Organizational context' and 'Information technology' are covered in the same way. The PORGI-team applied this Checklist in 8
interviews with the people in the CBIS-project who were most concerned with the
new system. Some of the results of this problem analysis were:

- Length of planning process: To an increasing extent the Board of Directors
  asks for plan-alternatives and puts forward 'What-if-questions', which can
  no longer be handled by the existing resources and within the allowed time.

- Problem level of planning: Financial planning was up to now a 'residual
  activity' not an area of strategic activity. The business trends led
  the Board of Directors to the expectation that there would be an urgent
  need for active strategic financial planning, but for that task the
  available tools were insufficient.

- In that context, the financial consequences of investments received
  much higher priority, but the existing information about production
  capacities supplied by the technical division were insufficient from
  the financial director's point of view. The technical director insisted
  that it was very difficult to define capacities and the financial director
  assumed that the possibility of losing freedom of activity could be the
  reason.

- The workload for the planners was too high, but they felt a need for
  more challenge to their intellectual abilities.

- Some members of the organization did not realize (at least from the
  Board of Directors' point of view) that the company had grown very
  rapidly in the last years and that patterns of cooperation and communication had not been changed appropriately.
  Therefore there was a tendency to isolate e.g. the manager of the
  financial accounting department from all design activities although
  he would have to play an important role in system use.

- The CBIS-project was primarily initiated by the vice-president of
  finance and his division dominated all design activities up to now.
  But the new system would be an integrated system covering all company
  functions and the interests of the other functions had up to now been
  insufficiently considered.

- The results of the organizational analysis showed that the organization
  structure did not have any organizational unit (staff, committee etc.)
  to handle an integrated planning process.

Characteristics of the problem situation	Possible causes
System component: TASK	
(1) Time structure of task	
· Planning horizon	too short; lack of long-range perspectives
· Length of planning process	too long; insufficient possibilities of coping with changes in market conditions.
· Initiative for planning process	unsystematic, ad-hoc, planning
(2) Level of task	
· Problem-level	only operative planning, no integration with strategic planning
· Considered units	isolated unit plan, integration with other units is insufficiently handled
(3) Complexity of task	
· Number of different activities	too high; cannot be handled with available methods and/or resources
· Intellectual requirements	too low; permanent coordination problems with other units performing similar activities
· Degree of detail	
(4) Work load	too high; permanent over-time too little challenge in job

PORGI	CHECKLIST PROBLEM DEFINITION AND ANALYSIS	PROB - 3.0 CONTINUED

Figure 5.
Part of checklist PROB

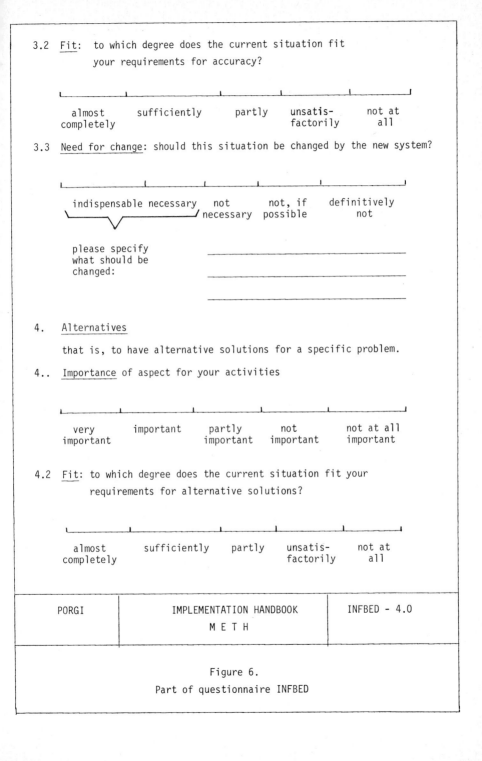

3.2 <u>Fit</u>: to which degree does the current situation fit
     your requirements for accuracy?

|_____|_____|_____|_____|_____|
    almost   sufficiently   partly   unsatis-   not at
  completely   factorily   all

3.3 <u>Need for change</u>: should this situation be changed by the new system?

|_____|_____|_____|_____|_____|
   indispensable necessary   not   not, if   definitively
                           necessary   possible   not

   please specify   _____
   what should be
   changed: _____

                       _____

4. <u>Alternatives</u>

   that is, to have alternative solutions for a specific problem.

4.. <u>Importance</u> of aspect for your activities

|_____|_____|_____|_____|_____|
    very   important   partly   not   not at all
  important   important important   important

4.2 <u>Fit</u>: to which degree does the current situation fit your
     requirements for alternative solutions?

|_____|_____|_____|_____|_____|
    almost   sufficiently   partly   unsatis-   not at
  completely   factorily   all

PORGI	IMPLEMENTATION HANDBOOK M E T H	INFBED - 4.0

Figure 6.
Part of questionnaire INFBED

These results were complemented by the results of the questionnaire INFBED which had to answered by the participants. The objective of this questionnaire (see an example in fig. 6) is to get an individual assessment of the <u>current</u> supply of information regarding the aspects actuality, availability, accuracy, supply of alternatives, possibility of what-if-questions, and planning horizons covered. Each of these aspects had to be assessed on a five-point-scale by the participants with respect to:

- <u>Importance</u> of an aspect (1 not at all important to 5 very important)

- <u>Fit</u> of current supply of informations and information need (1 not at <u>all</u> to 5 almost complete)

- <u>Need for change</u> (1 definitively not to 5 change is indispensable)

For some aspects the participants had the opportunity to specify the required changes. - Some of the results are shown in fig. 7:

Information aspects \ Problem aspects	Importance	Fit	Need for change
actuality	4.6	3.6	3.4
availability	3.8	3.4	4.0
accuracy	2.6	3.8	3.4
alternatives	4.8	2.6	4.2
simulation	4.8	2.8	4.4
planning horizon	4.2	3.8	3.4

Figure 7.

Mean Scores for INFBED

Most interesting are those information aspects which have a mean score in 'Need for change' of approximately 1 (should definitively not be changed) or 4 and more (change is necessary or indispensable). In this CBIS-project the aspects availability, alternatives and simulation show scores, which indicate that the participants are not satisfied with the current situation (low scores in Fit) and require appropriate changes. An additional possibility for analyzing these results is description by profiles which shows the differences between the answers of participants and therefore enables us to initiate actions which take into account individual needs and assessments.

All this information forms the basis for a project specification with the PORGI-Checklist ZIE. The objective of ZIE is to consider the major problem aspects together with the required changes and to translate it into operational design requirements. In this way we get a project specification which is accepted by all participants and forms the basis for the evaluation activities. These take place during the project at specific milestones in order that the fit of the different systems components is analyzed (by use of specific PORGI-tools not shown here) and in order that comparison with the planned status may be carried out. If variances exist, corrective action can be initiated early in the project. Furthermore at the end of the project when the system becomes operational, users as well as designers can evaluate whether the objectives of the project have been met.

3.3. SOME GENERAL METHODOLOGICAL EXPERIENCES WITH PORGI-INSTRUMENTS

In the preceeding sections we have discussed some preliminary results of the application of some of the PORGI-tools and instruments. This section focuses on some
experiences with the instruments themselves and problems in applying such instruments in real CBIS-projects. We shall evaluate these instruments with respect to
the following issues:

1. General applicability, i.e., the instruments should not only be tailored
    to one specific case. In our experience we have developed a general set
    of instruments consisting of questions, items and procedures which are
    generally applicable in CBIS-projects which have the objective to design
    and implement information systems for the support of planning activities.
    Additionally it may be necessary to tailor some of the instruments accord-
    ing to the individual terminology of the company or the specific CBIS-pro-
    ject (especially regarding the types of organizational units involved or
    the names of units of project organization). The checklists and question-
    naires are aimed at covering 'the whole (relevant) ground' which means
    that some parts may be irrelevant for the special case (like specific
    modules in a computer programme). Therefore in our experience a certain
    creative effort of the individual project manager, implementor etc. is
    indispensable in order to ensure the effective and efficient use of
    PORGI-instruments.

2. 'Valid' description of the situation, i.e. the siutations which are de-
    scribed and analyzed validly must be described so that it may be recog-
    nized by those involved and so that the major characteristics of the
    situation are covered. Our 'measure' for the success of the evaluation
    of this criterion was in general the feedback of our results to the mem-
    bers of the company and the discussion of these results with those indi-
    viduals who participated in the interviews. In all situations in the two
    CBIS-projects it could be stated that the main characteristics of the
    respective situations were judged by the participants as being valid.
    This holds true also in those situations where we diagnosed the existence
    of specific problems between different departments.

3. Basis for relevant action. Our aim in describing and analyzing implemen-
    tation situations is to diagnose potential problems early in the process
    (early warning) and to take corrective actions early enough. Therefore
    the evaluation criterion for our instruments is whether our diagnostic
    tools were able to translate our diagnostic results into action planning.
    We now have enough evidence to prove that our diagnostic results were
    sufficiently exact and operational to form the basis for planning specific
    actions. In case 1 the project team of the electro company changed the
    participation pattern after our first analysis and planned participation
    for the next phases by using the PORGI-criteria. In case 2 the partici-
    pation pattern initially intended by the DP managers of the pharmaceuti-
    cal company was changed completely according to our propositions and
    specific organizational design activities were initiated parallel to the
    technical design activities as a result of our problem analysis.

4. Economic aspects of applying PORGI-tools, i.e., the use of our instru-
    ments should not demand such an amount of manpower, time etc. that the
    results are not worth the effort. At this point we can only give some
    impressions of the costs we have experienced. Answering the questionnaire
    CAES-Q in case 1 took approximately 20 minutes per person and the indi-
    vidual tailoring of PORGI-tools to that situation, the analysis and
    interpretation of about 30 questionnaires and discussion of results took
    approximately two man-weeks. The activities with PROB and INFBED in case
    2 took approximately 2 hours per interview, and the analysis and inter-
    pretation of the results and discussion with the participants took appro-

ximately 2.5 manweeks. In both cases the members of the respective
project teams agreed that this was a reasonable amount of time with
respect to the outcome which in both cases was judged as very important.

From these preliminary experiences we can conclude that the PORGI-tools meet to
a reasonable degree the above-mentioned evaluation criteria. Some general prerequisites and implications of the application of tools of this kind will be discussed in section 4.

4. PREREQUISITES AND IMPLICATIONS OF THE PORGI-APPROACH

The PORGI-concept of organizational implementation of CBIS (mutually adjusting
the technical, organizational and social system components and adequate involvement of those organization members concerned) implies an understanding of system
development as a participative socio-technical (and therefore organizational)
change process.

Application of methodological instruments for a satisfactory organization of the
design and change processes (process fit) and adequate tuning of system components
(system fit) result in increase of system success, e.g. decrease of system development risks, but demands additional expenses (time, manpower etc.). Because of
the difficulties of evaluating the benefits of these tools in 'hard-dollar-terms',
management has to take account of these additional expenses if they are to make a
successful application of these instruments.

The applications of PORGI-instruments rigorously increases transparency of the
system development processes: it makes it possible to disclose technological and
organizational problems but, even more, it makes personal problems explicit and
conflicts in system design become apparent. What we have experienced is that problem disclosure and analysis demands a good deal of neutrality and independence
(professional expertise and experience are of course assumed), which possibly
only an external consultant may have. What we do not know as yet is whether and
how to avoid disclosure of problems or conflicts that cannot be solved or handled
adequately either because of a lack of appropriate problem and conflict solving
procedures in the practised management style or because of insufficient willing-
ness or capability amongst members of the organization to solve such conflicts.
In the cases described above we tried to anticipate problems potentially disclosed
in the analysis, and to discuss available problem solutions and possible consequences of either the conscious solution of the problem or the conscious 'non-
solution' of the disclosed problem. Also the neglect of possibly existing latent
conflicts was discussed. In every case the client organization, i.e. its management, has to take the responsibility for the application of PORGI-instruments.
Thus we are careful only to disclose problems or conflicts which could be solved,
but are not sure whether to disclose all of the existing problems which should be
solved for economic and socially satisfactory results in system development.

Traditional 'classical' activities of system design concentrate on the question
of the technological alternative which might best (i.e. most efficiently) solve
a given, predefined task. PORGI-tools concentrate on planning and control of the
fit between technological and organizational/human system components and presupposes that this question has been or will be attempted solved during system development. (A necessary limitation which has been chosen deliberately). The authors feel that the solution to the problems discussed in this paper are as crucial to system success as the organization of technological solutions. Our intention is not to substitute but to complement existing technological research and
design instruments with regard to certain variables which are extremely relevant
to system success.

REFERENCES

Kolf, F, J. Claus and H.J. Oppelland (1977). Grundlagen und Konzeption eines Modells zur Beschreibung organisatorischer Implementierungssituationen. PORGI-Projektbericht No. 1, Cologne.

Kolf, F, H.J. Oppelland, D. Seibt and N. Szyperski (1978). Instrumentarium zur organisatorischen Implementierung von rechnergestützten Informationssystemen. In Angewandte Informatik, No. 7, pp. 299-310.

Leavitt, H.J. (1965). Applied Organizational Change in Industry. Structural, Technological, and Humanistic Approaches. In J.G. March (ed.), Handbook of Organizations. Skokil, Ill., pp. 1144-1170.

Oppelland, H.J., F. Kolf and J. Claus (1977). Dokumentation der Ergebnisse einer Expertenbefragung zur Entwicklung und Einführung rechnergestützter Informationssysteme. PORGI-Projektbericht No. 5, Cologne.

Pounds, W.F. (1969). The Process of Problem Finding. Industrial Management Review, Vol. 11, No. 4, pp. 1-19.

DISCUSSION AND COMMENTS ON PAPER PRESENTED BY FRANK KOLF

ROLF HØYER

Some years ago systems departments in most companies, having a minimum of self-esteem, were developing comprehensive handbooks for system development. Some very large companies did it so well that their masterpieces were marketed as standard handbooks world wide, e.g. the ARDI-handbook here in Europe. Learned scholars also produced handbooks of different quality and size. But they all had one thing in common, the general claim that when following the prescribed procedures and using the appropriate forms, one would arrive at better systems, at lower costs and in a shorter time.

Parallel with this growing number of prescriptive models for the systems design process, a growing confusion followed among systems specialists about the most practical and useful handbook or model. So great was this confusion that $1\frac{1}{2}$ years ago three of my doctoral students were given a research assignment for Volvo Head-quarters in Gothenburg just to do an inventory of all the serious system develop-ment models available and of their most significant properties.

The final report of the group, covering some 800 pages, actually gave Volvo no answer to their question. Our reply was of course, "... the best method - well, that depends ..."

At this conference we are talking about social processes within the computer user community, and I feel quite sure that the nature of those processes requires far more skillful personnel assessment than any formalized procedural scheme may ever offer.

Having said that, I readily admit that I find it interesting that the PORGI group did not only include the traditional job design criteria, but also guidelines for how to design the design process, allowing it to be an independent variable adapted to the situation. This is not so often suggested in the literature within this field.

However, the basic question remains whether such formalized procedures are fea-sible. Obviously there is a need in systems design to follow some pre-planned procedure in order to coordinate the many efforts associated with the design pro-cess. And of course some standard forms and notation rules are mandatory to faci-litate documentation and communication among experts.

But we also know that different people and different situations require different tools and work models. No standard set of tools alone can ever be a guarantee for successful information systems. It all depends ...

What does it depend upon? First of all upon people. And I have a strong suspicion of handbooks, particularly the so-called socio-technical implementation handbooks, claiming that the problems associated with human and organizational problems in connection with systems design are so simple that they can be adequately solved simply by following a procedural scheme and using a battery of standard tools and standard knowledge.

Another critical issue is associated with the decisions about the important fac-tors to take into account, the kind of knowledge required to solve current ques-tions etc. This is not a static issue, - it is highly dynamic.

The basic nature of a true participative systems design process requires that the people affected identify the problems themselves, define critical factors and suggest relevant solutions. It is the core of every systems design process that it should be a learning process. If existing procedures and knowledge present ready-made solutions to these key questions, no learning process will take place.

However, genuine organizational learning and development as a prerequisite for innovation and progress, is a cumbersome exploration by foot through an undiscovered, virgin territory. Going by car on a pre-built highway is definitely faster and more efficient, but, as often happens, in an undesirable direction. I am also afraid that the mere fact that following some procedural scheme gives some fake impression or guarantee that the social aspects are taken properly into account.

I firmly believe that knowledge from outside and certain tools may be useful for line personnel involved in systems design for themselves. But it is a prerequisite that the procedures are administered and controlled by users as tools in an autonomous planning process administered by themselves. Unfortunately, I feel that the PORGI instruments to a large extent represent another form of pre-digested knowledge and that it invites outside expert control. In this area we need tools for the people, not for the experts.

A charming researcher from Lancashire
Ran a project which looked at the bank-
cashier
Participative planning
Got unexpected planning
From the woman as well as the mancashier.

THE PARTICIPATIVE DESIGN OF CLERICAL INFORMATION SYSTEMS
TWO CASE STUDIES

Enid Mumford

Manchester Business School
Manchester, England

This paper describes the participative
design of computer systems in two large
organizations. One a British Engineering
Company and the other an International
Bank. Both of these organizations wished
to use the introduction of new on-line
computer systems as a means for increasing
the efficiency and job satisfaction of
staff. They decided to use the clerks themselves as a design team. The organization
of work that was associated with the new
computer system was therefore a result of
the diagnosis by the clerks of their own
job satisfaction and efficiency needs.
Both design teams decided on autonomous
work structures.

The Human Side of Information Processing
N. Bjørn-Andersen, editor
© IAG
North-Holland Publishing Company, 1980

PHILOSOPHICAL APPROACH

The two case studies described in this paper represent the present stage of an evolutionary attempt to provide white collar workers with the opportunity and skills to redesign their own work systems. The catalyst for change has been the introduction of a new computer system; in the first case study to replace a manual work system, and in the second an existing batch system. This change of technology was seen as providing an admirable opportunity for the redesign of work so as to 1. increase the satisfaction of staff and 2. increase their work efficiency - a factor believed to contribute to job satisfaction.

PARTICIPATION PHILOSOPHY

A different level of participation was used in each organization. In the first, an international bank, the approach was through what the author calls 'representative democracy'. In the second, a firm in the aero-space industry, 'consensus democracy' was attempted with no changes being made until a large majority of the employees concerned agreed to these.

With representative democracy a design group is formed which is representative of all grades of staff in the department and, if a new computer system is being introduced, also includes the systems analysts. This design group assumes responsibility for diagnosing job satisfaction and efficiency problems and needs and for designing a new system of work, into which the computer system will be embedded, to increase job satisfaction and improve efficiency. The departmental manager may or may not be a member of the group depending on his own wishes. In the two case studies described here both departmental managers gave the projects their blessing but decided not to participate in the design activities in case their presence inhibited the ideas of their subordinates.

Consensus democracy takes the democratic approach to a higher level by attempting to involve all staff in a user department continuously throughout the systems design process. Once again a design group is formed from representatives of the user department and the computer systems analysts. With the consensus approach this design group, with the exception of the systems analysts, is likely to be elected by the staff of the user department, whereas with the representative approach it may be either elected or selected by management. The role of the design group using a consensus approach is twofold. It will have to develop a new form of work organization while continually receiving and giving ideas from and to departmental colleagues and allowing the final decision to be taken by the department as a whole.

DESIGN PHILOSOPHY

A participative approach to work design means that the employees of a department or their representatives construct a new form of work organization which is based on a diagnosis by them of their own needs. In order to carry out this diagnosis they need some analytical tools to enable them to identify technical problems associated with work procedures and administration and social problems associated with psychological needs. The tools used by the author, and communicated to members of the design group in training sessions, are based on the socio-technical approach developed by the Tavistock Institute in the 1950s. This incorporates an analysis of the technical components of the work system and the grouping of these into 'unit operations' or logically integrated sets of tasks related to the activities which a department or section must carry out to fulfil its principal function. For example a hospital ward dealing with coronary cases will have to handle the crisis stage of the heart attack; will have to maintain the patient in a state of stability once the crisis is overcome, and will then have to restore him to health. Unit operations will include reception of the patient at the crisis stage; activities to remove the crisis; activities to maintain a state of non-crisis; activities to ensure a return to normal health and so on.

The socio-technical method has a second important objective. This is the improvement of the efficiency of a work system through identifying and analysing system
variances. A variance is defined as a tendency for a system to deviate from a desired specification. This tendency arises as a result of some problem associated
with the work process itself in its normal operation. For example, in our coronary
ward, problems of co-ordination between ambulance services and the reception of
patients by the hospital. Variance analysis is not concerned with temporary problems such as machine breakdown or with people problems such as human errors; it
concentrates on system weaknesses associated with the organization of work operations. An important objective of this method is to identify clearly those key
variances that significantly affect the ability of a work system to pursue its
major objectives. These variances are often found at the boundaries of the system,
for example, where the work of one department interacts with that of another and
there are problems of co-ordination (Taylor 1975).

The tool for analysing the social system and identifying the job satisfaction
needs of staff has been developed by the author although it is based on the work
of many other researchers (Mumford 1972). The author defines job satisfaction as
the FIT between what an individual or group is seeking from the work situation
and what they are receiving from it, in other words the FIT between job needs and
positive expectations and the requirements of the job. Job satisfaction is seen
as being achieved when three kinds of needs are met in the work situation. These
are personality needs, competence and efficiency needs and needs associated with
personal values. If the philosophy of this paper is accepted, an improvement in
job satisfaction should always be made a design objective and a design group concerned with job satisfaction should be able to answer the following questions.

Needs associated with personality

1. Knowledge needs. To what extent does the existing organization of
   work meet the needs of the group of employees which the design
   group represents for work that fully uses their knowledge and
   skills and to what extent does it provide them with the opportunity
   to develop their knowledge and skills further?

2. Psychological needs. To what extent does the existing organization
   of work meet the needs of employees for recognition, responsibility,
   status, advancement, esteem and security? Does it also give them
   a sense of achievement? (Herzberg 1966).

Needs associated with competence and efficiency in the work role and the success- ful performance of work activities

3. Support/control needs. To what extent does the work situation provide
   employees with the kind of support services which enable them to carry
   out their job efficiently? These support services include the information and materials necessary to work at a high level of competence;
   supervisory help and encouragement and good working conditions. We are
   here making an assumption that an efficient and supportive work environment increases job satisfaction.

   To what extent also does the way work is controlled through checks
   and audits fit with employee ideas and wishes on how their work
   should be controlled? The level and structure of wages and
   salaries will be an important part of the control system.

4. Task needs. To what extent does the way in which work is organized
   and jobs designed meet employee needs for the following?

   (a) the opportunity to use a variety of different skills and
        different levels of skill.

(b)   the opportunity to achieve targets, particularly quality
      targets and to obtain feedback on how well these targets
      have been achieved.

(c)   Autonomy. The opportunity to take decisions, exercise
      choice and exert a degree of control over what is done
      and how it is done.

(d)   Task identity. The opportunity to undertake work which
      is viewed as important, which is organized in such a way
      that the work of one group is clearly separated from the
      work of other groups and which has a reasonably long task
      cycle so that an employee can look back with pride on the
      way in which he has solved a particular work problem or
      carried out a challenging set of tasks (Cooper 1973).

Needs associated with employee values

5. Ethical needs. To what extent does departmental management,
    and senior management also, treat employees in the way they
    think they should be treated. This applies particularly to
    issues such as communication, consultation and opportunities
    for participation in decisions which affect employee interests.

This job satisfaction information can usefully be collected by questionnaire provided that three important criteria are met.

1. The information is collected by an external consultant, as only
    in this way will employees be convinced of its confidentiality.

2. Aggregate data derived from analysis of the questionnaires is
    given to everyone who completed a questionnaire.

3. Questionnaire data is discussed with all employees who completed
    a questionnaire in small groups. This will check its accuracy,
    provide an understanding of the reasons for high and low satis-
    faction and get employees involved in improving the design of
    their own work organization.

Variance analysis and job satisfaction analysis provide essential diagnostic data
for gaining and understanding of existing efficiency and job satisfaction problems.
They can also be used to evaluate the success of the design task. A good socio-
technical task structure should have ensured better control over existing variances without the creation of new ones and a better fit between employee needs and
the requirements of their jobs on the personality, efficiency and value factors.

THE CASE STUDY SITUATIONS

International Bank

The author's introduction to International Bank took place in 1974. She was then
approached by a senior member of the Bank's Personnel Department who told her
that the Bank's Foreign Exchange Department was about to move from a batch to an
on-line computer system. Because the Bank had been experiencing some difficulties
in attracting and retaining staff there was a desire to associate this technical
change with a reorganization of work which would increase the job satisfaction of
staff. The Bank therefore proposed to make an increase in job satisfaction a specific system objective and to give the Bank clerks themselves responsibility for
designing an optimal form of work organization into which the computer system
could be fitted. The Bank had already created a 'Job Satisfaction Working Party'
from a representative group of Foreign Exchange clerks and asked the author if she
would assist this group to identify their needs and develop a work structure that
would meet these needs.

The Bank's Foreing Exchange Department consisted of two sections: the Dealing Room and the Exchange Department. The technical activities of buying and selling currency were performed in the Dealing Room while the Exchange Department was an administrative unit solely occupied with the processing of deals entered into by the Dealing Room. Currency was bought and sold by means of telephone communication to and from agents all over the world and customers, and the Bank itself aimed to make a profit from these transactions.

The organizational design project was to be primarily concerned with the Exchange Department as this had many more routine activities than the Dealing Room. Whereas dealers were essentially entrepreneurs who used considerable flair and skill in the buying and selling of currency, the work of the Exchange Department was controlling the paperwork. Management believed that the existing functional organization of work was underutilizing the talents of many clerks. Exchange Department staff consisted of 68 clerks of whom 25 were part-time. It has a tall grading structure ranging from grade 1 typists to grade 7 assistant managers.

AERO-SPACE LIMITED

The design project in this firm took place in two departments. These departments handled the accounts of firms which supplied goods and services to Aero-space Ltd., and they shared the same office. Purchase Invoice, the larger department, handled invoices from suppliers while the Treasurer's Department signed and despatched cheques for goods received and dealt with some suppliers' queries concerning payment. The work of the two departments was logically related but was kept separate because of the requirement that the Company Treasurer alone should have cheque signing responsibilities.

The Company was an experienced user of computers and was proposing to introduce a series of on-line computer systems into its accountancy functions. It perceived this as an opportunity for a form of office reorganization that would improve both job satisfaction and efficiency. The author was initially approached by two computer specialists from within the Company, the Systems Manager responsible for computer based accounting systems and a Systems Manager from the Central Management Services Department, who asked her to assist them with the design of a new on-line computer system for the Treasurer's and Purchase Invoice Departments. The initiative for work design therefore came from the computer specialist group within the Company.

The new computer system would have as its objectives both an improvement in efficiency and an improvement in job satisfaction.

The Purchase Invoice Department employs a staff of fifty clerks and handles the accounts of suppliers who have supplied goods and services to the Company.

Its original structure prior to the introduction of the computer system is shown below.

With the original manual system the work was routine and made more so by the functional organization of the Department in which staff were divided into four grades; the bottom grades carrying out very simple, routine activities associated with a certain kind of invoice. Because of the routine nature of the work the Department had difficulty in recruiting clerks and young people were reluctant to stay there. It was believed by management that job satisfaction was low.

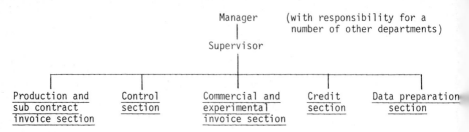

Purchase Invoice

Pre-computer Departmental Structure

TREASURER'S DEPARTMENT

The organizational structure of the Treasurer's Department is set out below.

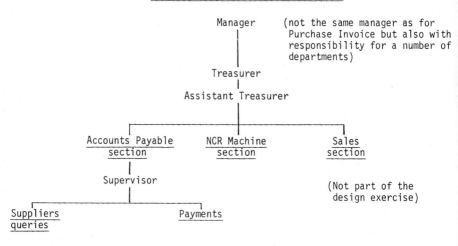

Treasurer's Department

Pre-computer Departmental Structure

The Treasurer's Department had a clerical staff of eleven clerks (including the two supervisors) and seven NCR machine operators. These machine operators would no longer be required once the new computer system was introduced and at the time the design exercise began they, their supervisor, and the two clerks in the machine section had all accepted transfer to other parts of the firm. This would leave the Treasurer's Department with a clerical staff of eight and one of these was very close to retirement.

The Treasurer's Department Accounts Payable Section had divisional responsibilities. It looked after the main company but also paid suppliers invoices for five subsidiaries scattered throughout Britain and Scotland. A major part of its function was liaising with suppliers and dealing with queries. It also controlled the monthly payment run for suppliers and looked after debits and credits. The Treasurer's Department claimed that it frequently had difficulty in obtaining information necessary to answer a supplier's query from Purchase Invoice and from the Buyer.

PREPARATION FOR CHANGE

In International Bank the design team was created before the author was invited to assist with the project, and was elected by the staff of the Exchange Department. One of its members was a dealer, to ensure that any redesign took full account of the needs of the Dealing Room; another member acted in a liaison role with the systems analysts who were not formally members of the design team.

In Aero-space Ltd., the project was started by the Systems Manager meeting the staff of the Purchase Invoice and Treasurer's Departments in small groups and explaining to them the nature of the project and its philosophy and objectives. The staff of both departments agreed to participate in the project.

FORMATION OF THE DESIGN GROUP IN AERO-SPACE LTD.

The Systems Manager in association with the departmental supervisor of the Purchase Invoice Department next selected a representative number of clerks to act as a Design Group. The Manager of the Treasurer's Department also nominated one member of his staff. This group would be responsible for the development of a new system of work, although this system would evolve on the basis of feedback and discussion with all members of staff in the two Departments. The Design Group was selected so that there would be a representative from each work section, from each job grade, from each age group and from men and women. When set up it consisted of six clerical representatives - four from Purchase Invoice clerks, one from the Data Preparation Group in Purchase Invoice and one from the Treasurer's Department - two systems analysts from the Management Services Department who would have responsibility for the design of the computer based part of the new work system, the author and the Systems Manager. One of the first steps was the organization of a one day training course for the Design Group so that the members could obtain some understanding of how work systems could be analysed and new alternatives constructed. A major feature of this course was a practical exercise in work design. This exercise took the Design Group through the steps they would need to follow to design a new system of work. It covered the following:

1. Diagnosis   An analysis of the job satisfaction and efficiency needs of the group of employees whose work was to be redesigned.

2. Objectives   How job satisfaction and efficiency objectives can be set in such a way that it is possible to later measure whether or not they have been achieved.

3. Alternatives   The alternative approaches for meeting job satisfaction and efficiency needs through the redesign of work that are available in a particular work situation. The way in which the human and technical advantages and disadvantages of each alternative can be set out.

4. Final Work Design   Specifying in detail the selected method for restructuring work.

5. The Design Process   Deciding on the best method for handling the process of design and implementation so that the enthusiasm and co-operation of employees is stimulated and maintained.

FORMATION OF THE STEERING GROUP IN AERO-SPACE LTD.

A Steering Group was also created consisting of the Head of Management Services, the Systems Managers who initiated the project, the Senior Manager responsible for the Purchase Invoice Department, the Senior Manager of the adjoining Treasury Department whose work would be affected by any reorganization of Purchase Invoice, one of the Company's Personnel Managers, the Factory Medical Officer, and the Trade Union Official. It was decided that the role of the Steering Group should be to provide encouragement and advice to the Design Group. The Steering Group would meet to review the progress of the project once a month but its members would make themselves available each Friday afternoon in case the Design Group wished to consult them. For example, if the Design Group became worried that decisions it was taking might not fit with Company policies it could ask the Steering Group for a ruling and receive an immediate answer. It was thought that this procedure would prevent the Design group spending several weeks developing an alternative system of work which would later prove unacceptable to top management. In fact, the Steering Group never had to intervene in such a negative manner. Its role turned out to be the more positive one of encouraging the Design Group to embark on a fundamental rethinking of the work system and not to be constrained by factors associated with the existing work situation such as the job grading system. Without this encouragement from the Steering Group the Design Group might have been too conservative in its approach, from fear that any radical design proposal would prove unacceptable to top management.

The setting up of these design projects was not free from problems although these were more apparent in Aero-space Ltd., where the 'consensus' democracy approach meant that there was constant communication to and from all staff in the Departments. Three problems emerged at this stage. First, that staff in Purchase Invoice were suspicious of the project. They could not believe that management was really permitting them to design their own system of work and suspected that management had a hidden ulterior motive. Second, although the Design Group had been carefully selected so as to represent all the different interest groups in the department, the fact that group members were selected by management meant that they were seen as 'management favourites'. Third, the fact that the Design Group had to be both 'designers' and clerks and when they were designing they were neglecting their normal clerical duties. Departmental Management was therefore anxious that they should not spend too much time in their design role.

This last problem was also found in International Bank where the Design Group complained that they were given responsibility for the project but not the time necessary to carry it out. The other problems did not show up so clearly as the 'representative' approach meant that the clerks as a group were not greatly involved in or identified with the design exercise, and were willing to leave the task to their representatives.

IDENTIFICATION OF WORK SYSTEM PROBLEMS

A first task of both Design Groups was to gather information as a basis for commencing an analysis of the job satisfaction and efficiency problems. This information had to be of three kinds.

1.   Information on work problems in the department that were impairing efficiency. In International Bank this was done by the Design Group. In Aero-space Ltd., all staff in the Purchase Invoice Department were asked to note any weaknesses in the existing system of work. For example, functions where delays occurred in receiving or giving information or where problems arose in co-ordinating one set of tasks with another. Staff were asked to describe these, to explain their cause and to provide suggestions on how they might be reduced or eliminated. This is the analysis of system variances described earlier.

2.   Information on job satisfaction needs and on the extent to which the existing system of work met these needs was obtained through a questionnaire based on the job satisfaction model described earlier. This questionnarie was completed by all staff, the data were analysed by the author and, in Aero-space Ltd., the results were fed back to all staff by the Design Group and later discussed in small groups. In both International Bank and Aero-space Ltd., work was perceived as too routine and there was a demand for more

challenge and for the opportunity to feel a greater sense of achievement. The clerks in both situations said that their work should provide them with better opportunities to develop their skills and knowledge and that they should be given more personal responsibility. They also wanted a greater opportunity to develop their own work methods, to take decisions and to have personal autonomy. This last need would, they believed, be assisted through the opportunity for seeing a piece of work through from start to finish instead of having to pass it on to another clerk.

3. The systems analysts in each organization provided information on how the new on-line computer systems could be developed so as to improve efficiency and to assist job satisfaction.

DEVELOPING AND CHOOSING THE WORK SYSTEMS

In both International Bank and Aero-space Ltd., the on-line computer systems were primarily for processing data and providing information through visual display terminals. They therefore imposed few constraints on the design of the human part of the system and could assist work interest throught taking over some routine activities. However, in order to facilitate the redesign of work organization, both groups of systems designers had to keep the technical systems as flexible as possible so that a variety of task structures could be associated with them.

In International Bank the pre-change structure of the Department was based on the different functions associated with the processing of deals and produced considerable work segmentation. Also the introduction of the batch computer system had brought with it a number of boring and routine jobs, for example the coding of input vouchers. It had also virtually eliminated ledger work which previously had been a source of satisfaction to many Bank staff.

Aero-space Purchase Invoice Department had a similar structure with individual clerks responsible for small accountancy tasks, most of which lacked challenge and interest.

Using the job satisfaction survey as a guide, the International Bank Design Group gave its attention to a number of alternative ways of reorganizing the department. Three alternatives seemed worth considering.

1. Maintaining the existing functional structure.

2. Eliminating fucntional divisions and organizing the department around the logical work flow.

3. Dividing up the department into groups based on currencies.

The first alternative had the advantage of minimising disturbance but had the disadvantage that it did nothing to improve job satisfaction. The Design Group also saw it as poor in meeting the staff needs for work variety. It was also inflexible and hindered staff mobility. If one section was very busy staff in other sections would not have the skills to help.

The second alternative would produce an improved work flow but would be very difficult to control and could lead to staff dissatisfaction as there would be no groups with which they could identify.

The third alternative, division by currency, was the one chosen. The Dealing Room was already divided by currency blocks and it seemed logical to divide the Exchange Department in the same way. This would give job variety to staff, since within each currency block all types of transactions would be processed. It would also give a sense of group identity to the members of each currency section. Also the supervision and control of such a system would be relatively easy.

Once they had selected a viable alternative the Design Group next had to set out
the detail of this form of organization. The most efficient currency breakdown
had to be worked out, based on the volumes per currency transaction, so that the
new sections would have similar work loads of one or more currencies. Details
of the organization of work within each section had also to be formulated and it
was decided that a multi-skilled group structure would be the most appropriate,
with each member eventually trained to do all the jobs of the section, from input
through to the final check before documents were despatched. This would increase
the interest of work and also enable a clerk to start a deal and effectively
monitor and complete its passage through the system. This approach would also
increase the clerk's knowledge, experience and responsibility. The Design Group
suggested that once the system was introduced job evaluation should be based on
knowledge and experience and not on grade as at present.

There would be four currency sections - dollars, sterling, Swiss franc/guilders/
sundry, Deutschmark/French francs, and a service section. Each section would require a staff of ten. The available mix of tasks comprised:

a. Tasks associated with computer input. Collecting information,
   adding to information, inputting information via the VDU's,
   checking the accuracy of input. When necessary establishing
   the integrity of input by using the VDU enquiry facility to
   check on customer status.

b. Tasks concerned with real-time computer output. Dealing with
   confirmations and payment documents such as cables and banker's
   orders. Checking the correctness of these before despatch.

c. Tasks associated with batch computer output. Identifying the
   reason for errors in printed output documents, balance lists etc.

d. Tasks still independent of the computer. Information coming
   into the Foreign Exchange Department from other Banks, e.g. confir-
   mation of deals handled by other Banks, requests for deposit
   guarantees etc. Problems associated with meeting customer
   instructions, reconciling documents, correcting errors.

e. Control procedures such as final check and signing before
   documents were despatched.

Staff within a section would have to deal with the three basic tasks of exchange
operations, fixed deposits/loans and sight and notice accounts, previously
handled in separate sections.

The Design Group also made recommendations about the environment of the Department, training, and implementation and designed a floor plan showing the layout
of the Currency sections. They also recommended that they should remain in being
once the new structure was implemented so that they could monitor it and iron out
problems. The Design Group's report was presented to the Bank Management at the
end of May, 1975, and was accepted.

The consensus democracy approach adopted by Aero-space Ltd., meant that a new
form of work organization would only be accepted for implementation after the
Purchase Invoice and Treasury Departments as a whole had given their approval.
This meant that the Design Group there had to provide a number of alternatives
for discussion. Three alternative systems were constructed and these were fed
back sequentially to all staff in the Department for their comments and criticisms.
These systems took the following form.

Alternative 1.   The Purchase Invoice Department would be split into a
                 number of autonomous or self managing groups. Each
                 group would take responsibility for all the activities
                 associated with handling the accounts and problems of
                 a group of suppliers. A group would consist of six
                 clerks, each of whom would be able to perform all the
                 tasks for which the group was responsible. The existing
                 grading structure of the department would be eliminated
                 and all clerks would eventually become the same grade.
                 Grading would in effect be based on job knowledge and
                 everyone who wished to do so would be able to acquire
                 this knowledge.

The response to this work design alternative was a great deal of hostility from the
higher grade clerks who felt that they would lose status if difficult and responsible work was available to anyone who wished to do it. The Design Group reacted
to this aggressive response with nervousness and moved back from their revolutio-
nary position.

Alternative 2.   This alternative was a modification of the existing work
                 system with the department organized in the same functional
                 way but with an enrichment of the jobs of the lower grade
                 clerks who, in the job satisfaction survey, were the group
                 with the least job satisfaction.

The response of the clerks to this work design alternative was that it did not improve much on the existing work situation. The Design Group tried again.

Alternative 3.   This alternative combined 1 and 2. The majority of staff
                 in the department would be organized in self managing
                 groups as in 1. In addition there would be a service
                 group with responsibility for handling mail and for other
                 activities which were common to all groups. The work of
                 the Service Group would be routine but the Design Group
                 was confident that a small number of staff in the depart-
                 ment did not want the responsibility of more complex
                 tasks. Some variety could be introduced into this work
                 through job rotation.

                 There would also be a small specialist group of high
                 grade clerks who would look after specialist suppliers
                 and activities. This would meet the needs of a group of
                 senior clerks who were extremely reluctant to change their
                 present role and responsibilities.

These three alternatives were presented to the staff of the Pruchase Invoice and
Treasurer's Departments at a meeting chaired by the Trade Union Branch Chairman.
He asked for a vote to be taken and alternative 3 met with general approval and
was selected for implementation.

During the design period the International Bank Design Group encountered few relationship difficulties with their colleagues in the Exchange Department. This is
not necessarily because these did not exist, although this might have been the case,
but the representative approach with its absence of feedback meant that they did
not come to the surface.

In Aero-space Ltd., in contrast, because the design alternatives were fed back sequentially and the first alternative was perceived as threatening by some of the
senior clerks a great deal of conflict broke out in the Purchase Invoice Department. The Design Group received considerable hostility from its own colleagues and
two now resigned as a result of the stressful nature of the interpersonal situation.

It became clear that there was no complete identity of interest amongst the Purchase Invoice clerks and that a number of those in the higher grades saw their
interests as different from those in the lower grades. Therefore a new work system
based on autonomous groups and work sharing was unacceptable to them. This critica
group were opinion leaders in the department and their objections caused a drop in
the morale of the staff of the department as a whole and of the Design Group. The
situation was rescued by the Systems Manager, Accounts, who sent a short questionnaire round to all members of the department asking if they wished the project to
continue or not and to give reasons for their answer. The response to this questior
naire showed that 60% of the department were in favour of the project continuing.
They gave as their reasons the fact that they wanted larger, more challenging jobs
together with the possibility of moving up to a higher work grade, a promotion
which would bring with it an increase in salary.

Before the design task was finished a further problem occurred which resulted in
the project being stopped for three months. This problem concerned the Trade Union
and arose because it transpired that the Trade Union Official on the Steering
Group had not informed the Union's area officials of the work design project that
was taking place in his firm. The higher levels of the Union Hierarchy heard about
the project as a result of a comment made at a branch meeting and they therefore
ordered it to stop until they had obtained the details of what was taking place.
Pressure of Union business made this investigation a slow process with the result
that the project was not able to recommence until three months later. By this time
morale in Purchase Invoice Department had dropped again. Staff interpreted the
Union's action as an indication that the Union did not support the project. This
situation was saved by the Trade Union Branch Chairman who came and addressed the
Purchase Invoice Staff. He told them that the project had complete Union support
and he urged them to participate fully and to make sure that the Design Group received their ideas for improvement. His message was 'here is an opportunity to
participate, do not lose it'.

IMPLEMENTATION

At this moment in time, September 1978, the new system of work is only settling
down in Aero-space Ltd., and a post-change evaluation of its efficiency and job
satisfaction consequences has not yet been made. In March 1978, however, the
author was able to carry out a post change evaluation in International Bank, once
again carrying out a survey of job satisfaction. The Exchange Department had now
been organized in currency groups since the beginning of 1976 although job evaluation to re-grade the new enriched jobs had had to be postponed until 1977, the
time it took for the on-line system to settle down. To the author's astonishment
the survey showed that <u>job satisfaction had decreased and not increased</u>.

How could this result, which is the opposite of the situation described in most
socio-technical case studies, be explained? The author tried to find out. It emergec
that dissatisfaction was a product of implementation rather than organization of
work. The delay in job evaluation had caused morale problems as staff became frustrated at having to wait so long for regrading when the new work structure meant
that they were undertaking larger jobs and carrying more responsibility. This frustration was increased by the fact that as staff were struggling to learn to operate the on-line systems attempts were made to gain some of the staff savings which
management had asked the Design Group to try and achieve through their reorganization proposals. Staff who left were not replaced and the Exchange Department reduced its labour force from 61 to 53 over a period of four months. Although staff
had previously agreed to run the department with fewer clerks this rapid reduction
in numbers at a time of major change caused stress, although management responded
to this by increasing the staff complement by two. Nevertheless this did not completely solve the staffing problem. Further problems had arisen at the end of
January 1977 when the job evaluation exercise was completed by the Bank's job evaluation officers. Many staff now found that despite the reorganization and the more
varied and demanding work, their jobs had not been regraded. These staff appealed

against this decision and as a result some were allotted a higher grade, but this dispute also damaged morale.

In addition to these grading and staffing problems other internal and external changes were affecting job satisfaction. First, there had been a tightening of Bank controls and a requirement that all transactions carried out on a particular day had to be processed the same way. Previously deals completed after 3 p.m. were processed the following day. This ruling was a consequence of a number of international banks sustaining heavy losses because dealing staff had not adhered to the procedures laid down by management but it had the effect of lengthening the clerks' working day. Second, the reorganization of work had not solved the department's promotion problems. Once a clerk became a section head at the age of about 25 promotion or an increase in salary could only be achieved through leaving. The two tier recruiting system adopted by most banks in recent years made the problem worse by creating one kind of promotion channel for graduates and a different one for school leavers. Third, the Bank had always tried to recruit bright staff and had succeeded in doing this. Now, however, the difficult state of the labour market for young people meant that very intelligent boys and girls wished to join the Bank and the routine nature of the work did not fit well with their expectations or ability. In the view of the Head of the Foreign Exchange Department the reorganization of work into currency sections had made work more varied but it had not reduced routine. Junior staff were doing more jobs but they were still doing 'junior' jobs. The vast amounts of money involved and the strictures of the Bank inspectors required that only senior staff signed documents involving the payment of money.

However the Head of the Foreign Exchange Department believed that the reorganization of work into currency groups had achieved the aim of enriching the job content of the clerks. Within each section each clerk was now able to deal with exchange operations, fixed deposits and loans and with sight and notice accounts, and all clerks could operate the VDU's. This meant that jobs were now more varied and this increased responsibility had led to most of them eventually being upgraded. He now had very few complaints from staff about the nature of the work they had to do. He was less certain that the on-line system had made any major contribution to job satisfaction. Both the batch and the on-line system had caused work to be more bitty and less integrated than the manual system. However he confirmed the view expressed by a majority of clerks in the post-change survey, that the VDU system enabled errors to be quickly identified and corrected and that queries could be handled more rapidly and efficiently as a result of the on-line system's enquiry facility. The designer of the system made the interesting suggestion that the clerk's ability to identify errors as soon as data was inputted might have reduced job satisfaction and removed some feelings of achievement. Previously a source of job satisfaction had been finding out the reasons for errors and discrepancies and rectifying these. This task had often involved quite complex search processes and some clerical detective work which the on-line system had eliminated.

CONCLUSIONS ON THE USE OF A PARTICIPATIVE APPROACH TO WORK DESIGN

One condition for a participative approach to work reorganization is that no-one must suffer and as many employees as possible should gain from the change. Because a computer system was being introduced into International Bank and Aero-space Ltd. there was a potential for reducing the number of staff and guarantees had to be given that there would be no redundancy and that any staff saving would be achieved by not replacing staff when they left voluntarily. If this guarantee had not been given the project would not have been acceptable to employees.

This participative approach has also to be acceptable to management and in both organizations management believed that they would gain from the increased efficiency of the new work system and from the fact that the reorganized Purchase Invoice and Exchange Departments would be more desirable work environments and therefore have less difficulty in attracting and keeping staff.

It is very clear that a major learning process is involved in the work design approach described here. A Design Group has to transform itself from a group of clerks whose knowledge is restricted to the performance of simple clerical operations to a group capable of creative problem solving and the generation of new, radical ideas. The fact that such groups appear to be able to undergo this transformation with relative ease suggests the extent to which their talents have been underutilized in their normal jobs. If the consensus democracy approach is used the department as a whole has also to learn a number of things. It too has to acquire skills in identifying work problems and suggesting improvements. It has also to be able to communicate these ideas to the Design Group and it has to learn how to participate in a new, democratic, process with which it is totally unfamiliar. The experience of this project suggests that learning how to participate democratically is more difficult than learning how to redesign work.

If a new computer system is being introduced as part of a reorganization of work then the computer systems analysts have to learn a new role. Instead of following their traditional practice of designing a technical system and then reorganizing the work system to fit this, they have to fit their technical system into the form of reorganization created by the Design Group. This means that they have to take a very flexible approach to the technical design processes and not insist on any technical solution that imposes constraints on the work of the Design Group. Ideally the systems analysts will develop the computer system as the Design Group is developing the new form of work organization. It is of course essential that the computer systems analysts are members of the Design Group. This raises the whole question of the training of systems analysts to enable them to assume this teaching and participative role. They need to understand how to design the human as well as the technical part of a computer system, they must be able to develop and communicate technical system alternatives to design groups and they must be able to work in a democratic situation where their ideas are only one of a number of inputs and have to be justified in terms of job satisfaction as well as efficiency needs.

The processes of change also have their problems. The lesson from International Bank is that work reorganization and socio-technical systems design can solve some problems but not all. A well designed system can be wrecked by poor implementation; changes in the internal and external environments may lead to tighter controls or new sets of job expectations.

Lastly, democracy is itself a difficult state. The representative approach seems to avoid conflict, but may do this by keeping it below the surface. The consensus approach brings conflict out into the open where it has to be handled. If this is not done successfully a worthwhile project may have to be abandoned. Democracy allied to a socio-technical design approach requires a particular set of values from all the participants. The systems designers must believe in the importance and viability of designing the human part of what have in the past been regarded as purely technical systems, and be willing to let the user assume responsibility for this area of systems design. Management must believe in participation and be willing to hand over an important design task to their subordinates, and the clerks themselves must be prepared to take on the design task and not see design as something for which only management or experts should have responsibility.

REFERENCES

Taylor, J.C. (1975). The Human Side of Work: the socio-technical approach to work design. Personnel Review, Vol. 4, No. 3.

Mumford, E. (1972). Job Satisfaction: a method of analysis. Personnel Review, Vol. 1, No. 3.

Herzberg, F. (1966). Work and the Nature of Man. Staples Press, London.

Cooper, R. (1973). How Jobs Motivate. Personnel Review, Vol. 2, No. 2.

DISCUSSION AND COMMENTS ON PAPER PRESENTED BY ENID MUMFORD

GERALD ROLLOY

I found Mumford's presentation extremely stimulating as in my country, France, the participative design of clerical information systems is still very unusual. More and more managers do seem to be concerned with the quality-of-working-life problems connected with computer design, but it is mostly a matter of: "Let's design once and for all a good work place and job content so that the Visual Display Units will not be rejected".

Such an attitude from managers seems to lead to an 'expert' rather than a participative approach with ergonomists being asked to help computer professionals in the design phase.

I would very much like to know, particularly for England and Scandinavia, how frequently during the design and implementation of a new computer system white-collar workers are provided with the opportunity to redesign their own work system?

My second question relates to the issue of designing flexible systems. Mumford mentioned that in order to facilitate the redesign of work organization, the designers had to keep the technical systems as flexible as possible: I think that this is a very interesting point for computer specialists, and I would like very much to have some details or examples of this technical flexibility? Does it for instance lead to what is called 'Modular Programming'?

In the Bank Case, staff agreed 'to run the department with fewer clerks', but it seems as if there was some kind of productivity pressure and stress caused by increase of work load. This raises at least two questions: In that specific case I wonder whether there was any Union Official involved in the design process, and if so, did he later on have any problems with the workers or with the Branch Union?

Thirdly, is it possible to use any method in the design phase which will help predict the future work load (especially the mental load associated with stress) for a given work place?

ENID MUMFORD

Participative design is not yet common but increasingly people are becoming sympathetic towards it. I believe that pressure from trade unions is likely to have a significant impact on progress. However, we have not seen this kind of union activity in the U.K. yet.

With regard to the second question, we encountered some conflict between senior and junior clerks and the trade union official was helpful in resolving this. He came into the department and held a meeting with the clerks in which he said: "This is your opportunity to obtain some control over your own work system, don't throw it away". So both the union and management took a very positive approach.

With regard to the last two questions, I really cannot answer them, and I should like to pass them on to the audience. Designers are always telling me that they are creating flexible computer systems which will accept any form of work organization the design group wants. So perhaps someone here could tell us what flexible systems are.

The last question abour reduction in staff and increased work load was actually negotiated. Obviously the negotiations were not very successful in the sense that the work load was not properly assessed in advance. Personally, I do not know any technique of finding out in advance.

A.W. ZIJLKER

I very much agree with what has been said in the presentation, and I am sure that many of us recognize the situation Mumford describes. She mentions the kind of problems we have all met and I believe we should be aware of the fact that there are no real solutions to problems and all we can do is to work on them constantly It is not a matter of finding the one methodology. What you presented was a strategy to cope with some of the problems arising in a particular situation. In othe words we were provided with a set of philosophically based guidelines and not with a rounded off methodology to solve all problems. This we hopefully have learned from.

I should like to know what would have happened, had Mumford not been there to diagnose and facilitate this project of participation.

Concerning flexibility, I believe that if you use a lot of procedures and precise methodology, you are bound to get stuck with the system and the methodology, and it is difficult to change. On the other hand, if you minimize the degree of systemisation and the amount of methodology, you remain as flexible as you wish. I thin it is as simple as that.

JAN C. WERKMANN

I wonder how reproducible is the exercise presented. If one is faced with a situation with geographically dispersed units and with a particular type of operation, is it possible to use a similar approach in the other places and get the same degree of user satisfaction?

ENID MUMFORD

Honestly, I do not know. I believe that the new work organization has been well liked despite the problems in Lloyds Bank International. But I think that the previous comment was an interesting one. Things never stand still. New groups of employees may at any time make different demands and desire different solutions.

H.C. PRICE

I have a comment on the grass-roots approach. At the hospital there is a myth that doctors know everything. There is a rulebook, but if one wants to find out what is going on in the ward, one should not look there nor ask the doctor. Patients and ward staff are really the only ones who know what is going on. So a grass-roots approach is absolutely essential.

JOHN BANBURY

With regard to flexibility, this straightforwardly depends upon the ease with which a system's hardware and software can be modified, new routines learned, and so on, in the short and longer term. However, I should like to support Zijlker's suggestion that, in practice, this may be more a matter of design philosophy than of technique. The extent to which flexibility is required in a particular system depends upon the characteristics of the particular context to which it significantly relates - and, obviously, the more this reamins stable, the less is the requirement for flexibility. However, if it is suggested that the relevant characteristics of a particular operating context (of or operating contexts in general, for that matter) cannot at present be forecast with sufficient accuracy to produce a tightly specifiable hardware and software design, then we must surely aim for a robust design. This may shift the emphasis in the direction of predominantly 'social' rather than 'hardware' based control links, for example, as might emerge from participative design approaches. Increased emphasis might also come to be placed upon semi-autonomous systems with a stronger user-orientation in both their development and their operation.

The philosophy underlying such approaches would tend to lean towards exploratory and evolutionary systems, rather than highly prescriptive 'once-for-all' ones, and towards a corresponding set of beliefs about the nature of organisation.

PAUL BLOKDIJK

I have had almost one year's experience with participative design. One characteristic of the approach presented was that it stopped with the implementation of the socio-technical design. In contrast we expect to continue re-developing the information system with the participants. This has the effect that flexibility is built in by the user himself and substantially alters the systems design approach. Among other things, we discovered that the complexity of the system had shifted. We had more complexity in one area and less complexity in another area. This shows that the participative approach is really improving the quality of the system.

MAX ELDEN

I should like to mention that we have had a number of experiences with participative design in the Scandinavian countries. We have about two dozen cases in eight European countries which are now being written up about participative research design, although they are not all directly related to computer technology. (Working on the Quality of Working Life, Developments in Europe, Martinus Nijhoff, 1979) There is also a collection of case reports from Western and Eastern Europe by Mumford and Cooper where a number of cases are concerned with participative design for Quality of Working Life published in spring 1979. Furthermore, Jim Taylor in the USA and Einar Thorsrud in a number of developing countries are pursuing similar kinds of activities. So in my opinion a lot has been going on in the last two years.

A Swede who is not a football Docherty
Is heading a large research hierarchy
Agreements and regulations
Industrial relations
With union involvement in computery.

USER PARTICIPATION IN AND INFLUENCE ON SYSTEMS DESIGN
IN NORWAY AND SWEDEN
IN THE LIGHT OF UNION INVOLVEMENT, NEW LEGISLATION,
AND JOINT AGREEMENTS

Peter Docherty

EFI, Stockholm School of
Economics, Sweden

The last ten years have witnessed major
efforts by the union movement in Norway
and Sweden in relation to the rapid development and application of computer technology, both as a means of controlling and
steering organisations and as a means of
rationalising and restructuring work. Union
efforts in the political sphere have led
to new legislation and joint agreements
with far-reaching implications for the
future development and application of this
technology. Key paragraphs from these and
their impact to date are presented. At the
same time various unions have been developing their competence, knowledge base and
policies in the area of computer technology
by conducting their own R and D and educational programmes. Several of these are
outlined in this article.

The Human Side of Information Processing
N. Bjørn-Andersen, editor
© IAG
North-Holland Publishing Company, 1980

1. INTRODUCTION

1.1. Aim and Scope of the Paper

In this paper I will present a general review of the growing involvement of the Norwegian and Swedish trade unions in issues and problems related to the development of computer technology. This interest is manifested in the development of new union policies and strategies, and marked investments in information, training, research and development. The developments in the seventies have been characterized by an intensive interaction between the unions and the political parties on the one hand, and the unions and the employers'confederations on the other hand. This interaction has led to legislation and the formulation of joint agreements which have, in their turn, stimulated further development.

This article concentrates on the impacts of legislation and joint agreements on union activities and thinking regarding their roles in the development and utilization of computer based systems. In this context I shall give primary attention to the issues of work organization and work environment and shall not specially treat the issue of personal integrity (which has also been the subject of much legislation in Scandinavia).

I find it somewhat easier to present the developments separately for each of the two countries. Different issues have naturally been emphasized at the same time as there has been an extensive exchange of ideas and experiences between them. The paper is written from a Swedish perspective in which the experiences, interactions and parallel developments from Norway are presented although not in a historical sequence.

The following subsection gives a general background indicating the structure of the following sections. These deal with the three main points: relevant legislation and joint agreements, experiences to date, and current developments. These are first presented for Norway and then for Sweden. In all cases the legislation and joint agreements are very recent and there is little systematic documentation of their impact. I can only report relatively isolated anecdotal evidence or results from studies initiated as part of the union reorientation in this sphere before the new legislation and joint agreements came into force, or, results from progress reports of projects initiated since these came into force. Thus the legislation and the joint agreements have not as yet had such radical influence on current practice as they have had on aspirations and expectations which naturally imply marked changes tomorrow.

I conclude this paper with some observations and thoughts regarding unions' reorientation towards systems development and utilization and a number of the problems which can already be discerned in this context.

1.2. General Background

The close of the sixties was marked by a chronic deterioration in the economic climate in Sweden. There no longer existed the possibilities for an automatic improvement in the standard of living for all groups in society. This was one factor which led to an increased interest within union organisations in a review of strategic planning and policy development. A defence of the ground won regarding standards of living and security of employment required other forms of influence over societal planning, and development in business and industry. New forms of cooperation emerged between different white-collar unions, e.g. the formation of the cartel of salaried workers in industry and commerce (Privattjänstemannakartellen:PTK) and between white collar and blue-collar unions, for example the joining of forces between PTK and LO (Landsorganisationen - Trade Union Congress) in their negotiations with the Swedish Employers' Confederation (SAF).

At the same time as it was essential to defend what had been achieved, there was also a marked increase in the interest and priority given to conditions of work,

for example the work environment regarding both the physical environment, i.e. ergonomic and chemical factors and the social environment regarding such factors as
self- and co-determination, and stress in work.

Efforts to create suitable conditions for the desired strategy development were
channeled through the social democratic parties in government in a comprehensive
programme of labour market legislation. These covered such issues as security of
employment, co-determination, the rights of shop stewards and a work environment
law. The attainment of independence and control over research and development led
to the abandonment of joint efforts with the employers confederations in favour of
union projects concentrating on their own specific issues.

The new emphasis accorded issues concerning conditions of work, for example work
environment and work organisation, places new and heavy demands on the means at
the unions' disposal (Berg and Docherty 1975). New legislation and joint agreements
gave the union the rights to take action on issues which were previously 'out of
play'. Research could be expected to supply information and knowledge necessary
for the development of goals and policies. Other vital issues were, however, the
development of compentence and skills, for example in the field of computer technology, the need for a rapid expansion of union resources - not least in terms of
the numbers of members actively involved in union work - and even in the internal
reorganisation of unions to deal with issues concerning conditions of work.

Thus new legislation and joint agreements which extend the possibilities for union
involvement in development and utilization of computer based systems present the
unions with many new and difficult but challenging tasks. They are already meeting
these tasks with enthusiasm.

2.   INSPIRATION IN THE WEST: NORWEGIAN DEVELOPMENTS

There is a depressing saying, well known to many innovators that "No-one is a
prophet in his own land". It may, however, be of some consolation to Norwegian
colleagues that innovations in the sphere of systems development and the organization of work in Norway have been followed with great interest in Sweden and in
many cases have been applied there.

2.1. Legislation and Joint Agreements

The Norwegian experiments regarding industrial democracy sponsored by the Norwegian Employers' Confederation and Trade Union Congress in collaboration with
researchers from the Work Research Institutes (WRI) were the object of much emula-
tion in Sweden at the end of the sixties. In Norway, however, the industrial democracy movement was soon replaced by the work environment movement in which important and operative needs for the majority of employees were more clearly seen
(Gustavsen 1976). The WRI were involved in the formulation of the Norwegian work
environment law which was intended to promote the following changes:

- To make the development of the work environment an integral
  part of the general developmental work at the enterprise,

- To bring the employees into this work through their unions
  and the work environment committees,

- To establish the employees' right to take part in decisions
  relating to the work environment,

- To inforce planned development of the work environment and

- To bring the factory inspector into the supervision of the
  implementation of these plans.

This piece of legislation is probably unique in that it explicitly formulates social needs for meaningful work for the individual in the legislation. The needs

enumerated are those from socio-technical theory regarding variation in tasks, social contact, personal development and discretion in work (Emery and Thorsrud 1974). Paragraph 12 of this legislation also stipulates that the employee should have information (insight) and training in systems to be utilized in the planning and execution of work and that they should also participate in the design of these systems.

An ongoing study of participation (Qvale 1977) shows that workers in manufacturing industries maintain that although the work environment is the decision area over which they already have highest influence, it is also the one where they want the greatest increase in influence/level of participation.

This law have been followed by one of the most intensive training programmes in Norwegian industrial history. In 1977 already 90,000 of Norway's 1,3 million workers had attended the course. Ødegaard (1977) has made the first plant level follow-up study of the impact of the new law, departing from the use of the training course 'Better Work Environment'. In this study he compared the analysis of work environment made by study circles analysing their own workplace compared with those analysing other workplaces in the same organisation. (The composition of the study circles was the same in both cases, i.e. they included managers, supervisors shop-stewards and workers).

Type of problem	Model for analysis	Causes in % of total			Total	
		Technical	Human	Organizational	%	(N)
Physical	Study of others' situation	75	25	0	100	(36)
	Study of own situation	65	13	22	100	(23)
Accident hazards	Study of others' situation	8	92	0	100	(13)
	Study of own situation	39	44	17	100	(23)
Psycyological/social	Study of others' situation	100	0	0	100	(5)
	Study of own situation	45	0	55	100	(11)

Table 1.

Causes of work environmental problems according
to type and model for analysis (Ødegaard 1977).

The difference between the results obtained by the two types of analysing the environment were:

- The inspection of other's jobs only leads to the tracing of technical and human factors while the analysis of own situations <u>also</u> indicates the way work is organized as a cause of problems, and

- Inspections of others attribute accident hazards almost entirely to human error, while own situation analyses focus to a considerable extent on technical and organisational factors.

From a union viewpoint this is concrete evidence that it is essential that those workers who use a system in operation or will come in contact with that system must be directly involved in the analysis and development work producing the system.

Joint agreements regarding computer based systems have been signed between the various parties in the Norwegian labour market in the mid-seventies. A paraphrase of some of the paragraphs in the central agreement in the government sector from 1975 indicates the kinds of issues they cover:

1.1 The agreement covers computer based systems affecting the employees and their working conditions. It also covers the storage and use of personnel data on the employees.

2.3 The relevant union officials shall be informed of the introduction or alteration of such systems so that they may present their viewpoints as early as possible and before possible decisions are taken.

2.4 Information shall be presented in a comprehensible form and in a language which may be understood by people without an expert knowledge of the area.

3.2 Data processing shop-stewards shall be given the opportunity of penetrating the general issues regarding computer based systems and their influence on the working conditions of the employee. They shall have access to necessary documentation and shall have the opportunity of consulting with individual employees and other union officials.

3.3 Other union representatives and employees participating in specific systems projects shall have access to current documentation regarding the project.

4.1 The government shall be responsible for giving personnel representatives a general training in computer technology.

4.2 The government and the unions shall together decide on the need for further training of union officials and other employees who will particiapte in specific projects.

4.3 The government shall defray the cost of all such training.

5.1 It is the duty of government authorities to control that the utilization of personnel data takes place in a safe and satisfactory fashion.

Local joint agreements in individual government authorities specify in greater detail the information to be given, and the forms for employee and union involvement. Thus for example they may specify as in one case (Norska Lånekassan) that discussion takes place between management and union when the feasibility study is completed and that this shall specify expected changes in manning levels and job content. The same agreement specifies that the union official for computer issues (Datatillitsman) be consulted in decisions regarding investments in computer equipment and that the union may utilize the available systems for union administration - and even other tasks - as long as the authority concerned is satisfied that this does not entail unreasonable economic costs and the work may be fitted in the production schedules for the computer centre. Similarly no change which is not accepted by the majority to the work environment committee may be enforced without the approval of the board.

What impact has this type of joint negotiation had in practice on systems development in Norway? There is little evidence available at the present which is directly coupled to these agreements. Marthinsen (1978),himself a union official responsible for computer questions, reports his own experiences. He experiences the reactions partly as an anticlimax and that the agreement is something quickly for-

gotten or regarded with little respect. He feels that this is partially explained
by the fact that managers are suspicious towards the computer officials on account
of their previous records as shop-stewards and 'natural opponents' to technical
development. Managers do not seek going into a clinch with experienced shop-stewards specially trained in computer issues. Their status in the union would appear
to be a typical expert role in which they are regarded as the only ones competent
to express an opinion in this area.

The role of the union data processing shop-stewards is still evolving and is as
much an issue of aspirations as of confirmed practice at the present time. Aspirations and expectations include direct participation from the outset in all project
affecting workers with respect to the design of training programmes, organisationa
changes, the work environment, computer print-outs and VDU-displays, layout of per
sonnel suggestions. The DP-shop-steward will also assume responsibility for the
election of personnel representatives, information to personnel and the coordination with other union officials that other joint agreements and legislation are
adhered to.

SAS have also reported their experiences of such joint agreements (Korsvold 1978).
A general reflexion is that it is very difficult for people to understand developments if they solely receive written documentation. Both management and unions fel
at the outset that it was not necessary for unions to participate in the group
responsible for planning systems development in the organization. However the unio
in both Norway and Denmark have recently voiced interest in these issues - an aspiration which has not been positively received by management. Management also feels
that the vast majority of the employees are lukewarm to the idea of personally
participating in systems development.

Systems development staff feel that the quality of the products in the feasibility
and specification stages of systems development has improved as a result of the
joint agreement. More work is put into these stages although union action is not
regarded as having affected the solutions chosen. The quality of user participation
has improved, attitudes to union involvement are positive and time schedules have
not been extended.

Management has not experienced any problems. Occasionally they have questioned the
union representatives technical competence and passivity. They felt that communication with the union so far has mainly been a one-way process.

The union is generally positive although they experience difficulties regarding
the defrayment of costs for union representatives' participation.

2.2. Current Development Projects

The developments on the Norwegian scene have been characterized by a series of
innovative experiments initiated by individual unions. Probably the most influential of these was that started by the Norwegian Iron- and Metalworkers' Union
(NJMF) in collaboration with researchers from the Norwegian Computing Centre (NCC)
(Nygaard 1975). The cooperation began in 1971 with a study of planning methods in
the union. In 1972 the project group wrote two basic textbooks for union rank- and
file members on data processing, planning and control. In 1973 roughly 90 union
members and officials participated in study groups in four union clubs. These groups
evaluated systems recently introduced in their companies. The workers themselves
examined what decisions had been taken and why, and how the relations between
different groups in the workforce had changed as a result of the systems.

This development project was also very important with the respect to the influence
it has had in Scandinavia on the concept of research. Nygaard's group abandoned the
idea that their research reports were the products of the research project. They
felt it was truer to say that the important results were all the actions taken by
the union, centrally and locally, which were based on experiencies in the project

and which aimed to support the union and its members' efforts to attain greater influence on computerization and production planning and control in the organizations.

An essential point in the development strategy was that it was the union members themselves who analysed what they thought were the important issues in the company and its relation to its environment. In so doing they were developing their own language, concepts, models and theories of organization, work content and society which reflected their interests and values.

The pioneer work of Nygaard and his colleagues at the NCC has inspired a series of other union projects in Norway and in the other Scandinavian countries. Two further Norwegian examples are projects by the Norwegian Commercial and Office Workers Union (NHKF) (Pape 1977) and the Norwegian Chemical Industrial Workers Union (NKIF) (Elden et.al. 1978), both of which utilized a strategy centred on study groups of active union members and officials. In the first stage of the NHKF project the work group administered a survey questionnaire at different levels of the organization in a self-service chainstore. A next step is to carry out a number of intensive studies of different clubs. One of the aims of the research group is to formulate a programme of action for the union which will cover suggestions for incompany training and a more politically orientated programme of action regarding change processes in companies.

The work place democracy approach developed at the Institute for Industrial Social Research in Trondheim, Norway and the Work Research Institutes in Oslo is being combined with the self-development strategy of the NCC in a new large scale action research project for the NKIF. Amongst the research issues being studied are union influence on systems development, the implications for unions of increased automation in factories, union goals with respect to automation and the utilization of computers, the influence of computerization on job design, work environment and social contacts within the company and on employment patterns in a local community. The work is also based on work groups consisting of members officials and researchers and aims to build up a contact network between different clubs. The project is organizing a series of workshop seminars and courses for union officials as means to establish this network.

Thus legislation and joint agreements in Norway have provided the opportunity for new forms of union involvement in systems development and individual unions are giving high priority to developing their competence and resources 'across the board' in this area.

3. DEVELOPMENTS IN SWEDEN

3.1. Legislation

For over thirty years the Swedish government pursued a policy of nonintervention in the labour market. This changed radically in the seventies in which we have experienced a spate of labour market legislation. Much of this legislation has direct implications for systems development and utilization. The two most important are the co-determination law and the work environment law.

The co-determination law came into force on the 1st January 1977. The aim of the law was to restrict management's prerogatives concerning the running of an enterprise. According to paragraph 10 in this law the unions have the right to negotiate on all issues in the company. There is no restriction regarding issues which may be raised or the form for the organization of the negotiations.

According to paragraph 11 the employer must automatically initiate negotiations when he plans 'important changes' either in the business as a whole or for any single employee.

According to paragraph 12 the unions have the right to demand negotiations before decisions affecting relations between employers and employees which are not covered by paragraph 11. Decisions may not be taken or executed before negotiations are completed - except in 'exceptional' or 'special' cases.

According to paragraph 19 the employer has the duty to continuously inform workers on such issues as personnel policies and practices, budgets, plans, prognoses as well as work and production methods.

According to paragraph 33 of the act the unions have the right of precedence of interpretation within the law.

According to paragraph 38 employers must negotiate before engaging consultants or subcontracters, for example to conduct computer systems development. Exceptions to this paragraph are assignments of a short-term and temporary character, assignments which demand special knowledge and skills not available in the company and assignments which do not constitute any deviation from previously established practice.

According to paragraph 38 of the same law unions have the right of veto against the hiring of consultants or subcontracters if such assignments may be considered in conflict with good practice or with other laws and joint agreements.

The work environment law came into force on the 1st July 1978.

According to chapter 2 paragraph 1 the environment 'shall be satisfactory with regard to the nature of the work and the social and technical development in society. Conditions of work shall be adjusted to people's capacities regarding both physical and psychological aspects. Possibilities to arrange work so that the worker himself can influence his work situation shall also be taken into consideration in this context.

Some critics have maintained that this definition is unsatisfactorily vague. The government investigation which preceded the proposed legislation itemized the following points regarding social aspects of work: job content, social contact, cooperation between individuals and groups, personal discretion and influence, and possibilities for personal development. The legislators did not feel that they could be more precise at this time regarding social job criteria taking into consideration the individual variations which have been observed.

Chapter 6 in the law provides garantees for employee influence on the work situation and gives them the automatic right to negotiations when changes are being considered. This same point is also covered in the co-determination law.

According to the work environment law (1978) the work environment joint agreement (1976) between SAF, LO and PTK and the co-determination law (1977) discussions and negotiations shall take place at such an early stage that the unions have a real chance of influencing the employers' decision. According to the proposals preceding the co-determination legislation the negotiations should take such a form that their outcomes would constitute a natural step in the employers decision making.

According to the letter of the law the employer has the right to carry out necessary investigations for him to be able to make up his mind on a specific question. Thus according to a strictly formal interpretation of the current legislation the employer is only dutybound to take up the issue of introducing, changing or developing a computer based system in connection with the decision to actually produce the system. The preparations may however not proceed so far that it may be justifiably maintained that the employer has in fact taken a tacit decision before entering discussions and negotiations with the union. Furthermore the unions can demand complementary investigations and further information in order to be able to form an opinion in the negotiations or in the handling of the question in the joint industrial safety committee in accordance with paragraph 19 of the co-determination law and paragraph 20 of the work environment joint agreement. In order to avoid the disruptions in a decision process and possible postponements in the projects which this would imply it is clearly practical, from a union viewpoint, that management enter into negotiations in accordance with the eleventh paragraph of the co-determination law and enter into discussions with the industrial safety committee throughout the entire decision process (Olausson 1978).

The unions maintain that negotiations should take place between the local union organization and the employer as soon as their plan for the system is drawn up or when it is changed. Furthermore these negotiations should cover the composition of, and assignments to those groups responsible for the preliminary and main studies for different projects included in the plan. These investigations will then form the basic material in the negotiations between unions and management.

Negotiations should take place between management and the local unions in the company when the main systems development study has been carried out and a decision is to be taken on the production of the system. The proposals shall also be discussed in the industrial safety committee which shall make pronouncements on the organizational production, work methods, and work organization in the company in accordance with the third section of the 22 paragraph in the work environment joint agreement. Primary negotiation may not be concluded before the pronouncement of the industrial safety committee is available. Worker representatives in this committee may demand further investigations on the implications and effects of proposals for the work environment.

If agreement cannot be reached in the safety committee these questions become the object of further negotiations in the light of the paragraph 11 in the co-determination law. If agreement cannot be reached in local negotiations, the union has the right to take up the issue at the central level in accordance with paragraph 14 of the co-determination law.

Over and above these regulations the union can at any time raise questions regarding the utilization of computer based systems in the work place in the light of the paragraph 10 in the co-determination law and the regulations in the work environment law and the work environment joint agrement.

3.2. Some Developments to Date

The Swedish Trade Union Congress (LO) set up a work group for industrial democracy and computer questions in September 1974. This initiative was mainly the result of a motion past at the Metal Workers Union's annual congress in 1973 which underlined the relationship between industrial democracy and computer based systems. This motion was presented by the Gothenburg district which maintained that it was more important for unions to exercise influence and co-determination in steering committees controlling systems development than it was for them to be represented on company boards. The author of the motion, Göran Johansson, senior shop-steward at SKF, Gothenburg, stated:

> "We can achieve rather good results as union negotiators in
> our discussions with management. But we have noticed lately
> that our agreements have been shortcircuited in the company
> organization. The line has been broken somewhere. What has
> happened? It is the systems people who sit there with their
> own ideas. We do not reach them in the traditional union work.
>
> Influence over systems must be channeled via influence over
> systems development. We must make demands both on the forms
> for systems development and on the actual systems.

The specialists take the initiative all too often, instead the
users ought to shoulder greater responsibility for their own
involvement in these issues".

This working committee presented its suggestion to a programme of action to the
LO-congress in 1976. This programme of action indicated the need for increased
efforts in the areas of information and training. Since then LO has produced two
popular pamphlets on systems and computer utilization in the work place which have
been widely distributed within the local unions. In addition a special training
package for use in study circles has been produced. This deals with the applicatic
of the co-determination law in the context of the development and utilization of
computer based systems. In addition a series of articles have appeared in the LO's
weekly journal presenting case studies of computer applications in different sectors of industry.

The committee also suggested that the unions build up their resources of technical
experts in this field. The concept of wage-earner consultants had previously been
launched and there are already concrete examples of development projects in which
the local unions have access to systems consultants whose fees are paid by the
employers. Such an example is the development of a new online system for matching
vacancies and applications in the Swedish labour exchange. The union has a full
time official coordinating union representatives in different subprojects and
work groups and has at his disposal a consultant paid by the ministry.

Another suggestion concerned the formation of a 'bank' of experiences, case studies
evaluation reports from individual companies regarding the outcome of different
systems development projects and the effects of implemented systems. The committee
also suggested that the unions conduct their own research into these issues.

The confederation of unions of salaried employees, TCO, formed a similar data processing committee in autumn 1975. They presented a first listing of problems in
this area the following spring. They have just written a proposal for a central
policy and plan of action which will be presented at the annual congress in 1979.

3.3. Current and Planned Union R and D Projects

Unions' interest in pursuing R and D activities independently of employer organizations has grown as recently and as rapidly as their interest in systems development. The need for research in work environment and work place democracy issues
was taken up in the LO-congress in 1971. In 1975 LO was very critical of the government white paper on research councils and this led to a general discussion of
research policy at the 1976 congress. Once again the Swedish Metal Workers' Union
played a prominent role in pushing this issue. Bert Lundin (1977), the union president, maintained that alongside the issue of economic democracy, research constituted the most important question for the Swedish union movement at the turn
of the seventies.

The 1976 LO-congress decided:

- That a proposal for an integrated union research policy be
  prepared for presentation at the next congress and,
- That LO should draw up proposals for and demand increased
  union influence over research questions at both a local and
  central level.

At the moment union influence over research is limited to co-determination over
the finances distributed in certain research funds. All in all the union movement
can exercise influence over the allocation of approximately 300 million S.kr.
This constitutes roughly 7.5% of the total research resources in the country.

LO's (1976) main criticism of the conduct of research today is that management exercises dominant influence over research questions, i.e. they can determine the research to be carried out, the problems to be given attention, and the utilization of research resources. This is regarded as unacceptable partly because todays research determines to a large extent the scope and direction of possible reform tomorrow (PUFRA 1978) and partly because practically all the major and decisive issues regarding the democratization of business and industry have in common that they are characterized by strong conflicts of interest between labour and capital. Meaningful research on these issues can hardly be a joint venture, (Ehn and Sandberg 1976).

In 1975 a group of researchers at Stockholm university began an extensive research project in cooperation with LO, the so-called DEMOS-project (Democratic Planning and Control in Industry). The research design followed that of Nygaard and his associates at the NCC in Oslo. An action research approach was adopted to help local unions investigate their own situations with the aim of activating individual members and developing their competence. Other goals in the project were to develop methods and instruments which would help the unions:

- To formulate their demands on computer based planning and control system
- To facilitate the control of the fulfilment of such demands
- To analyse possible conflicts and
- To indicate alternative solutions.

The project was carried out with local unions on four sites:

- A heavy-duty vehicle maintenance yard in which management has plans to introduce a new production planning system and where the union are developing an alternative solution as a basis for negotiation,
- A newspaper in which a new type-setting technology is to be introduced and where the union are developing concrete proposals regarding manning levels, job design, work organization and work environment,
- A steelworks in which a new production planning and control system is being introduced and where the union is studying job design and the work environment, and
- A department store in which the union is studying personnel policy and administration especially with respect to working hours, the environment and the eventual introduction of computerized cash registers.

The project utilizes the 'work group' approach. The aim is that these groups shall continue their activities after the researchers have withdrawn from the scene. Experience so far would seem to indicate that researchers and systems specialists should have a low profile in such groups and that a small group of active union members should conduct the first feasibility study before a larger group is formed for the main study.

The DEMOS-group have developed a negotiation model for union development work in connection with computer based systems. This is shown in figure 2. The essential point is that the unions should exercise co-determination in the decision process at every stage in the development of the system. This is achieved by negotiations between management and unions.

In this model the local union may appoint representatives in the systems project group. These participate in the development work but are not bound by decisions made in the project group, i.e. union positions in the negotiations are not restricted by representative action in the project group. These project group representatives form a link with a union work group which is studying what demands the union should place on the system on the basis of their values and interests

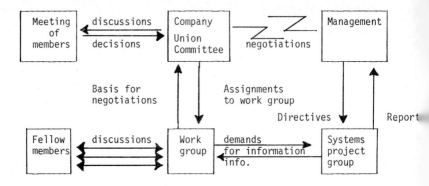

Figure 2.
A negotiation   model for union development work
(from Carlsson et.al. 1977)

and, should the issue arise, what alternatives there may exist to the line of development being pursued in the project group. The work group conducts parallel di
logues with its fellow members in the company and with the union committee.

The union committee defines the assignments to the work group, presents proposals
to meetings of the members, which meetings also constitute a dialogue. The commit
tee conducts negotiations with management on the basis of these activities.

This model has not in fact been tested in full scale in the DEMOS-project but the
are current discussions between LO, PTK and an employers confederation regarding
the launching of a project which will investigate when, how and on what basis suc
negotiations shall be carried out in the course of a systems development project.

The PTK data processing committee is also conducting a research project in collaboration with researchers from the Stockholm School of Economics. This is also an
action orientated project although the conditions existing for the project are
somewhat different from those in the DEMOS-project:

- Management, specialists and endusers are all organized within the
  same union,
- The project is geared to the endusers direct involvement in the
  design of given systems and
- The project has been launched after the co-determination legislation
  has come into force.

The researchers are working together with representatives of management and the
unions in the development of a materials administration system in an industrial
company and an personnel administration system in a service company. Two aims of
the project are:

- To develop meaningful forms for participation and co-determination
  for personnel and their unions in systems development, and
- To develop means to integrate social and organizational development
  with technical development in the context of designing computer
  based systems.

The day-to-day work in the specific systems project group and the departments involved in each company is concerned with evolving new roles and a new division

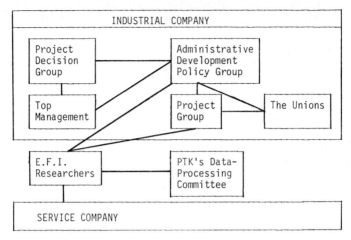

Figure 3.

The organization of the PTK research project

of responsibility between management, systems (and other) specialists and personnel and their unions. At the same time administrative development policy groups consisting of representatives for management, specialists and the unions are evaluating the experiences from these and other projects with the aim of developing policies, development paradigms and design principles which will facilitate and support personnel participation in the development process. The project started in February 1978 and is expected to continue until the middle of 1980.

4. SOME OBSERVATIONS AND REFLECTIONS ON THESE DEVELOPMENTS

In summary there can be no doubt that there has occured a strong union reorientation towards efforts in the area of working conditions in which active steps are being taken to play a more influential role in the development of computer based systems in organizations. This reorganization is characterized by an 'across the board' effort which includes:

- The development of specific policies and programmes of action,

- The initiation and support of independent R and D projects,

- The development of union competence through members' participation in specific project groups, the conduct of workshops in computer issues for union representatives from different companies, the development of study circle materials and the publishing of textbooks and other educational material for non-expert members,

- Concrete efforts to systematize the experience gained within different companies and to make it available to other clubs, and finally,

- Efforts to reorganize union resources in individual companies by, amongst other things, appointing special committees for administrative development or special officials responsible for data processing issues.

Available evidence indicates that the unions have a strong mandat from their rank file members for these efforts. For example, Docherty et.al. (1977) found that practically 100% of personnel questioned about the implementation of systems felt that the union should be involved in the projects to safeguard and promote their interests. Similarly Bjørn-Andersen and Jappe (1978) found that 79% of clerical staff in savings banks in 1977 wanted influence on systems development as compared to only 30% for the same group in 1974.

At the same time as the unions would like to conduct research, there exists in many quarters a marked uncertainty regarding the formal role of research (Docherty and Callbo 1978). The unions' experience of researchers is not simply positive: many researchers are regarded as either too theoretical, 'too neutral' or too management orientated. They are regarded as having little understanding of unions' viewpoints needs and values. The work group approach adopted in many of the development projects in Norway and Sweden would appear, however, to offer good possibilities for the integration of academics and non-academics.

Another aspect of this dilemma in Sweden today is that it is difficult for many unionists to assess the relative benefit of pursuing research as against simply negotiating. Negotiating is a traditional skill in which the unions have a marked competence and it is difficult to assess whether or not more rapid progress could be made or greater freedom of action could be retained at the bargaining table without engaging in the course of research which may be seen to offer serious risks to the pace and form of the development of the unions' position and possibly little benefit in terms on practically usable results.

The circumstances facing white-collar and blue-collar unions would appear to be quite different in several respects. It is easier for the blue-collar unions to see the question of systems development as a relation between two parties: labour and management. On the other hand, the fact that many white-collar unions in Sweden have a vertical structure, i.e. organize members throughout almost the entire hierarchy puts the issue in a different light. For example, Docherty and Herber (1977) report a case in which the manager commissioning a system was the vicepresident of the local union, the system specialist was a member of the local union committee, the personnel specialist responsible for personnel transfer and training was the union president and users of the systems were the union's rank and file members. Hedberg (1974), in a study of a Swedish bank, found that the local union officials felt that their interests coincided practically entirely with those of management. They experienced no distinctive issue on which it was necessary for them to make a stand against management. Berg and Docherty (1975) observed a similar phenomenon in the insurance sector: union company officials regarded such issues as systems development as vital to the company's internal efficiency to the extent that they constituted a means of competition. Given this view they regarded experience concerning systems and organizational development as something which should be concealed from union colleagues in other companies. They had a direct loyalty to management in these issues.

First experience from the PTK-project would seem to indicate that systems development is a highly complex drama in which many different parties interests are at stake. For example in the service company there are at the present moment over 20 groups working on different aspects of the problem complex at different levels in the organization. It is quite clear that there is no one 'union' or 'management' view of the system.

The locus and clarity of awareness of the importance of computer based systems varies in the unions. There is considerable clarity and singlemindedness of purpose at the central level in some unions. The picture would appear to be very uneven however at the company union level. Many local unions do not perceive these issues as critical today and have not awarded them high priority. It is not unusual in the white-collar unions that it is the systems specialists themselves who are the driving forces in these matters. It is not even unusual in some cases for professional specialists who are not active union members to be more actively engaged in these issues than union officials.

There are of course a number of sources of strain and possible conflict which hamper the development of union involvement in systems development work. One such compli-cating factor is the wide diversity of interests which may arise in the given pro-ject - even within the unions. For example, Docherty and Strååt (1977) report a case in which the union faced a dilemma of advocating the introduction of a system which would help to strengthen its members security of employment at the same time as it constituted a marked threat to the self-determination of its members in their work situation. Similarly, many studies have shown that even in a systems context, 'one man's meat is another man's poison'.

Another complicating factor is that technical development and social and organiza-tional development are characterized by markedly different rates of change. While technical change may be rapid social change is often a slow and painstaking process. The social changes demanded may often be difficult to achieve. For example many specialists' self selection to their profession may have been based on the attrac-tion of being a technical backroom boy. Current admonitions to such specialists to become socially extroverted change agents are hardly realistic.

Developments in Sweden at the present time are hampered by the pervading uncertain-ty existing in the labour market: the joint agreements envisaged in the co-determi-nation law have as yet, two years after the legislation came into force, to be signed. Similarly, there exists little previous experience, policies or codes of practice, for example regarding union research. The tendency to innovative behaviour is countered by the fear of precedential action, and the fear of diminished freedom of action or room to manoeuvre in negotiations.

The current developments with their revision of responsibilities have naturally given rise to frustrations and irritation, especially on the part of systems spe-cialists and researchers. Many specialists feel that they are being made scapegoats by management and unions for the deficiencies of yesterday. Management and unions can reach new understanding in the light of the knowledge that both have been mis-led by the specialists (Steele 1975). They are also alienated in the general media debate: they have little chance of making their voice heard (RDF-Nytt 1978:3).

Other obstacles in this development process are management's view of the work force, current systems development paradigms, current design principles for organizations and the ways in which organizations plan systems development activities (Docherty et.al. 1977).

In the flood of legislation, for example in Sweden, it is hardly surprising that inconsistencies arise. For example a union computer centre reported recently that it was having distinct difficulties in matching the demands of the work environ-ment law regarding the working conditions of computer centre personnel on the one hand with the demands on the safety and integrity of personnel data in the system included in the data law on the other hand.

Despite such inconsistencies, legislation and joint agreements are seen as essen-tial means of improving the prerequisites to enable employees and their unions to engage in a broad and coordinated programme to develop their competence and in-fluence on systems development in which the initiation of and participation in R and D projects provide both design skills and impact knowledge.

REFERENCES

Berg, H. and P. Docherty (1975). Fackliga Strategier i en Föränderlig Situation. Stockholm: EFI, PA-rådet and URAF. Report No. 14 in the series 'New Forms for Worker Influence in Companies'.

Bjørn-Andersen, N. and L. Jappe (1978). Computer Impact and the Demand for Partici-pation. Paper to the seventh IFAC World Congress, Helsinki, June.

Carlsson, J., P. Ehn, B. Erlander, M.L. Perby and A. Sandberg (1977). The Demos Project - A Short Presentation. Stockholm University TRITA. IBADB - 6007.

Docherty, P. and K. Callbo (1978). Establishing a Union Project: A Case Study Regarding the Computerization of Office Work. Paper to the EIASM seminar on "Research on Management Issues from the Perspectives of Workers and Their Unions" Oxford Centre for Management Studies. March.

Docherty, P. and S. Herber (1977). System QB på Kockums. Economic Research Institute, Stockholm School of Economics, Research paper 6076.

Docherty, P., A. Magnusson, B. Stymne, K. Callbo and S. Herber (1977). Hur man lyckas med systemutveckling. Economic Research Institute, Stockholm School of Economics.

Docherty, P. and C. Strååt (1977). ADB i konstruktionsarbete på Jacobsson & Widmark Economic Research Institute , Stockholm School of Economics, Research paper No. 6079.

DUE-Group (eds.) (1977). Systemarbejde og fagbevaegelseprojekter: Materiale fra marts-seminaret. Computer Science Department, Aarhus University, Denmark.

Ehn, P., B. Erlander, B. Göranson, M.L. Perby and A. Sandberg (1975). Demokratisk Styrning och Planering i Arbetslivet. Stockholm University TRITA. IBADB 1023.

Ehn, P. and A. Sandberg (1978). Forskarmakt åt löntagere! in A. Sandberg (ed.): En Ny Företagsekonomi. Liber, Stockholm.

Elden, M., J. Fjalestad, M. Levin and G. Myrvang (1978). Fagbevegelsen og EDB i Prosessindustrien: For projektrapport. Institut for Industriell Miljöforskning, Trondheim. Rapport No. STF82 A7800CD.

Emery, F.E. and E. Thorsrud (1974). Form and Content in Industrial Democracy. Social Science Paperbacks No. 144, Tavistock Press, London.

Gustavsen, B. (1976). Design of Jobs and Work Organisations in a Changing Political Context. Paper to Dubrovnik Interuniversity Centre Conference on 'Shop Floor Participation', February.

Göranzon, B. and J. Andersson (1975). Arbetstagarnas ansvar för och interesse i den tekniska utvecklingen (Del 1). SINFDOK, Stockholm.

Hedberg, B. (1974). Humanized Computers or Computerized Humans? A Case Study of the Design and Impact of a Real-time System in a Commercial Bank. International Institute of Management, Berlin. Preprint Series 1/74-24.

Korsvold, T. (1978). Medvirkning og medbestemmelse: Systemarbeitet - Erfaringar fra SAS. Paper to OA-Consulting Conference on 'Experience of the Effects of Computer Based Systems on Work Environment and Organisation'. Oslo, February.

LO (Swedish TUC) (1976). Utbildning för arbete och demokrati. LO and Prisma, Stockholm.

Lundin, B. (1967). Samhällsforskning och arbetslivet. Paper to the seminar on 'Samhällsforskning och Arbetslivet', Folksam, Stockholm, May 1978.

Marthinsen, P.J. (1978). En datatillitsmanns praktiske erfaringer. Paper to the OA-Consulting Conference 'Experiences of the Effects of Computer Based Systems on Work Environment and Organisations', Oslo, February.

Nygaard, K. (1975). Kunskapsstrategi for fagbevaegelsen. Nordisk Forum, Oslo, 6 Vol 10, No. 2.

Olausson, E. (1978). Hur påverkar lagar och avtal utvecklingen av datasystem? MBL, Förtroendemannalagen, Arbetsmiljölagen. Paper to the NordDATA Computer Conference, Stockholm, August.

Pape, A. (1977). Metodlogiska erfaringar fra NHKF-projektet. Paper to the DUE-Conference 'Systemarbejde og fagbevaegelseprojekter', Aarhus, Denmark, March.

PUFRA (1978). Medbestämmande och Arbetsliv: Kartläggning och analys av forsknings-
behov m.m. Arbetarskyddsfonden, Stockholm, Rapport 1978:2.

Qvale, T. (1977). The Impact of the Work Environment Law. Work Research Institutes
Oslo. AI Doc 44/7.

RDF-Nytt No. 35, March 1978: 'Externa Relationer'. Riksdataförbundet, Stockholm.

Rundqvist, A. (1978). Arbetsmiljölagen. Utbildningsproduktion AB, Malmö.

SAF (1976). Lagen om Medbestämmande. SAF, Stockholm.

SFS (1974:358). Lag om facklig förtroendemans ställning på arbetsplatsen. Stockholm.

SFS (1976:580). Lag om medbestämmande i arbetslivet. Stockholm.

SFS (1977:1160). Arbetsmiljölag. Stockholm.

Steele, F. (1975). Consulting for Organisational Change. University of Massachusetts
Press, Amherst.

TCO's Arbetsgrupp för datafrågor (1976). Datorn i Arbetslivet. TCO, Stockholm.

TCO's arbetsgrupp för datafrågor (1978). Datorerna och arbetslivet: Rapport til
kongressen 1979. TCO, Stockholm.

Ødegaard, L.A. (1977). Arbetsplatsundersökelsene i miljöarbeidet. Work Research
Institutes, Oslo.

APPENDIX

General Agreement of 1978

between the

Norwegian Federation of Trade Unions

and the

Norwegian Employers' Confederation (N.A.F.)

on

COMPUTER BASED SYSTEMS

The Norwegian Employers' Confederation (N.A.F.) and the Norwegian Federation of Trade Unions (LO) agree that the development, introduction, and use of computer based systems shall be carried out according to this General Agreement which is based on Part A, Section 9, and Part B, Section 32 of the Basic Agreement.

This Agreement covers computer based systems which are used by the planning and carrying out of the work, as well as systems for data storage and use of personal data. By the latter is meant all data which either by name or by other identifying code may be traced back to concrete persons employed by the individual undertaking

I.   Computer-based systems can be useful tools in the planning of methodical use of the total resources of an undertaking. Such systems may affect the work place and working conditions of the employees.

Where this is the case it is important that computer-based systems are evaluated not only from technical and economical, but also from social angles, in order that total considerations are made the basis by the development, introduction, and use of such systems. Such total considerations shall include changes in organisation, employment, information routines, human relations, etc.

II.   Management shall, through the shop stewards, keep their employees informed about all matters which are covered by this Agreement, so that the shop stewards may express their views as early as possible and before the decisions of management are effected. Cp. Section 12, par. 3 of the Working Environment Act.

The information shall be given clearly and in a language easily understood by persons lacking special knowledge of the area concerned.

Furthermore, management and the shop stewards, both separately and jointly, shall attach importance to furnishing the employees with sufficient information in order to gain insight into and understand the fundamental features of the systems which they themselves either use or are affected by, and to understand the importance of the use of such systems both to the undertaking and the employees and their work situation.

The two central organisations recommend that in addition to the shop steward representatives, also employees who will be directly affected by projects covered by this Agreement, should to the greatest practical extent be involved in project work. This is desirable so that use may be made of available knowledge in all parts of the undertaking, and in order to ensure that the employees, through their elected representatives, may influence the development, introduction and use of these systems. It is presumed that sufficient time is allowed for this work, and that both lost earnings as well as any expenses needed for information according to this paragraph (II) will be covered.

III. If the employees of an undertaking so desire, they may elect, preferably among the existing shop stewards, a special representative to safeguard their interests and to cooperate with management within the scope of this Agreement.

If the size of the undertaking and the extent of the use of computer-based systems so require, the employees may elect, in agreement with management, more than one special representative. It is recommended that these representatives form a working group, and it is presumed that the time needed is made available.

It is a prerequisite that the representative(s) of the employees be given the opportunity to become generally acquainted with the conditions pertaining to the influence of computer-based systems on conditions concerning the employees. The representative(s) shall have access to all documentation on programmes and machine equipment within the scope of this Agreement. The representative(s) shall, on the basis of their particular qualifications, be at the disposal of the employees and the other shop stewards, e.g. in connection with their involvement in concrete projects. The representative(s) shall also contribute to the coordination of the employees' involvement in matters covered by this Agreement.

Shop stewards and employees participating in concrete projects shall have access to <u>all necessary</u> documentation within the project area.

IV. The undertaking shall secure that the special representative(s) of the employees be given the necessary training in general data processing techniques so that they may fulfil their duties in a proper manner.

Moreover, management shall evaluate, in consultation with the representatives of the employees, the need for training shop stewards and employees who will be engaged in concrete projects within the scope of this Agreement.

An example of such training are courses on system work and project administration sufficient to develop the competence needed for participating actively in system design.

V. As regards systems for storage and use of personal data reference is made to the forthcoming/existing law on personal registration etc.

The collection, storage, processing and use of personal data shall not take place without due cause out of consideration to the activities of the undertaking. In each undertaking it should be collected, stored, processed and used by means of computer equipment.

In each undertaking in cooperation with the shop stewards instructions shall be prepared for the storage and use of personal data. Failing agreement, the matter may be submitted to the central organisations.

VI. The parties within the individual undertaking shall seek to arrive at the most appropriate forms of cooperation and organisation within the area of this Agreement. In accordance with the guidelines drawn up in this General Agreement a special agreement may be concluded in the individual undertaking, if the parties so request. If agreement is not reached, each party may submit the case to the central organisations.

VII. The parties in the individual undertaking who are affected by the provisions of this Agreement, undertake to make it known to the employees.

VIII. As far as the duration and termination of this Agreement are concerned, the same rules shall apply as those governing the Basic Agreement.

DISCUSSION AND COMMENTS ON PAPER PRESENTED BY PETER DOCHERTY

HASSE CLAUSEN

First of all I shall suggest that the title of the paper is changed to "Some
Consequences of Union Activities in Norway and Sweden", not only because this
better reflects the contents of the article, but also because the unions are the
ones to present a real challenge to the computer specialists and the managers.

Had it not been for the pressure from unions, we would never have seen the Acts
and Joint Agreements in connection with developing and using computer systems, e.g
the data agreements in Norway came as a result of the Norwegian NJMF-project. This
research project was steered by and carried through by the trade unions.

I find that the unions carry out a very important function in questioning and
challenging the work by computer specialists. For example the union can easily -
by asking simple questions about budgetting, steering and documentation in the
design process - get the specialists nailed by their own belief in rationality.
If the unions demand that the design process should be carried out according to
the rules described in the text books or in agreed company standards, the specialists would find it impossible to ever develop a reasonable system.

Therefore, if we are interested in Acts and Joint Agreements we should not only
look at the documents in isolation. We need to study the different documents as
part of the union activities.

In my opinion the following kinds of union activities must be taken seriously in
the context of designing and using computer systems:

  1. Activities aimed at acquiring political influence.

  2. Research activities done for and by the unions.

  3. Educational activities aimed at changing attitudes to increase
      self-reliance/self-consciousness and at giving the employees a
      greater knowledge about problems in connection with edp.

  4. Activities supporting the purpose of activating the members.

  5. Activities which will result in the introduction of acts or agreements.

All these activities support each other and serve the overall union objective of
strengthening the possibilities of their members gaining influence in their own
working situation.

If I should characterize the situation in Denmark today, I would say that the
unions have not reached as far as is the case for Norway and Sweden. But there is
an ever growing number of activities within this area. Whereas the unions in
Norway and Sweden have primarily chosen political activities resulting respectively in Data Agreements and acts, the unions in Denmark have chosen educational activities as the chief activity area.

But I want to underline that the set of activities should be seen as a whole, and
therefore there are also union activities within other areas. There is for instance
a growing interest among the unions in Denmark in becoming involved in political
life. The Danish TUC (LO) has started the DUE-project which will follow the same
model as the NJMF and DEMOS projects. There are also activities in the unions
supporting local working groups. The data agreement as a possible solution to problems with computer technology has been and is discussed in most of the unions in

Denmark.

The only data agreement which exists in Denmark today is the data agreement in SAS (Scandinavian Airline System) which came out on the initiative of the management in SAS who wanted a uniform agreement for all of Scandinavia. The unions in Denmark have not rejected the idea of entering into special data agreements, but they find the Norwegian Data Agreements insufficient.

SVEN KJELDSEN

I found the paper presented very interesting and should like to ask a few questions.

Firstly, it is claimed that according to the Swedish Co-determination Act, the employer has the right to carry out necessary investigations in order to clarify issues before they are put up for decision. Do you think that this fact is influencing the communication pattern between employers and trade unions?

Secondly, it is not clear from the paper how the Co-determination Act is limiting the rights of the employers to manage and plan the work of the plant. Are there any specific examples by now?

Thirdly, Docherty estimates that the unions control approximately 7.5% of the total funds for research in Sweden. Would you consider that a fair share?

Fourthly, is it likely that the Co-determination Act will lead to economic democracy or are these separate issues?

Fifthly, is it correct to say that the laws and agreements mentioned in the paper are less concerned with the specific issues about computer systems and are more concerned with the general issues of influence, democracy and redistribution of ownership?

PETER DOCHERTY

A strict interpretation of the Co-determination Act is that the employer has the obligation to inform the unions about what he is up to, but he does not have to involve the union until he is going to make the decision whether to acquire the system or not. The tricky point in this issue is that at the same time he is not allowed to make preparations which may be interpreted as a tacid decision. No doubt unions will question just how far an employer has gone in specific cases. Are there real alternatives or has the employer in reality already made up his mind?

In all events the unions have the right to demand complementory studies when they come in. The unions might claim that issues a, b and c are not covered in detail and that they should like to have them investigated. It is quite clear in relation to systems development that the unions feel that in order to make the co-determination feasible, union participation must take place from the outset. Otherwise there is a great likelihood that unions will demand such studies, resulting in their turn in delays in the implementation of the system. So there are methods by which the unions can apply pressure.

Some employer confederations are actively planning with the unions to evolve a negotiation approach to union involvement in the whole life cycle of a project.

The second question concerned the ideas behind the Co-determination Act. There is no doubt that the basic aims of the Act are to curtail management prerogatives such as the right to hire and fire workers. The law does not specifically regulate

the relations between management and the unions but form a basis for central and
local joint agreements in most areas. The unions maintain that the development of
systems is such a key area that it must be regulated by a joint agreement.

The third question relates to the union control of research funds averaging approximately 7.5% today. In Sweden the general impression is of course that the proportion will grow.

About co-determination and economic democracy I think they are seen as parallel
objectives by unions in Sweden and that they are not directly related.

The fifth question challenged me to evaluate whether democracy or better systems
was the prime objective. Computer systems are essential tools in the control
systems of the organization. Seen from a union point of view you do not want to
concentrate on the tool but on the general philosophy for control in the organization. This is why LO's DEMOS project for instance is concerned with the economic
planning and control of companies.

PER GRØHOLT

I should like to give a few comments on the Norwegian scene. Nygaard had a very
important function as a trigger, but the so-called Nygaard-movement is in my opinion a side-step as it has little support from unions and key companies. Therefore
I hope that he will not succeed in exporting his conflict models to Sweden, Denmark or anywhere else.

I do not feel that Docherty emphasized one of the most central areas of the joint
agreement we have in Norway. It is that social aspects must be explicitly evaluated in addition to the technical and economic aspects. I think that has tremendous importance.

My third comment relates to what Docherty called the anticlimax of the introduction
of the joint agreement. I can confirm that probably only 5-10% of middle and large
size companies are in practise working according to the joint agreement, others do
not understand it or do not want to follow it. It is of great importance, however,
that the LO (TUC) and unions are using the joint agreements as tools for increasing
their influence. Therefore we shall see improved systems design as a result of
union pressure. Perhaps this is the only hope for further development in this area.

Finally, I think that there will be some key companies with very close cooperation
between management and unions which will be the leading companies.

PETER DOCHERTY

I fully agree with the statement that the issues of social effects of computerization has a very strong back up in the working environment law and working environment joint agreement in Norway.

CHRISTIAN GRAM

I understand the unions are pressing for increased influence. Are they doing that
on behalf of and in order to support the rank and file members or are they doing
it in order to strengthen the union organization?

PETER DOCHERTY

There has been quite a lot of research and discussion about that issue within political science. Recently a book called "Who Steers the Unions" (Lewin 1977, Vem Styr Facket?) has been strongly debated in Sweden. That was a survey of the relations between the values and aspirations of central union officials at the LO in Stockholm and the rank and file members in clubs around the country. Many people interpreted the results as showing a very high level of agreement between central leaders and the broad membership on views, rights, and issues. So in the Swedish LO one hopes to have eradicated the misconception that bright intellectuals running LO were more concerned with their own ideas than with the problems of the rank and file members. There seems to be a very strong mandate from the grassroot level for what the top is doing, even though some critics maintain that the results have been obtained by a prudent selection of the results.

Mr. Eason what a conspiracy!
With ideas of specialised Ergonometry
Management today still rules the way
Tomorrow micros will win the day
Unless someone cries cease this piracy.

COMPUTER INFORMATION SYSTEMS AND MANAGERIAL TASKS

K.D. Eason

Department of Human Sciences
Loughborough University of Technology
Leicestershire

An international research project (CISM:
Computer Information Systems and Management) is described in which eight case
studies were completed using a multi-level, multi-disciplinary framework. Partial results are presented which show widespread impact upon the manager's perception of his task and the degree to which
the computer information system supports
and constrains the task. An analysis is
also presented of changes in the manager's
roles with respect to his subordinates,
superiors and colleagues.

The Human Side of Information Processing
N. Bjørn-Andersen, editor
© IAG
North-Holland Publishing Company, 1980

THE DIVERSITY OF COMPUTER IMPACT

Investigations of the impact of computer based information systems upon management are beset by many difficulties not the least of which are that the impact may take many forms and that many different theoretical frameworks may be appropriate to assess the variety of potential impact. Some investigations have focussed upon potential impact at the organisational level of analysis, e.g. Whisler and Meyer (1967), whilst others have concentrated upon the impact on the individual manager, e.g. Licklider (1965).

Observers have used theoretical frameworks derived from cybernetics (Beer 1968), man viewed as an information processor (Eason 1977) and the organisation as a social system (Stewart 1971). As a result of this fragmentary approach and the lack of dialogue between the different specialities, the current literature is bewildering in the variety of terminology and in the apparent contradictions to be found in the findings.

In an effort to stimulate a dialogue between the different approaches and to investigate the relations between the different levels of analysis, the author and his colleagues have been engaged in an international collaborative study. The purpose of this paper is to report the aims and philosophy of this study and to present an initial analysis of data on one complex and central issue: the impact of computer information systems upon the nature of the managerial task.

ACKNOWLEDGEMENTS

I am indebted to the following who contributed to the research design and data collection of the CISM project: H. Lippold & E. Reindl (West Germany), N. Bjørn-Andersen & P.H. Pedersen (Denmark), G. Wieser (Austria), D. Robey (U.S.A.) and L. Damodaran & T.F.M. Stewart (Great Britain). The project team wishes to acknowledge the support of the funding bodies in each collaborating country who provided funds for the respective teams.

THE C.I.S.M. INTERNATIONAL PROJECT

Since 1974, principally through the initiative of Professor Niels Bjørn-Andersen (and as a result of international links facilitated by the Vienna Centre for the Coordination of Research and Documentation in the Social Sciences) research teams from Denmark, West Germany, Austria, Great Britain and the U.S.A. have been engaged in a joint project on the impact of Computer Information Systems on Management (CISM). The project staff constitute both a multi-national and a multi-disciplinary team, the disciplines of organisational theory, computer science, sociology, social psychology and ergonomics being represented in the group. The aim of the project has been to make a multi-level, multi-perspective analysis of the impact of computer information systems upon management.

In pursuing this objective it was necessary to eschew the traditional strategy of examining a small number of variables in many organisations carefully selected for comparability. To embrace all of the variables of concern to the different theoretical formulations, a case study approach was adopted in which a small number of cases were examined in depth according to a common, and therefore comparable, methodology. This approach means that it is not possible to make valid, statistical tests of theoretical propositions although any proposition will derive considerable support if it predicts a tendency which is found to be common across eight very diverse cases. The project should be viewed as a hypothesis generating rather than a hypothesis testing exercise: it is the intention to suggest causal links between variables at different levels of analysis and in different theoretical formulations. The project team has no illusions that it will produce an all embracing, integrated framework which will explain all forms of impact: the joint publication which will result from this study will take the form of a series of papers addressing the same cases from different perspectives and focussing upon different aspects of each case, hopefully to illuminate the many facets of computer impact.

As a result of this approach, the study consists of data from eight cases in organisations as diverse as banks, manufacturers and hospitals. The criteria for the selection of the cases were primarily that the system should be designed at least in part to serve management funcitons and that it should be used by management at different levels in the hierarchy and in a number of departments. It is salutary that, some years after the excitement of 'total' and 'integrated' management information systems, these criteria did not prove easy to meet. The ideal of a longitudinal study covering the periods before and after system implementation did not prove feasible and data was gathered by intensive interviewing of managers about their past and present jobs and their perceptions of, and attitudes towards, the impact of computer information systems.

The variables upon which data was collected covered a number of levels of analysis. At the micro end managers were questioned about the quality of the service they received, the ease with which they could obtain this service and the support they received in using it. They were also asked to make an assessment of the impact of this service on the tasks they performed. At the inter-personal level of analysis data was gathered about the impact of the computer system upon the manager's relations with his superiors, subordinates and colleagues. A special aspect of this level of analysis is the investigation of possible effects upon the distribution of power and influence in the organisation. At the organisational level of analysis attention is focussed upon possible changes in the nature of coordination and control systems and in such variables as specialisation and formalisation.

ORGANISATIONAL FUNCTIONS AND MANAGERIAL TASKS

The collection of data at these different levels of analysis has been dominated by the concept of task. One reason for this is that the task concept appears at all levels and offers the opportunity of relating findings at one level to the findings at the other levels. A second reason is that computer systems are usually designed to support specific organisational functions rather than every aspect of organisational life. Studies which do not take explicit account of this factor but which ask respondents to report the impact of computer systems upon the organisation in general run the risk of obtaining a view of impact which is insufficiently sensitive to variations due to the nature of the functions being supported by the system and the kinds of support given.

In this study therefore the strategy was to first identify two organisational functions which the computer system was designed to support. Two functions were chosen in order that we could examine whether there was a differential impact upon management within the same organisation and caused by the same computer system, which we could attribute to differences in the nature of the function and the way it was handled by the organisation. A function was considered suitable if it was a major organisational task to which managers from different departments and at different levels made a contribution. In the study examples of functions investigated were as diverse as the daily scheduling of production, the patient admissions process of a hospital and the creation of an annual marketing plan. The total list of 16 functions includes both long term planning functions and very short term operational functions and it includes functions which are performed under conditions of considerable environmental uncertainty and others which are performed within a fairly certain environment. All of the questions posed to managers were related to the contribution they made to the two selected organisational functions. As a result we hoped to bring into sharp focus the manner in which a computer system made its impact on an organisation by a detailed examination of how it influenced the way in which the organisation handled two of its major tasks.

COMPUTER IMPACT ON THE MANAGER'S PERCEPTION OF HIS TASK

One of the issues examined was the impact of the computer upon the task as it was perceived by the manager. The literature offers a variety of views on the form this impact is likely to take. Theorists who discuss computer control systems with an organisational frame of reference cf. Leavitt & Whisler (1958) emphasise the greater formalisation that results and suggest that the manager will perceive himself operating under greater constraint. In contrast theorists who discuss the impact of interactive computer aids for management tasks such as planning and resource scheduling (e.g. Licklider 1965, Morton 1971 and Simon 1965) emphasise the way in which the richer information base and the possibilities for information manipulation free the manager to explore his task more deeply and to examine more possible actions. Although these views appear to be in conflict some authors, notably Blau and Schoenherr (1971), conclude that both can be correct. The diversity of management tasks, types of organisation and types of computer system are such that the nature of the impact may vary substantially from one manager to another.

To examine these questions managers were asked whether they perceived any changes in nine aspects of the tasks they undertook as their contribution to the organisational functions under investigation. If they reported a change they were asked to evaluate it on a satisfaction rating scale. The nine questions covered task dimensions which, on the basis of the arguments presented above, may be either supported or constrained by the use of computer information systems.

The results from six case studies are summarised in figure 1. There were different numbers of respondents for each organisational function and, in order to equalise the contribution of each function to the results, the average value for each function has been calculated and the mean of these averages is presented in figure 1. The questions are presented in rank order according to the incidence of change reported. Respondents were asked to indicate whether a change represented an increase or a decrease in the relevant dimension and the overwhelming response to all question was 'increase'. The diversity of the questions means that the overall direction of change is of methodological interest only and the direction of the change has to be considered for each question separately.

The investigators of each case study were asked to classify the organisational functions they studied as either conducted in a relatively certain or a relatively uncertain environment. Figure 1 presents a subsidiary analysis for each question of the average incidence of change for 5 functions conducted in a relatively certain environment and 7 functions conducted in an uncertain environment.

The four questions which identified the highest incidence of change were primarily concerned with the support the manager received in appreciating his task, for example most managers saw their tasks as more complex and as being composed of a greater number of sub-problems. It is possible to interpret this as meaning that the tasks had actually changed. However, the managers' comments which supported these responses suggest that it is their perception of the task which has changed rather than the task itself. The results for the second question give indirect support for this interpretation because the managers are reporting that, as a result of the computer system, they are receiving more feedback on the results of their decisions and it is widely recognised that feedback is the most powerful force for changing one's understanding of one's task. Finally, there is evidence that the computer system leads to new ideas and methods for tackling the task, again an indication that the manager's response to his task is changing.

The most plausible interpretation of this data is then that the use of computer information systems leads to widespread reconsideration of the nature of the task. The general comment made by managers was that the improved information base gave them a better view of their task and stimulated new ideas for tackling it. An example from the Hospital case study may illustrate this point. A doctor reported that he used to base his decisions to admit patients almost exclusively on clini-

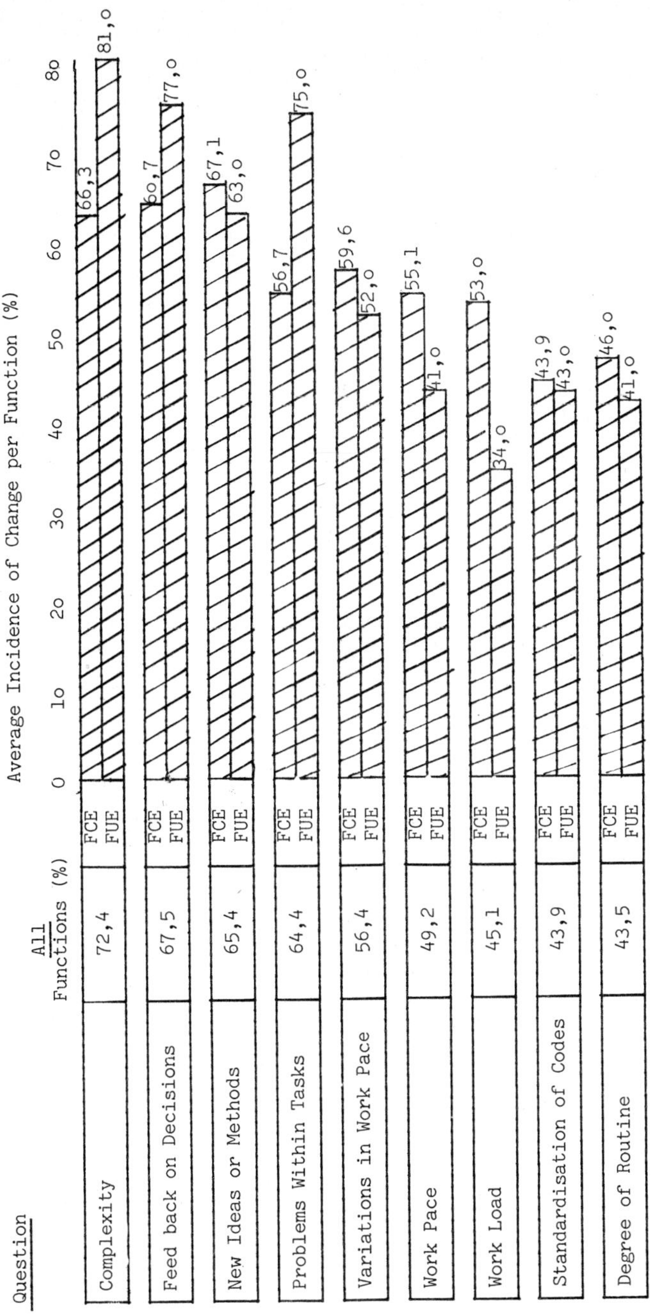

Figure 1.

COMPUTER IMPACT ON TASK PERCEPTION

Question

Average Incidence of Change per Function (%)

Question	All Functions (%)		FCE / FUE	0	10	20	30	40	50	60	70	80
Complexity	72,4		FCE								66,3	
			FUE									81,0
Feed back on Decisions	67,5		FCE							60,7		
			FUE								77,0	
New Ideas or Methods	65,4		FCE							67,1		
			FUE							63,0		
Problems Within Tasks	64,4		FCE						56,7			
			FUE								75,0	
Variations in Work Pace	56,4		FCE						59,6			
			FUE						52,0			
Work Pace	49,2		FCE						55,1			
			FUE					41,0				
Work Load	45,1		FCE						53,0			
			FUE				34,0					
Standardisation of Codes	43,9		FCE					43,9				
			FUE					43,0				
Degree of Routine	43,5		FCE					46,0				
			FUE				41,0					

Key: FCE = Functions in Certain Environment
     FUE = Functions in Uncertain Environment

cal criteria. As a result of being able to access information about the bed-state
of the entire hospital he was now much more aware of the consequences of his actions for hospital staff. He now found himself making the decision to admit on
clinical criteria but arranging the admission to minimise disturbance to others.
As a result of the computer system he now undertook a more complex task than hithe
to.

Although they show a smaller incidence of impact, the remaining questions also indicate a substantial amount of change. The common element in these questions is
that they concern sources of constraint upon how and when the task is undertaken
and the most common response is that there has been an increase in all forms of
constraint. The greatest degree of impact is upon work pace and in particular upon
variations in work pace. It was commonly reported that the availability of data
through the system for example, determined when managers could undertake their
tasks. The managers also reported more standardisation in the terminology of the
tasks and an increase in the degree of routine. The question concerning workload
produced the highest number of 'decrease' responses. This was for the functions
involving relatively certain environments where 37% of change responses specified
that there had been a decrease.

These results show that managers experience a general increase in the degree of
constraint affecting when and how they conduct their tasks. The overall results
are therefore that computer information systems support the manager by offering
an improved view of the task but they can also introduce greater sources of constraint. It could be that these results are the product of the operation of different kinds of system. However, further analysis reveals that, whilst the amount
of change varies across functions, the pattern is common to all; the managers are
reporting the simultaneous occurrence of both kinds of effect.

Before attempting to explain how these two kinds of impact can co-exist, it is
useful to summarise the results of the manager's evaluation of these changes. As
might be anticipated the majority of responses to the first four questions were
positive (62.5% improvement, 8.0% deterioration and 27.5% no difference). More
surprisingly perhaps, 33.4% of the ratings for the last five questions were also
positive, there being in addition 18.4% 'deterioration' and 48.2% 'no difference'
responses. The majority of the negative evaluations were associated with increase
in workload and workpace plus, especially, variations in work pace. This is in
line with the results of many studies which have shown that, of all task factors,
the one that human beings most dislike to lose control of is the pacing of their
work; managers are apparently no exception to this rule and do not like to see
the demands that they already experience, added to by computer information systems

Having accounted for the negative evaluations we are left with the finding that
increases in standardisation and routine (and to some extent workload and workpace) are either evaluated as positive changes or are regarded neutrally. The
unstructured comments of managers suggest that the new constraints were either
regarded as affecting inconsequential aspects of the task or they served to provide order and structure that had hitherto been absent. This made it easier to
perceive the nature of the task and, because of the shared framework provided by
the system, to communicate about the task with colleagues.

To interpret these results it is first appropriate to question their validity. The
prevalence of positive evaluations is in conflict with the general mood of management disenchantment with the computer which is conveyed by the literature. This
may be attributed | to the fact that managers in this survey have tended to be posi-
tive in order to give a favourable image of their organisation. It is difficult
to evaluate the extent to which this is true but, if it is, it casts doubt largely
upon the evaluative comments because the change comments are substantiated by the
managers' description of the change and this provides a good basis for judging the
change to be real. If we concentrate therefore upon trying to explain the changes
reported by managers, the most important task is to explain how managers can ex-

perience improved perception (and possible better understanding) of their task at the same time as experiencing greater constraints in the execution of the task. From the manager's comments it is apparent that they do not always regard an increase in constraint as necessarily an important loss of task freedom. It is possible that this would be the case if the task was closed: if every aspect of the task was known then the task performer might experience an additional constraint on any dimension as a serious diminuation of the task. Managerial tasks are, however, not usually of this kind. They tend to be open-ended tasks in which the manager is continually striving to improve his grasp of the variables at work and to predict the consequences of possible actions. He may experience a constraint upon how he engages in his tasks as an inhibition of his freedom or he may see it as controlling an aspect of the task which permits him a clearer view of the important issues. On the admittedly limited evidence presented here a constraint in work pace is regarded as inhibiting whilst a constraint in how information is presented is regarded as an acceptable way of giving a clearer view of the nature of the task.

Additional insights into the managers view of his task may be gleaned from examining the reported impact of the computer systems upon relatively more open and relatively more closed tasks. The classification of organisational functions into those that have a relatively certain and a relatively uncertain environment provides a crude but perhaps useful way of categorising managerial tasks into relatively closed and relatively open tasks respectively. From figure 1 it may be noted that, for the first four questions concerned with the manager's perception of his task, there is more evidence overall for a change in tasks conducted in an uncertain environment than for tasks conducted in a certain environment. This appears to mean that it is just as possible to clarify the information base of a relatively open task as it is for a relatively closed task and it may in fact have more effect, possibly because there is more room for improvement, with the relatively open task.

Figure 1 shows a cross-over effect in that there is overall substantially less constraint upon tasks in an uncertain environment then those in a certain environment. This would seem to mean that it is more difficult to constrain how tasks conducted in uncertain environments are to be undertaken.

It is apparent therefore that the impact of a computer information system varies according to the nature of the task at the individual level of analysis. It is appropriate then to ask similar questions at the interpersonal level of analysis.

COMPUTER IMPACT UPON MANAGERIAL ROLES

Management is pre-eminently about conducting tasks with and through others and the task impacts discussed above are unlikely to be limited to the manager's own work experiences; they will be reflected in his relations with his superiors, subordinates and colleagues. Using a different theoretical formulation we may search for the impact of computer systems in the task relations that exist between a manager and other members of the organisation. It is useful to express these relations in terms of role theory and Mintzberg (1973) has provided a framework which identifies three groups of roles the manager performs; inter-personal roles, where the manager, by virtue of his position, is the figurehead for his department and leader of his staff, informational roles, where he is the focus for information into and out of his department, and decisional roles, where he is the principle maker and implementer of strategy for his department.

Most of the speculations about computer impact upon these roles have centred on the informational and the decisional roles. With respect to the informational roles the speculations focus upon the possibility of the computer system providing an alternative flow of information. Mintzberg divides the informational roles into the roles of desseminator and monitor and both may be affected. The need for the manager to act as desseminator may be reduced because other members of the

organisation may have access to information about his department which was not
available to them before the computer system was implemented. Similarly, in his
role as monitor, the manager may make less use of traditional sources of information because the information is directly available to him through the computer
system. Mintzberg shares with others some doubts about this interpretation because
in his own studies he found that most of the information monitored and desseminate
by managers was of a qualitative nature not readily processed by the computer.

There are many hypotheses that can be advanced concerning possible changes in the
decisional roles of the manager beginning with the issue examined above; will the
manager find his decision making powers constrained as a result of the system or
will he find he can evaluate new possibilities? With respect to his subordinates
there is the possibility that the system will provide an impersonal control system
which will free the manager from regular intervention in the daily routine of his
department. Alternatively the information he receives from the computer system may
encourage him to intervene more frequently. The reverse of this process applies
to decision making outside the manager's department; he may find he loses some of
his autonomy because his superiors intervene more frequently, he may be allowed
more freedom or he may find himself more actively engaged in decision making with
his superiors and colleagues. - To examine these possibilities managers were asked
about changes in each of the above roles as a consequence of the implementation of
the computer information system. They were asked whether a change had taken place
and, if so, to describe the nature of the change and to evaluate it using a satisfaction rating scale. Possible changes were sought within the manager's department
i.e. with respect to his subordinates, and betweeen departments i.e. with his superiors and colleagues. All questions referred to changes in the organisational
functions under investigation and, as a result, the data permits a comparison of
tasks conducted in relatively certain and relatively uncertain environments.

The results form six cases are presented for the informational roles in figure 2
and for the decisional roles in figure 3. As before the average response for each
function has been calculated and the mean of these averages is presented for each
function. - From the results presented in figure 2 it can be seen that there is a
considerable incidence of change in the informational roles of the manager, the
most frequently cited changes being in the dessemination of information to subordinates and to superiors and colleagues. Figure 2 gives the incidence of change
but not its direction and a review of the unstructured reports by managers reveals
that many different kinds of change are being experienced. The picture is not
therefore a simple matter of examining whether the manager is more or less involved
in information dessemination and monitoring. Inasmuch as the changes can be summarised, they are in line with Mintzberg's suggestion: computer based information
does not replace traditional forms of information flow to and from the manager but
it does tend to change the content of this information flow. For example, the
manager finds that his subordinates, superiors and colleagues are already informed
of the facts of a situation and seek explanation, interpretation and discussion.
Similarly the manager can use the computer system to monitor <u>what</u> is happening in
his department but when he wants to know <u>why</u> he tends to use <u>more</u> traditional means
of gathering information. Furthermore, since the data is presented as averages, it
does not reveal that there are substantial differences between cases which suggests
that an explanation of the data will have to make recourse to organisational and
system variables.

Management attitudes to these changes were positive for all questions (77% of responses indicated satisfaction with the change). This could be said to reflect a
general desire to report the organisation favourably but unstructured comments
conveyed the general feeling that computer information systems tended to provide
a sounder, agreed basis upon which task discussions could take place. People
ceased to argue, for example, about how much had been sold and, with the evidence
clearly before them, concentrated upon deciding how to sell more or finding good

Figure 2.
COMPUTER IMPACT UPON THE INFORMATIONAL
ROLES OF THE MANAGER

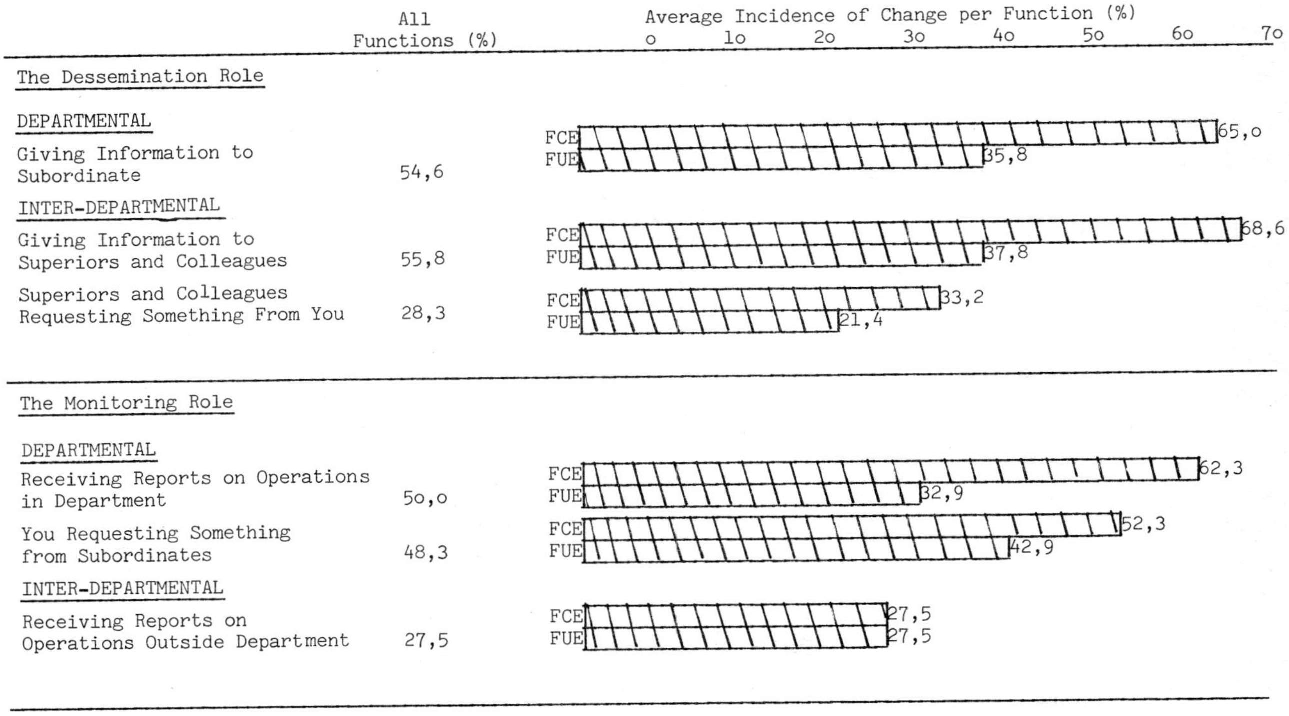

	All Functions (%)
The Dessemination Role	
DEPARTMENTAL	
Giving Information to Subordinate	54,6
INTER-DEPARTMENTAL	
Giving Information to Superiors and Colleagues	55,8
Superiors and Colleagues Requesting Something From You	28,3
The Monitoring Role	
DEPARTMENTAL	
Receiving Reports on Operations in Department	50,0
You Requesting Something from Subordinates	48,3
INTER-DEPARTMENTAL	
Receiving Reports on Operations Outside Department	27,5

Average Incidence of Change per Function (%)

FCE: 65,0 / 68,6 / 33,2 / 62,3 / 52,3 / 27,5
FUE: 35,8 / 37,8 / 21,4 / 32,9 / 42,9 / 27,5

Key: FCE = Functions in Certain Environment
FUE = Functions in Uncertain Environment

Figure 3.

COMPUTER IMPACT UPON THE DECISIONAL
ROLES OF THE MANAGER

	All Functions (%)
DEPARTMENTAL	
Subordinates Requesting Authorisation	38,3
Subordinated Requesting Action	49,7
Decision Making	61,3
INTER-DEPARTMENTAL	
You Requesting Authorisation from Superiors/Colleagues	3o,3
You Requesting Action from Superiors/Colleagues	39,7
Decision Making with Superiors/Collagues	5o,5

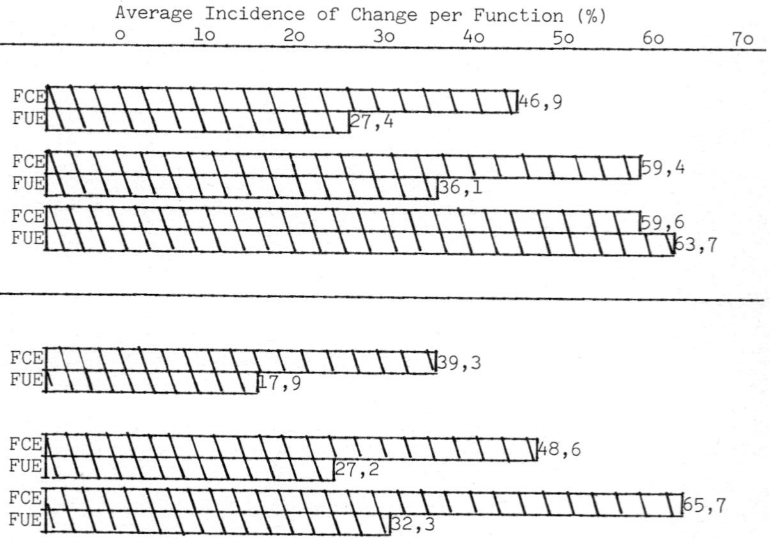

Key: FCE = Functions in Certain Environment
FUE = Functions in Uncertain Environment

excuses for why they were not to blame.

A rather similar incidence of change was found for the decisional roles, with the most frequently cited changes occurring in activities directly related to decision making. The unstructured comments about the nature of these changes again displayed great variability, the most general comment being that managers were now able to take their decisions using a better information base and this agreed information base also improved the quality of decision making discussions with other members of the organisation. Once again the evidence does not give unequivocal support for a theory that says the locus of decision making will be moved up or down within the organisation. It suggests instead that there is a qualitative shift in the nature of decision making.

The evaluation of these changes was 72% positive and probably the most interesting responses came from a group of managers (in different cases) who indicated disquiet with respect of changes in decision making and in their roles with respect to their subordinates. The managers were reacting to pressures from subordinates to be more involved in decision making because they now had access to information which was previously under the manager's control.

Probably the most important finding with respect to this data is that there are substantial variations from one organisational function to another, and it is appropriate to ask what variables are responsible for this. Figures 2 and 3 provide an indication of two variables which may make a contribution. In 10 questions out of 12 the incidence of change is higher for functions in a relatively certain environment than it is for functions in a relatively uncertain environment. Similarly the questions were asked for both departmental and interdepartmental roles and in 5 cases out of 6 the highest incidence of change is in departmental roles. We have then some basis for predicting where a computer system is likely to have its greatest impact but we need to speculate about possible reasons for these variations.

One avenue to explore for a possible explanation is in the nature of the organisational functions under investigation. The focus of this research on sepcific functions means that each case study yields a detailed map of how the organisation handles the functions under investigation, i.e. how the functions are subdivided into component tasks, who is responsible for these tasks and what kinds of task dependencies result from this allocation of responsibilities. These analyses show that, for most organisational functions, the strongest task relations exist within rather than between departments. It is not perhaps surprising therefore that computer impact upon task related interpersonal roles is strongest within departments, where there is, in effect, greater mutual concern for the task. Preliminary examination of the data on other variables also suggests that a variety of organisational forces seek to protect organisational territory which may also serve to reduce the impact of computer systems across departmental boundaries.

To interpret the finding that there is relatively little computer impact upon interpersonal roles in organisational functions dealing with uncertainty it is useful to examine how organisations cope with uncertainty. Thompson (1967) has identified a number of strategies an organisation may employ and one of these relates to the way responsibilities are allocated to members of staff. In the case studies, the method of allocating responsibilities associated with the functions in uncertain environments is primarily to establish specialist staff who are experts with respect to each aspect of uncertainty and who filter this source of uncertainty for the organisation. As an example a marketing plan was established by specialists in product and regional markets pooling their specialist predictions of market trends. Task relations between such specialists tend to be weak because each has his own information base and his actions have limited consequences for his colleagues. In contrast, where the envrionment is more certain , division of responsibilities tends to be on functional lines with sequential interdependencies between component tasks with the result that, unless buffers are introduced, one person's task behaviour can have direct repercussions for other people.

On the basis of this analysis we may speculate that the impact of a computer system upon interpersonal task relations is directly related to the strength of task relations within the relevant function. Thus, where there are strong interdependencies of the kind we have found in the functions conducted in a relatively certain environment, the way an individual's task changes as a consequence of the use of a computer system may have considerable 'spill-over' effects in his inter-personal roles. When individual tasks within a function are more independent, as they tend to be in the functions conducted in relatively uncertain environments, there can be considerable change in the way a task is undertaken with only minimal impact upon interpersonal roles.

Whilst these propositions need more direct testing we can find some specific support for the general argument in the data presented here. In the first four questions presented in figure 1 there is evidence that there is slightly more impact upon task perception for functions in relatively uncertain environments. The same can be seen in figure 3 where direct decision making activities within the Department are seen to be more influenced in the functions involving relatively uncertain environments. However, the rest of the questions in figures 2 and 3 tell a different tale: they show that the impact on the individual task is not carried over as much into interpersonal roles within the functions conducted in a relatively uncertain environment whereas there is considerable impact in the functions conducted in relatively certain environment.

CONCLUSIONS

This paper is inevitably only a progress report on the CISM project and, even within the context of computer impact upon managerial tasks, it is incomplete. There remain, for example, the questions of how different types of computer system influence managerial tasks and whether the impact is different for managers at different levels of the organisation. The analysis presented here has made use of data and concepts from individual, inter-personal and organisational levels of analysis and is therefore a good indication of the character of this multivariate research project.

The analysis makes plain that it is simplistic to expect all computer systems to have the same impact on all managerial tasks. The most common kind of impact, found to some extent in all of the functions investigated, was that the computer system provides a better information base which permits managers to make a better appreciation of their task. In passing, it is worth adding a cautionary note to the general satisfaction evinced by managers with respect to this finding. It may be that a computer information system provides a better 'window' upon the task but it may also be that, as Weizenbaum (1976) has so plainly warned us, it is not so much a 'window' as a 'tunnel' which may blind the user to other views of his task. We have no direct evidence to support this view in our data but then the data comes directly from users and, by definition, blind men do not see. The simultaneous presence of improved task perception and additional sources of constraint in the way the task is undertaken should serve as an indirect warning that there may be effects of this nature.

The many other forms of impact found in these cases are not common to all managers or to all functions. In attempting to identify where and why these effects occur, two contributing variables have been isolated. The first is a distinction between work roles within and between departments where it would appear that organisations have many ways of keeping the impact of a computer system on relations between departments to a minimum and the strongest effects are felt within departments. Analysis of the way in which organisations conduct the functions investigated suggests that one of the reasons for this finding is that there are stronger task interdependencies within than between departments and the computer system has greater possibilities for impact where there are strong task interdependencies.

The issue of task interdependencies arises again with respect to the second contributing variable; the environmental uncertainty of the organisational function. Where there is a substantial degree of environmental uncertainty the computer information system offers minimal constraint to the way the task is undertaken and there is rather limited impact upon interpersonal roles. One interpretation of this finding is that it occurs because the computer system only has marginal effects upon weak task interdependencies and these tend to be the rule rather than the exception in work organisation strategies to cope with high environmental uncertainty.

One general point about the nature of the models used to explain computer impact is raised by this analysis. The results relating to task perception and to the importance of environmental uncertainty have demanded that we recognise that the manager's task is essentially open-ended. However, much of the literature on computer impact involves closed system thinking and appears to be based on a finite quantity model of organisations. For example, when such variables as discretion, power and influence are considered, computer impact is usually seen as causing a redistribution of finite quantities of these variables. It has been necessary in this analysis, in order to interpret the findings, to employ a more open-system approach in which both the individual and the organisation is seen as seeking better ways of coping with an uncertain task environment. Viewed from this perspective the important questions relating to tasks become not so much who loses or gains task autonomy but the extent to which the computer system supports individual and organisational attempts to cope with environmental vagaries and to what degree it introduces new forms of constraint to this coping process.

REFERENCES

Beer, S. (1968). Machines that Control Machines. Science Journal, Vol. 4, No. 10.

Blau, P.H. and B.A. Schoenherr (1971). Structure of Organisations. Basic Books, New York.

Eason, K.D. (1977). The Potential and Reality of Task Performance by Man-Computer Systems. In A. Parkin (ed.). Computing and People. E. Arnold, London pp. 55-62.

Leavitt, H.S. and T.L. Whisler (1958). Management in the 1980's. Harvard Business Review, Nov.-Dec., pp. 41-48.

Licklider, J.C.R. (1965). Man-Computer Partnership. International Science and Technology, May.

Mintzberg, H. (1973). The Nature of Managerial Work. Harper & Row, New York.

Morton, M.S.S. (1971). Management Decision Systems. Harvard University, Boston.

Simon, H.A. (1965). The Shape of Automation for Men and Management. Harper & Row, New York.

Stewart, R. (1971). How Computers Affect Management. Macmillan, London.

Thompson, J.D. (1967). Organisations in Action. McGraw-Hill, New York.

Weizenbaum, J. (1976). Computer Power and Human Reason. Freeman, San Francisco.

Whisler, T.L. and H. Meyer (1967). The Impact of EDP on Life Company Organisation. Personnel Administration Report No. 34, Life Office Management Association, November.

DISCUSSION AND COMMENTS ON PAPER PRESENTED BY KEN EASON

H.F. GEERDINK

The findings of the CISM project team on the subject of the impact of computer information systems upon the nature of the managerial task, is very interesting and very valuable. I believe that these can be of great help in developing methods for designing computer information systems in such a way that it will result in systems having an impact very close to the intended one.

However, I have some remarks:

1. It is stated that computer systems are usually designed only to support specific organisational functions.
    This leads to the following question:

    Should we not always design computer information systems in such a way as to take into account every aspect of organisational life? And would you not say that a structural design of the organization should precede the design of the computer information system?

2. It is also stated that the tasks of a manager tend to be open-ended and that he is continuously striving to improve his grasp of the variables at work and to predict the consequences of possible actions. Accordingly, we might expect that the manager is taking the initiative himself to have computer information systems developed for his specific needs based on his specifications.
    From the presentation it is not clear if such a case was present in the investigation. If so, it would be of great interest to know whether there was any difference in satisfaction between managers who made the specifications for the information systems themselves and managers who did not.

3. There were indications that a variety of organisational forces will lead to reduction of the impact of computer systems across departmental boundaries.
    I believe this is a very premature conclusion.
    If one looks to the theoretical model of an organisation as a whole with one overall computer information system for all information needs, this organisation is subdivided into departments and these departments have their own information system as a subsystem of the overall information system. In such a situation I would expect that the number of people who experience impact of the subsystem inside the department is higher than outside. But I think it is not correct to conclude that this means lower impact of computer systems across departmental boundaries.

4. In the CISM research project the impact of computer information systems has been measured by asking managers what they perceived about the change of their task and about the change of their roles. However, the perception of change is very much influenced by factors like:

    - how the computer information system was introduced? For instance did somebody tell the manager one day that he from now on had to use the system or did he have the possibility of growing mentally from the use of the old information system towards the use of the new system,

- whether the manager himself participated in the
  design and the development of the computer information system?

KEN EASON

I feel as if I need to start on a new paper and need to go back to the data base
to do it. However, one of the first questions was whether we should use computer
systems to making structural design changes in the organization. I feel we should.
We should take that viewpoint and ask ourselves whether we wish the particular
changes to occur or not. And the decision should be taken by the people who are
going to be in there trying to operate the new system afterwards. They should be
asking themselves those questions. Unfortunately in the companies investigated
we found that even though a number of organizational changes were planned in advance, a lot of the more subtle changes occured accidentally.

I was also asked whether the managers actually involved gave more positive responses to the impact on them. I cannot answer that one because I have not looked at
the data across all cases, but I can tell you that in the hospital case there was
a very distinct difference between the doctors involved in the process of systems
design. They were very enthusiastic about it, but all around them when the system
was implemented, there were a lot of doctors who felt very hostile about it primarily on privacy grounds. The lesson to learn from this is that it is no good
getting one or two users into the design team. Their likely enthusiasm is no
guarantee that all the users will be behind the system.

JAN BENDIX

It is my opinion that it is not really what we do to or for an organization or
its employees that counts but the fact that we do something. Any organizational
change with or without computers could create exactly the same kind of results as
presented in the paper. The type of changes reported on I could have found in my
own organization without any introduction of computer systems. Therefore, I should
like to ask what is so specific about computer systems? Is it possible to point
to just one important difference between the type of change in managerial work
enforced by computer systems compared with the type of change introduced into managerial work by any other environmental factors.

My second point is that I understand from the paper that a computer system is a
vehicle for change, and since we can work with that vehicle we naturally do it
and think it is fun. We use a lot of excuses to work with it and sometimes we are
lucky that people think what we are doing is valuable. But I feel that it does not
have to be valuable for anybody else as long as we are in the organization.

My third point is that computer systems in themselves are sources of limitations
for managerial innovations. This has somehting to do with the idea about the
window and tunnel vision. That is a problem which ought to be given more attention.

Finally, I feel the paper rightly discusses the managerial task instead of the
managers' task. To me it does not matter who is carrying out the managerial task
but that there is a task to be done.

Therefore the research objective of looking into the changing aspects of managerial
task be they introduced by computers or any other organizational change is very
important.

KEN EASON

I am reminded about a comment by Rosemary Stewart after she had done a series of
studies of the impact of computer systems on managers. She wrote that the organizations perhaps would have done better to engage in the systems design process,
to really look carefully of what they were doing and then decide not to use the
computer. I have a lot of sympathy for that statement as it is the act of looking
carefully at what is going on and coming to new conclusions about what to do which
perhaps is half of the story revealed by our data.

I was also asked whether there are any changes which we attribute to the computer
system which could not have been caused by something else. That is hard because
these things are really too intermeshed to be pulled out, but I believe that ther
are potentials for information handling which only the computer can give us, e.g.
in the Danish case, because of the new system, they could now centrally control a
stocks and that meant that they did not need to hold bufferstocks of components.
This could not have been achieved successfully without a computer.

NILS H. MØLLER

Focussing on change one will invariably hit at the problem about whether it is
practically possible to carry out comparisons between conditions before and conditions after the change. My question is whether you have come across some cases
where managers to some extent resent answering questions about changes, for the
single reason that they were not aware of their roles before.

KEN EASON

We have had very lengthy discussions about the problems of measuring the before
and after situation. In an ideal world we would have stayed with the organizations
from the very beginning when the new system was being discussed right through to
several years after it was implemented and traced what happened. However, we did
not think we would get any support from funding bodies to do that, so we had to
abandon this ideal strategy.

So we had to base our assessment of change on the perception of individuals of
what had happened over the years. We tried to handle this difficulty by being very
specific about changes in particular tasks. That gave us all sorts of replies like
"yes, there has been changes but do not go and say it has anything to do with
computer systems" and "there has been a change which partly may be associated with
a change introduced parallel with the introduction of the computer system". - We
are obviously faced with the problem of the world not standing still while the
computer system is introduced and we carry out our research. The computer system
is used within a set of changes so that some things occur faster and some things
are inhibited in occurring.

In assessing the before situation I am very conscious of the fact that people
learn something about their tasks over the years, and indeed many of our respondents would have gone through a process of change whether the system was introduced or not. But we asked them "whether the system had contributed to ..." and
we have to rely upon what they said. I share the doubt about whether all of them
could adequately analyse the before situation, but there is little choice, and I
am still in the world of believing what people tell me.

H.C. PRICE

Eason mentioned that in the case of the hospital he found some doctors who were very enthusiastic about it, but when the system was implemented there were a lot of doctors who were hostile. My advice to you is to throw out the enthusiasts before you start!

The other thing I should like to ask is that you quoted the managers for claiming that there had been a saving in using the computer system. Are they applying this criterion to the management system or the productive system?

KEN EASON

When they talk about savings they normally talk about savings in resource allocation of one sort or another. When they talk about understanding their own task better they very seldom quantify this issue, and I do not think that they should.

Bob Tricker's from O.C.M.S.
Where he's the Director, no less.
Oxford's the place,
Where intellects race,
So his paper is sure to impress.

ORDER OR FREEDOM - THE ULTIMATE ISSUE IN INFORMATION SYSTEMS DESIGN

R.I. Tricker

Oxford Centre for Management Studies
Oxford, England

Concerns about system developments perceived by senior executives are reviewed.
It is argued that many apparent problems
stem from a failure to distinguish technical, operational and organisational levels
of systems. At each level vignettes of
problem cases are used to illustrate the
differences. - Three broad determinants of
corporate culture are suggested - technological, physical and managerial - that
also determine the structure of information systems. The fundamental issue is
seen to lie at the organisational level
and to involve the balance between individual freedom and corporate control. It
concerns the locus of decision-taking
power. This classical dilemma is becoming
specific and potentially soluble by the
elaboration of computer and communication
based information systems.

The Human Side of Information Processing
N. Bjørn-Andersen, editor
© IAG
North-Holland Publishing Company, 1980

INTRODUCTION

For nearly twenty years now I have been working with executives as they grapple
with the effects of computer-based technology in their organisations. In the private and the public sectors of business, in local authorities and government departments, each year or two seems to bring its particular set of issues that concern the senior executives involved.

In the early '6os the predominant concern was the application of the new technology - could it be made to work? Would the staff savings and improved efficiencies
really emerge? Then the worries were about the training for systems analysts and
how to keep them. By the early '7os the problem area was the application of tele-
processing and remote access.

Gradually the focus has shifted from the CPU centered system to the present preoccupation with distributed processing, intelligent terminals front-ending widespread systems, mini-computers ..... How often the current concerns are referred
to by that glorious over-simplification as questions of centralisation or decentralisation. And what might the dominant concerns be in the '8os?

In this paper issues that are currently being voiced by systems executives and
their Board level colleagues are reviewed. Their perceptions of the problems, it
is argued, often stem from a failure to distinguish different system levels; and
short vignettes of case examples are used to illustrate the differences.

Then it is suggested that the structure of information systems is, increasingly,
dependent on determinants of the corporate culture - technological, physical and
managerial - and not on computer technology. The real issues and opportunities,
as we plan for the '8os, though totally dependent on computer and communications
facilities, lie with organisational and managerial decisions about the locus of
decision-taking power.

BASIS FOR THIS PAPER

For some years I have been running a series of discussions in Oxford with senior
executives, among other things about the managerial and organisational aspects of
information systems. These confidential discussion groups, Top Management Briefings as they are called (Lincoln 1976) provide a continuing forum for the exchange of experience. Queen's University in Canada have also mounted a similar
series of seminars which I have chaired.

In the past eighteen months IAG have held two workshops in Denmark, drawing executives from various European countries; and the Chairman of IAG, Mr. Paul Dixon,
and I have run similar seminars in South Africa, Australia and New Zealand, under
the auspices of the national computer societies.

This paper draws on the accumulated experience of these Briefings. Necessarily the
discussions were confidential, thus ensuring that the real personal and organisational questions were fully explored. Consequently the ideas are presented here in
a generalised form, and the examples have been disguised to ensure anonymity.

PROBLEMS PERCEIVED

Inevitably a wide range of topics are discussed in a Briefing. For this paper those
involving organisational implications of information system developments have been
identified.

The following comments are typical of the problems being faced:

> "It is obvious that some systems are better handled locally and
> some centrally. But which should we locate where? What criteria

should we use to decide?"
(a large company with autonomous manufacturing and selling
divisions, with some central marketing - the systems executive)

"We are faced with the need to upgrade our mainframe. We could
shift towards distributed processing. What are the real implications?"
(a company in the service sector - director of administration)

"Important organisational implications have followed our system
developments. There have been changes in managerial power and
authority. The difficulty is predicting the effects".
(a major bank - a general manager)

"The computer is a way of life in our business. There is no way we
could now operate if the systems go down. But how do I really know
if we are getting value for money? It is one thing to measure
efficiencies in the computer department; it is quite another to
assess the effectiveness of our systems in organisational terms".
(a multinational company - the finance director)

"The systems we are implementing now will mean that the divisions'
information will be more readily accessible, more visible. But
will this mean a shift towards the centralisation of management? I
am not sure that my top management are competent to handle the
situation we are, in effect, creating".
(an international manufacturing company - the executive responsible
for computer system developments)

EXTENT OF KNOWLEDGE

Issues posed in this way are not, for the most part, explored in the current literature. Articles in the practice-orientated journals tend to address specific
matters in the design and implementation of computer and telecommunication based
systems. Only rarely do they embrace the organisational or strategic issues: yet,
from the problems perceived by executives, these are the significant areas. The
scholarly literature, on the other hand, does not permit ready extrapolation from
the abstraction and generality to an appreciation or resolution of specific questions within the enterprise.

Theories of inter-personal behaviour and organisation structure tend to be remote
from the problems perceived by the executive. Knowledge deriving from practical
experience is ahead of the literature's ability to identify and explain the organisational implications of information system developments. But inevitably, therefore, the wheel is being reinvented by different organisations, whilst other organisations remain in the cart that is wheelless.

The work done by Leavitt & Whisler (1958), Hofer (197o) and Stewart (1971) has focused on the impact that the computer has had, or might have, on the organisation.
Unfortunately these studies were undertaken before the computer and telecommunications technology reached its present stage of development. The question now is
much less about the impact of computers on the organisation; it is how to compare
and evaluate alternative organisational forms and possible locii of decision-
taking power that become feasible with different designs in information systems.

Nolan's (1973) study in which he characterised four distinct stages of computer
system development, has an intuitive appeal. It has been well received in many
companies, which can identify the evolution he postulates in their own experience.

Nolan's successive stages are:

I Initiation. The computer is introduced into the organisation.
Applications are orientated towards cost reduction. Controls are
non-existent. The initial impact is substantial. Computer
management is located at a relatively low level in the department
introducing the equipment - frequently in accounting.

II Contagion. Management appreciate the advantages in computing
and become committed. Applications proliferate, development costs
are heavy and controls lax.

III Control. There is a crisis; costs have tended to run away.
There is a moratorium on new applications. Planning justification
and budget controls are imposed. Co-ordination and control re-
emphasises central authority. Data-processing moves away from
the accounting function.

IV Integration. The role of computing is re-examined in the
light of the organisation's objectives. Longer term planning
is introduced. The importance of computing is recognised by
top management.

But, despite the intuitive appeal, the use of the stages as a predictive device
for organisational change has to be challenged. The stages seem more likely to reflect thresholds in the development of computer-based technology than inevitable
stages of organisational and managerial development. Withington (1974) would rather
support this suggestion.

Moreover Nolan (1973) himself has suggested further stages in the evolution, recog
nising the implications of mini-computers and intelligent terminals front-ending
large distributed systems.

Nolan and Burnett (1975) argue for integration and the exercise of central control
in a discussion of the role of mini-computers. They recommend a central function
to establish standards and co-ordinate the development of software, application
programmes and data-bases. At the same time they recognise the need for the involvement of the user department. The actual organisational implications are not
developed.

In Nolan (1977) the potential disagreement between data processing personnel and
users, about which activities should be controlled by whom, is recognised. The
solution offered is a separation of "function" for which the user would be responsible, whilst data processing organisation has a responsibility for managing the
"data" resource.

AN ALTERNATIVE FRAME OF REFERENCE

In this paper it is argued that much of our interest in the impact of computers on
organisation, or the right place for the computer in the organisation, has been
misplaced. The important questions, though brought into focus by the potential of
computer and telecommunication-based systems, are not about computers at all.

When messages were carried by bearers in a cleft stick and thence by sailing ship,
in the early days of, say, The East India Company, six to eight weeks might pass
before a reply came. Consequently organisational forms and patterns of managerial
authority arose that were appropriate. Today, with reliable voice and telex telecommunications throughout much of the developed world, different organisational
forms, managerial responsibilities and networks of authority for decisions are
created. But the managerial discussion is about organisational and management
matters. Whether the routing of the telecommunications is by micro-wave link, land
line or satellite is immaterial, providing the service is satisfactory: similarly
with information systems and computers.

Confusion is arising from a failure to distinguish different types of problem. The three level framework, introduced in a paper at the IFIP Congress in Toronto (Tricker 1977) is developed further here. It is postulated that the issues being faced by executives can usefully be considered at an organisational, operational or technical system level.

THE TECHNICAL LEVEL

The task of the technical level systems is to provide facilities for the communication and processing of data for legitimate use anywhere in the organisation. Consequently they cover all telecommunications, computers and related input/output equipment (with the possible exception of equipment dedicated solely to process applications such as numerical control of machines), and the relevant software and support systems. In other words, the technical level covers the "plumbing".

> Case example: In a large manufacturing company related components are produced in plants around the world. The supply, manufacturing and assembly logistics are co-ordinated centrally, against the demands from customers internationally.
> The company have a head office executive, at a high level in the organisation, with responsibility for the entire computing and communication systems world-wide. His approval is required before any division can lease or buy equipment for computing or telecommunications. A recent expenditure approval for corporate-wide systems was for over $2o million.

Proper concerns at the technical level are for the creation of mechanised systems that are effective and efficient, bearing the loads demanded with appropriate levels of service, reliability and cost. There are likely to be attempts at determining an optimum structure for the communication and computer systems, recognising the changing load patterns and communication costs between locations. Concern will be felt for uniformity in operating protocols and input/output devices. There is likely to be an overall plan for network operations. Dealings with vendors can be co-ordinated.

The sort of problem being faced is whether to use private lines or direct-dial facilities in parts of the telecommunications network; or if one division's request for a mini-computer for a specific application is consistent with the broader corporate strategy for a larger distributed processing facility in that country.

Essentially, at the technical level, we are talking about the management of computer and communications technology. Micro-processors, mini-computers and massive interrelated computing networks are all included.

There are further impressive technological developments on the way - the "electronic mailbox", text editing and word processing, reducing data storage and communication costs, voice recognition and so on - leading towards the more automated office with significantly reduced paper-work.

The need for proper management planning and control at the technical level is fundamental. Increasingly computer and communications technology is becoming as fundamental to the operation and survival of any business, as aircraft are to an airline, or ovens to a bakery. Professional management of the systems at the technical level is becoming anonymous with operational and financial viability. In some industries, notably insurance, airlines and commercial banking, this is already the case.

But, it is argued, the problems and opportunities at the technical level are different in nature from those at the operational or organisational levels. We confuse them at our peril.

THE OPERATIONAL LEVEL

The task of the operational level systems is to ensure the availability of relevant data, for the enterprise to transact its business and for the decision-takers to be informed. Consequently they are concerned with the capture, storage, processing, retrieval and presentation of data. Questions about the contents of data bases and rights of access, about security, privacy and priority ratings, and application-orientated programmes are legitimately the focus at the operational level. The more traditional transaction based systems are included, so are the decision support systems whose purpose is to facilitate the provision of information for decision-takers.

> Case example: A senior executive in a large financial enterprise commented: "Our systems seem to be set like concrete. We wanted to introduce a new service to some of our existing customers with particular needs. We found it was very time-consuming and difficult, both to reorganise our files to identify them and to prepare the systems for the new product". Such matters are problems at the operational level.

Although obviously, the facilities that are available at the technical level will affect what can be attempted at the operational level, many operational systems will be quite independent of the equipment on which they are run. In some cases problems are perceived by executives in terms of the technical level - "upgrading the mainframe or decentralising processing with minis" - whereas the reality of the issue lies at the operational level.

Management at the operational level involves administration of the data resource: it is different from management of computer and communications technology. Attention is directed to the user rather than to the equipment; in many cases the user will be responsible for the development of systems and will have a sense of ownership.

ON OWNERSHIP OF INFORMATION SYSTEMS

The importance of user involvement in the design and implementation of computer-based systems, has long been recognised. The literature is replete with ideas on steering committees, joint design teams and user-designed systems to ensure identification and commitment. But something different is being suggested in this paper.

> Case example: An airline reservation clerk was asked about the system by which she could enquire about seat availability on a flight between two distant locations. "It's here in my computer" she replied. Questioned further she had no comprehension of the system into which her terminal was hooked. To her it was irrelevant that three main-frames in the United States, Australia and Europe were linked by a complex network of computer switching and data-based systems. For her the computer was the desk-top display and keyboard; that was "her" system; with it she could fulfil her task.

In operational terms the mark of success in user involvement and commitment has been achieved when he refers to my system. At that stage the technical level system by which his data is handled and processed is immaterial. At the operational level the user, whether he be shop-floor operative, counter clerk, manager or corporate director, is thinking in terms of the data which is necessary to fulfil his function and which is available in "my system".

> Case example: Previously telephone operators in an insurance company took messages from policy holders and agents and passed them on hand written forms to the clerks who handled that class

of business. Now they sat at terminals which gave them access to
the files themselves. They were able to relate to the callers
in a new way. One of the things they asked management was whether
they could take responsibility for a wider range of policies and
include the claims side as well as the premium. Their field of
interest had widened because they had access to the files of
"their own customers".

Case example: A large manufacturing plant introduced data-capture
devices on the shop floor. Operatives were required to key in
details of machine states and work-in-progress. Error rates were
high. Now they are considering giving information to the operative, by means of a visual display, so that he will see the relevance to him at his work station of the data he is inputting. He
would be able to discuss the work load, to compare performances,
to see the effects on his pay. In other words, he would be given
his own set of information. The outstanding question now is not
the technical feasibility, but the effect on the shop stewards
and foremen, who are traditional communication channels on the
shop floor.

There is effectively no technical limit now, and within the next few years no cost/
effective limit, to the provision for each management decision-maker of terminal
access to his own files. A desk-top device, or a portable coupler to use over the
public telephone lines, can link him into any corporate files that are to be open
to him, give him computational facilities, and enable him to create his own files.
The proverbial little black-book of the manager will have been computerised. Each
manager will have an information system which he thinks of as his own, as well as
linking in to the corporate and local systems. It is outside of the scope of this
paper to speculate further - except to highlight the significance of an outside,
non-executive director, or other representative of corporate stake holders being
able to access and pursue enquiries within corporate files. The real implications
are then focused at the organisational level of systems.

THE ORGANISATIONAL LEVEL

The task at the organisational level is the management of the enterprise, structuring the relationships between its parts, identifying goals for achievement, and
allocating resources. The concerns at the organisational level will include the
definition of boundaries and groupings in the organisation structure, introducing
management control systems and performance measures, ensuring appropriate checks
and balances in accountability, and achieving the corporate goals.

The massive range of alternatives now available at the technical level and the
implications of information system ownership at the operating level provide a
major set of issues and opportunities at the organisational level.

Case example: A government department is considering putting cost
data-collection into the geographically remote regions. It is
recognised that this will enable the regional managers to control
costs more directly. But it also implies a passing of authority
from the centre to initiate actions previously requiring central
sanction. Some officers at the centre are opposed to this development, arguing that it implies a loss of control.

Case example: An insurance company with highly centralised technical level systems sees the head office as "the administrative
factory doing the paperwork, with the regions responsible for
selling". The regional executives argue that they are not getting
the information they need to do their job efficiently. If they
are given this information, which technically and operationally

would be straight forward, the head office would be faced with demands for wider discretion being exercised in the local offices.

>Case example: A grocery chain is introducing point of sale termi-
>nals at its check-out stations. It has received a union demand for
>upgrading the job of the operators, as they are now responsible
>for inputs to the corporate systems.

The changes that are now feasible at the technical and the operational level provide new opportunities at the organisational level for creating the structure and
adopting the management style that the executives think consistent with their strategies. They may shift towards greater central oversight of corporate affairs or
devolve power to decide out towards the periphery of their organisation. Provided,
that is, that the executives can recognise the opportunities and are competent in
selecting appropriate alternatives.

An effect of developments at the technical and operational levels is to destabilise
the organisation. There was a consistent feeling in briefings, that many board-
level executives, having been brought up in conditions in which such issues did
not arise, were potentially incompetent organisationally, despite their unknow-
ledgeable enthusiasm and confidence in computing. It was also pointed out, significantly, that one of the more conservative functions in some organisations was
the data-processing department which could be loathe to move to new alternatives
and shift the balance of power over computing and data.

The potential for changes to organisation structure is not confined to relationships within the existing enterprise. Another effect of developments at the technical level is to alter the boundaries of the enterprise itself. Consider, for
example, the organisational implications in an airline if clerks in agents offices
could not only enquire about seat availability from remote locations but actually
up-date the file making a reservation. The customer would be directly amending the
order-book.

>Case example: A bank is installing terminals in a retailer's
>stores. Customers may now transact business with the bank from
>these remote locations. If the bank goes further and enables the
>retailer to debit the customer's account directly where does the
>boundary lie? Is the bank involved in the retailer's business or
>is it the reverse?

>Case example: Another bank is now technically able to provide
>an accounting service for its corporate customers, in effect
>maintaining their pruchase and sales ledgers for them. It is
>considering offering this as a new service. Where do the boun-
>daries between banker and customer then lie?

It is apparent that at the organisational level there are many issues to be faced.
But, it is asserted in this paper, the questions are fundamentally about management and organisation, not about computers. The key question is becoming how do
you want to run your business? The opportunities at the technical and operational
levels open up a wide vista of organisational alternatives. No longer need organisation structures and management styles emerge as a reaction to recurrent crises.
But the choices need to be driven by the business needs, not those of computer
systems. It is a matter of corporate culture.

THE CORPORATE CULTURE

So what does affect the design and development of organisations and their information systems? Are there any clues that might help executives?

A review of the case notes from the briefings, which now cover presentations by

over 2oo senior executives around the world, seems to suggest three broad criteria
- technological, physical and managerial. Further elaboration of these factors
must await detailed study. But in the context of this paper some relevant features
emerge.

The technology of the business, indicated for example by its industry and market
sector, its capital intensity and product cost structure, seems to be relevant
both to the patterns of organisation structure and the technical level systems.
(Thus following the arguments of the Woodward school of management thought.)

> Case example: In an electricity supply utility the basic tech-
> nology is based on central and regional controls over an inte-
> grated supply network. The focus of the information system was
> described by an executive as "supporting the utility as it tried
> to meet the demands for electricity in the short and long terms".
> At the technical level responsibility for systems development
> was centralised, with longer term systems planning integrated
> with the capital development plans of the utility.

> Case example: In a company which manufactured shoes in various
> factories for sale through company retail shops there was a
> central facility, at the technical and operational level for lo-
> gistic control over stocks, re-ordering and manufacture, but lo-
> cal plant control over local systems such as personnel. The plant
> managers were held repsonsible for performance against budget
> and had some autonomy over expenditure.

> Case example: A food products company was divisionalised by pro-
> duct with divisional managers being responsible for production,
> distribution and marketing of specific product ranges. They
> also had considerable degrees of freedom in the design of ope-
> rating level systems and the choice of technical level facili-
> ties.

Despite the tendency to generalise about business management, it is the case that,
technologically, businesses can be very different. In considering the corporate
culture and the implications for the design of information systems, it is apparent
that such differences, and their implications at organisational, operating and
technical system levels have to be recognised.

Another set of criteria that seem to influence information system design might be
termed 'physical criteria', for example, the scale of the enterprise, its geographical location and international spread.

> Case example: A multinational company in the motor industry had
> made a major investment at the technical level to facilitate
> world-wide communications in voice and data. Consequently each
> operating division transmitted its monthly operating statements
> directly to head office, where the message switching computer re-
> cognises the type of message and relays it directly to the com-
> puter data-base in which the results are being formulated. By
> contrast a motor manufacturer operating predominantly in one coun-
> try can use the postal service for that link in the information
> system.

Finally the impact of management style, that set of influences stemming from the
key executives and past corporate history and experiences, can be very influential
in conditioning people's expectations about the business and determining the way
it operates.

> Case example: The Chairman and Chief Executive of a company in
> the dairy industry that had grown quickly under his leadership
> by acquisition, was in favour of information system developments
> when they promised to give him more relevant information about
> each separate company. He stopped developments when managing
> directors of some subsidiaries complained at the head office
> controller's interference in their production planning and
> control systems.

The corporate culture provides the setting for the design and development of information systems, at each level - organisationally, operationally and technically.

There has been some discussion about the relationship between the different levels.
Whether, for example, the effect of centralising facilities at the technical level
automatically leads to a centralising effect at the operational level with a centralisation of files, and at the organisational level with a centralisation of
managerial authority.

The conclusion argued in the IFIP paper (Tricker 1977) is that the levels are
neither dependent on one another, nor are they independent. In other words, though
a shift at one level need not be mirrored at another level, it will have an effect.
The system levels are inter-dependent, changes in one causing effects at another.

With the new technology and facilities potentially available at the technical level, there are new forces open to those who would shape organisations and society.
There are consequently new responsibilities for those with managerial, executive
and political power.

ON ORDER AND FREEDOM

But the underlying issues are ancient. Information, and the right of access to it,
is a source of power in any society, as anthropologists will confirm. For centuries the privilege of information in Western societies has been a function of
one's place in the social hierarchy. In corporation or government department, for
example, the right to information has been determined by the corporate culture and
one's perceived place in the power hierarchy, on one's position in the organisational decision-taking structure. So secure has this underpinning been in Western
management thought, that neither the words "information" nor "power" appear with
any frequency in the management literature until about fifteen years ago.

Two factors are now causing those in authority to reappraise their position. The
first is the pressure for openness, disclosure and accountability, for participation and involvement. Examples are legion - in the health services, in parent-
teacher associations, in local and national government and at the work place. The
second derives from the potential availability of information through the extension
of information systems at the technical and operational levels.

A new managerial and executive competence is needed to create organisations which
can meet the challenges for accountability and participation, whilst maintaining
sufficient freedom and discretion to act decisively in the achievement of corporate goals. Achieving such a balance at the organisational level is likely to
feature prominently in the problems perceived by executives in the '8os.

The central issue is as old as civilisation. Political philosophers have always
been concerned about the balance between centralism and devolution of authority,
between the whole and the parts, between state and individual. Plato, More, Jef-
ferson and Marx all recognised the essential dilemma and addressed it in ways they
thought appropriate to the circumstances of their time.

The issue facing the executives in a large multinational corporation, as they decide how much authority to allow to a remote division and what controls to exer-

cise centrally, has similar dimensions. As they push authority to decide out from the centre towards the periphery of the organisation, with all the concomitant paraphernalia of divisional performance measures, allocation of costs, transfer pricing and reporting systems, they recognise the potential benefits that can stem from a devolution of authority - the motivation that comes from a sense of involvement and participation in the control of one's own situation, the commitment that is associated with the recognition of worth and trust, the creativity and imagination that can be released, the discretion and thoughtfulness that can be exercised, the experience and training that can be given, as well as the avoidance of some of the diseconomies of scale.

But the price of freedom can be high for the enterprise as a whole - potential benefits of scale economies may be lost, failure to co-ordinate activities can be wasteful, opportunities for standardisation and co-ordination may disappear and heavy costs can be associated with a loss of order in the whole. In a word these are the effects of suboptimisation, by which the parts, in seeking to achieve their own objective, take action that is detrimental to the interests of the whole. Suboptimisation can always be avoided by moving authority to decide to the next higher or more central level; with, of course, the diminution of local autonomy.

Designers of any social organisation face the balancing act between freedom for the local decision-maker and the greater social control of the whole, between autonomy for the parts and centrality of control. Whether the organisation is a business enterprise, a social service department, a law enforcement agency, a state or a meta-state (like the EEC) the issues arise. The organisational form is chosen that, in the opinion of the designers, has the highest probability of sufficiently optimising the goals of the parts, whilst contributing to the achievement of the purpose of the whole. The textbook refers to goal congruance, Anthony (1965) or compatible aims, Tricker (1976); but the implications for organisational design and the creation of appropriate management control systems have still to be explored in the context of the new opportunities for providing information.

There seems little doubt that the potential at the technical and operational levels to provide access to information has, at present, hardly been tapped. When the opportunities are pursued significant and fundamental changes may occur in the power structure of organisations and societies.

If this sounds grandiose consider two cases. When the worker in manufacturing industry has access to the production and financial information he wants and can determine his own contribution to his colleagues, what role would there then be for the shop steward and trade union? At an entirely different level consider the nation state. When multinational companies operating within its borders can operate world wide information networks, they can model the economic advantages of operating in any location at any time, and allocate resources accordingly. Why is there such interest in monitoring cross-border data flows to protect national sovereignty?

These are great issues brought about by computer and communications technology. The implications demand management and executive decision-makers of new orders of competence. They have to grapple with the late 2oth century's equivalent of the age-old balance between order and freedom. Schumacher (1973) put it most succinctly:

> "In the affairs of men, there always appears to be a need for at least two things simultaneously, which, on the face of it, seem to be incompatible and to exclude one another. We always need both freedom and order. We need the freedom of lots and lots of small, autonomous units, and, at the same time, the orderliness of large-scale, possibly global, unity and co-ordination".

> ".... most people find it difficult to keep two seemingly opposite necessities of truth in their minds at the same time".

REFERENCES

Anthony, R.N. (1965). Planning and Control Systems - a Framework for Analysis. Harvard University Press.

Hofer, C.W. (1970). Emerging Edp Pattern. Harvard Business Review, March/April.

Leavitt, H.J. and T.L. Whisler (1958). Management in the 1980s. Harward Business Review, Nov.-Dec., Vol. 36, No.6, pp. 41-48.

Lincoln, T.J. (1976). Impact of Changing Business Environment on Management and Their Information Needs. Management Datamatics, Vol. 5, No. 3.

Nolan, R.L. (1973). Managing the Computer Resource - a Stage Hypothesis, Communications of the Association for Computing Machinery, July.

Nolan, R.L. (1977). Restructuring the Data-Processing Organisation for Data Resource Management. In B. Gilchrist (ed.), Information Processing 77. Proceedings of the IFIP Congress, Toronto. North-Holland Publishing Company, Amsterdam.

Nolan, R.L. (1977). Controlling the Costs of Data Services. Harvard Business Review, July/August.

Nolan, R.L. and G.J. Burnett (1975). At Last - Major Roles for Mini-Computers. Harvard Business Review, May/June.

Schumacher, E.F. (1973). Small is Beautiful. Blond & Briggs, London.

Stewart, R. (1971). How Computers Affect Management. Macmillan, London.

Tricker, R.I. (1976). Management Information and Control Systems. Wiley, London.

Tricker, R.I. (1977). The Impact of Information Systems on Organisational Thinking. In B. Gilchrist (ed.), Information Processing 77. Proceedings of the IFIP Congress, Toronto. North-Holland Publishing Company. Amsterdam.

Withington, F.G. (1974). Five Generations of Computers. Harvard Business Review, July/August.

DISCUSSION AND COMMENTS ON PAPER PRESENTED BY ROBERT I. TRICKER

A.W. ZIJLKER

As long as we have organizations they will be managed so the perceptions and the problems of managers are important. But I feel that Tricker missed a chance to escape from the cage the computer professionals have been in since the invention of the computer.

Tricker stated as a fundamental problem the balance between the individual freedom and corporate control. Furthermore, a three-level system model is introduced which can be summarized in the following way; on the organizational level the organization is controlled by management, they use an information system on the operational level and the actual processing of data takes place on the technical level.

OK, but why this emphasis on control? Control of what and by whom. The question seems too obvious, but obvious questions are not always asked.

Let us have a look at an organization. I consider it as a set of manned processes executed by people. I see types of processes, planning processes, administrative control processes, operational processes where the actual production is taking place, and the processes involved with renewal. It was made quite clear by Tricker that he is concerned with the first two processes which is the area of information systems. This is the area where planners are outguessing others and where 'accountants' are doing normative data handling whether done by computers or by hand. On the operational level it is essentially communication taking place. People say "I am ready, you may go". This is message transfer or communication (and not control) going on at the shop floor between people doing their job.

I should like to go into this communication aspect of data. If we take:

- Tricker's balance between individual freedom and corporate control,

- Mumford and Hedberg's participative approach

- Brief's 'worried workers',

and if these issues are taken seriously, then we should not stick to control only. We should try to break out of the standing preoccupation of the edp profession that computers are there to control others. I claim that computers are there primarily to be used as mechanisms for communication, and we should start to pay specific attention to data-handling within operations. In other words, we should stop worrying about information systems and start working on communications systems. Therefore, we must pay specific attention to the way in which people communicate in operations; or in other words: to the way in which human beings send messages to each other.

I should like to present my thesis that

- if we introduce 'good' communication and

- do that according to existing insights into linguistics, then we are really talking about this main human capacity of:
  .. almost total freedom of expression
  .. within a framework of normalized grammar and lexicon
  .. based on a strictly common logical underlying structure

- then we may make use of modern electronics to gain effectiveness (including flexibility, motivation, self-control etc.) in operations,

- and we might even find that the need for vertical information (control) is reduced (cf. Jay Galbraith).

The outcome may of course well be decided upon by 'micro-political games' (Pettigrew). But that constitutes no excuse for not including aspects of data-handling in our studies concerning a field on which most of the emphasis will be concentrated in the near future. So the game is to introduce electronic gadgets to facilitate people-to-people communication (that is freedom) instead of having man-machine interfacing based on the systems fed into the computer (control); because the latter might introduce too much order for people to stand. And even if they stand it, it might not even be effective.

MOGENS D. RØMER

I think the paper very precisely points to some of the basic issues in information systems design. It provides a conceptual framework which I feel can be useful to those of us involved in the development of information systems at the executive level, in structuring our conception of the problems, and thus helping us identifying the real opportunities of the information and communication technology for solving management problems.

I should like to comment upon the concern aired by Tricker that executives and computer specialists lack the competence to recognize the opportunities and select the appropriate alternatives. Indeed, the data processing department is often one of the more conservative functions, reluctant to move to new alternatives and to shift the balance of power over computing and data.

At this point in time, very few organizations and institutions, whether in the public or the private sector, have used the computer as a decision supporting tool. And very few organizations have to any degree of completeness systematically discussed the decision structure and thus the information needs of the organization.

As is pointed out, one of the major problems in this connection is the fact that the actual information needed among other things, is a function of the manager himself as a person. Therefore, to a very high degree the needs have to be defined individually by the particular organization and by the manager himself.

On January 1st, 1977 the Danish Local and Regional Authorities started the implementation of a financial management system which is supported by one of the largest computer systems ever developed in Denmark. One of the goals defined for this system is to change the managerial and organizational behaviour in order to improve radically the possibilities of effective and efficient management of huge economic resources.

The actual experience is that this change in behaviour will take several years to accomplish not because of deficiencies in the technical system but because of the vast adjustment processes involved in the organizational and managerial implementation of the system, in the administration of each local authority, and in the political systems of elected politicians.

The data processing specialist is also in a difficult position. So far, he has primarily dealt with the technical problems of system design and implementation in an environment where the boundaries between the edp-activities and the user-activities have been pretty well defined.

With the current change from the traditional record handling systems towards information systems, the boundaries are disappearing, or at least changing drastically. This problem of lack of knowledge and experience is not easily resolvable. One dilemma is that we cannot organize ourselves out of the problems.

As the author states, the three system levels he identifies are inter-dependent. Changes in one cause changes at another. We cannot completely leave it to managers to deal with managerial and organizational problems, and we cannot completely leave it to computer specialists to deal with the technical problems.

The manager has to understand, to quite some depth, the opportunities created for him by the technology; and the computer professional has to understand the managerial and organizational implications of his technology.

Neither are really prepared for this. Even though Tricker has contributed to our knowledge, the problems of utilizing this and other knowledge in the practical world are tremendous. The realization of the managerial and organizational opportunities of information technology might require the breeding of a new generation of managers and computer professionals.

R.I. TRICKER

As to the comment about control, I agree with Zijlker if control is defined as stopping, preventing, prohibiting and so on. But I suggest that managerial control and guidance should be a creative process.

As to the comment by Rømer about the lack of top management knowledge, I agree. But it is also my experience that top management shows a remarkable enthusiasm and is very supportive of expenditures in systems.

I should like to raise one problem which so far has got almost no attention. It seems to me that the more successful we are in developing and exploiting these technologies, the more work will disappear.

However much commitment we get from the employees for the reformulation of the office of the future or continued automation on the shop floor, however much participation we get, however much employees take the initiative, we have to face the economic realities. Survival may be extraordinarily difficult in a competitive world with countries outside the Western world who adopt the technologies and have different work ethics. Half of the employees in our countries will have to plan for their own displacement. I have heard nothing about that in this conference, and it is a very, very significant issue.

PER GRØHOLT

I should like to rephrase the title of Tricker's paper to read "freedom through order" instead of "order or freedom".

R.I. TRICKER

I think the rephrasing captures my meaning. It is a question of balance in our society. That is a balance that we have not yet achieved in Western societies. That is what the challenge really is. Providing sufficient freedom has been the thrust of our discussions in this conference; but at the same time we must recognize that there is an enormous price involved with the maintenance of the personal freedom and the improvement in the quality of working life.

H.C. PRICE

As to the problem of working oneself out of the job, I wonder whether it would be of value to define the job concept. Are we talking about the existing job being constrained by the manual means of communication in the past, the residue of the industrial revolution, or can we conceive of some other sort of job which is more constructive and innovative and might have more control from below than control from above.

R.I. TRICKER

The concept of a job generally accepted in western cultures, based on puritan work ethics is that a job is the work you do; it is noble; it enables you to be the breadwinner; and to support a family; and to be out of the job is a social disgrace. That is the sort of view that should be in the process of being reformulated. And this must take place within a short time span given the technological developments ahead of us.

Tony Hopwood from L.B.S. comes.
His accounting is more than just sums.
He includes matters social,
And behaviour is crucial.
He's far from twiddling professional thumbs.

TOWARDS DESIGNING MANAGEMENT ACCOUNTING SYSTEMS FOR THE SUPPORT OF NEW CONCEPTS OF ENTERPRISE ACCOUNTABILITY

Anthony G. Hopwood

London Graduate School of Business
Studies, England

Recently there have been enormous pressures
on corporate management to explicitly recognize the interests of a broader range
of stake holders. Concerns with employment,
energy, and environment are increasingly
being seen as complementary to, and at
times conflicting with, those of economic
effectiveness. As yet, however, accounting
and information systems within the enterprise tend to ignore the new concerns.
The paper considers the possibilities for
designing management accounting systems
that strive to support new concepts of
enterprise accountability. Organizational
and social roles are given particular consideration. And, on this basis, some constraints on change and ways of facilitating
change are discussed.

The Human Side of Information Processing
N. Bjørn-Andersen, editor
© IAG
North-Holland Publishing Company, 1980

INTRODUCTION

Patterns of enterprise accountability currently are being debated and reappraised throughout Europe. Not too long ago it was taken as self-evident that the position of the shareholder vas supreme. Business enterprises were seen as not only having a primary economic mission but also a mission that was defined in terms of the economic interests of one particular social group. But the pressures and debates of the last two decades have started to change that position. In a comparatively short period of time the broader concept of the stakeholder has become a much more frequent feature of corporate discourse even if its implications still have to per-meate corporate strategies and actions. Increasingly the enterprise is being seen as a constituent part of a wider society, its actions having ramifications that extend far beyond the domain of the narrowly economic and, in consequence, its obligations being defined in terms of a far wider array of social interests and groupings. Although a new concept of enterprise accountability may be far from being crystallized, it is clear that the accepted limits of prior conceptions have been challenged and that the search for a new understanding is underway.

A wide variety of social pressures and interests have played a role in such deve-lopments. Not least in importance has been the growing power and confidence of the labour movement. In striving to articulate their interest in such matters as securi ty of employment, the right ot meaningful work and, increasingly, in some countries at least, the overall governance of the enterprise, the pressures emanating from labour have started to question prevailing conceptions of the corporate economy and the formulation of strategic options. However the labour movement has not been the only force for change. The last two decades have witnessed a growing concern with the interests of the community at large. At least some environmentalists, consumer advocates, energy experts, development economists and community activists have succeeded in at the very least highlighting the wider consequences of corporate behaviour and, perhaps more importantly, pointing to the ways in which options for corporate action are currently constrained, being assessed and debated in all too circumscribed a manner.

No doubt debates of this nature will continue for decades to come for the issues which they raise are fundamental to the values and the institutional strucutres of the societies in which we live. Already, however, at what might be quite an early stage in the development of a new social consciousness, quite explicit considera-tion has been given in many countries to at least some of the ramifications of these debates.

Legislation on such matters as health and safety at work, employment protection, consumer concerns, energy conservation, pollution and the protection of the envi-ronment has been a dominant feature of the programmes of so many European legisla-tive assemblies in the last few years. At least to this extent the corporate en-vironment is indeed in the process of changing. An ever growing array of obliga-tions and responsibilities are being given quite explicitly to the modern business enterprise and, in consequence, expectations of its accountability to different social groups also are changing. And, at the corporate level itself, related dis-cussions on the forms of corporate governance are starting to reinforce these patterns of change. Indeed, in retrospect, it is perhaps surprising how rapidly the debate on employee participation has moved from its early focus on the social psy-chology of satisfaction and happiness, and indeed even greater commitment to the unquestioned interests of the managing group, to a more fundamental concern with those institutional and structural issues which are central to the governance, di-rection and accountability of the enterprise.

CHANGING PATTERNS OF SOCIAL CONTROL AND THE MANAGEMENT OF INFORMATION

The nature and type of information, including accounting information, which either eminates from the enterprise or flows within it, and the social and organizational roles which information serves, are partly dependent upon the way in which the business enterprise is socially controlled. Different forms of corporate governance and different patterns of enterprise accountability make different demands on the management of information within the enterprise. For the form of social control influences the scope of information dissemination, the directionality of the information flows, the institutional forms through which and to which it flows, the parties within and outside the enterprise that can influence the management of information and thereby those control concerns which play a role in determining the dimensionality of the information and accounting flows. Furthermore different patterns of enterprise control can influence the relative importance of different roles that can be served by information. Not only can there be more or less emphasis on the decision rather than the control orientation of information but information can be used to either create or reinforce different patterns of organizational visibility and legitimacy.

In fact discussions of corporate accountability are already starting to influence the nature of debates on information and accounting. The potential for designing information and accounting systems which increase the power of employees and their unions is being investigated (Briefs 1975; Moore 1977; Sandberg 1976) and attempts also have been made to move towards strategies for designing information systems which give more explicit consideration to the social as well as technical aspects of the design task when delineating and selecting design alternatives (Mumford and Henshall 1978). Experiments also have been conducted on the design of information systems which facilitate rather than constrain new forms of organizational structure (Galbraith 1973; Knight 1977). And there is also an emerging interest in forms of social accounting, reporting and auditing. At first in the USA (Epstein, Flamholtz and McDonough 1976) and later in such European countries as France (Accounting, Organizations and Society, 1978), Germany (Dierkes 1974; Ullman 1978), The Netherlands (Dekker 1976), and Sweden (Gröjer and Stark 1977) a number of enterprises have strived to develop ways of reporting on their social as well as economic performance. Indeed in France the publication of an annual social report is now legally required of all enterprises employing over 750 people.

As yet it is far too early to assess the meaning and value of such developments. Many critics point to the primary legitimizing role of many of the experiments undertaken to date, seeing them as defensive responses to the threat of social change rather than more positive reflections of the reality of change and the evolving nature of information and accounting practice. Regardless of such conflicting views, however, at least the concept of alternative practice might well have entered into organizational discourse. And by themselves stimulating new approaches to the design of information and accounting systems by, in many cases, very different social groups, the inadequacies and partialities of the initial endeavours might have provided a basis for further experimentation and progress.

Many of the new developments in information systems design and alternative forms of accounting are illustrative of the way in which struggles over and changes in the social control of the enterprise can influence the nature of what is problematic and important in the information area. Alternative forms of social information processing and, in turn, alternative forms of accounting can be seen as reflections of more fundamental debates over alternative forms of the social control of the business enterprise, as is illustrated in Figure 1. And because of such a relationship, current pressures for changes in the accountability and control of the enterprise are likely to stimulate an even greater questioning of what has been taken for granted in the information area.

THE NEGLECTED ROLE OF MANAGEMENT ACCOUNTING

Until now very little consideration has been given to the ways in which the changing social environment of business might influence approaches to the provision of accountability and control information within the enterprise. When contrasted with the emerging interest in different approaches to the management of information in organizations and in social accounting, such a neglect of management accounting is

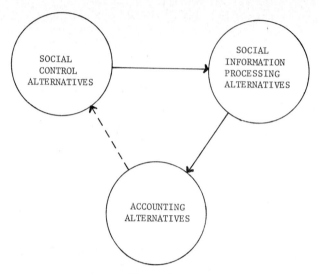

Figure 1.
Alternative Patterns of Social Control,
Information Processing and Accounting.

itself of interest. For it is, I think, a reflection of a view that sees current
approaches to management accounting as being organizationally self-evident and necessary and socially neutral.

Surely, such a line of reasoning would argue, a cost is a cost is a cost. And equal
ly surely, do not all organizations have a need for such essential management accounting procedures as costing systems and standards and budgets and plans? Well
possibly, but in a much more complex way than is commonly reflected in the cannons
of conventional wisdom. Not only can costs vary with circumstance and problem definition, a fact that is now well known to all, but the economic framework from
which they are derived is dependent on rather specific and quite debatable social
assumptions. In other words costs are neither organizationally self-evident or
socially neutral. And similarly the apparatus of management accounting is less of
a necessity but merely one aspect of an organization's more general approach to
the management of its internal and external environments. When seen in such terms
rather fundamental organizational options most certainly exist.

Rather than being organized as a design orientated body of knowledge, which is explicitly adaptive to the circumstances of particular enterprises and responsive to
the evolving needs of business, for some reason accountants have tended to conceive
of a much more static body of management accounting knowledge, many of the practices, routines and procedures of which are codified in student texts and manuals
of practice.

Yet in practice management accounting systems are not invariant to organizational
circumstance and they have evolved over time. Historically modes of accounting
have adapted to the advancing rate of both technological development and organizational complexity (Chandler 1962). Often their form has followed and indeed facilitated the aims and development of new forms of organization structure both in
the public and private sectors. And, as one might expect in the light of such historical responsiveness, management accounting systems also vary across organizations at the present time reflecting not only varying technologies, organizational

uncertainties and forms of management but also different evnrionmental pressures for internal efficiency, economising and the creation of order (Khandawalla 1972).

Increasingly however even the realm of practice reflects the ambiguities of our present body of management accounting knowledge. Whilst there is indeed evidence of adaptiveness to circumstance, increasingly there is also a growing realisation of the constraints implicit in present approaches. Their emphasis on regulation, the manufacturing of order and the consequent reduction of internal uncertainty, for instance, are now seen as increasingly problematic when applied in innovative organizations or in enterprises whose very existence depends on their ability to cope with rather than eliminate the uncertainties of their environment (Hedberg, Nystrom and Starbuck 1976; Grinyer and Norburn 1975). Similarly the role which present management accounting systems play in establishing the dominance of internal economic visibility is also questionable in enterprises which are primarily dependent upon technical, social or environmental ingenuity. More recently, moreover, the constraints inherent in so many management accounting systems have become even more visible as enterprises have strived to more radically change their management structures to meet the requirements of today's technological, managerial and social environments. The development of matrix structures of management created its own need for new insights and procedures - a need that was first met in the public rather than the private sector (Hopwood 1977). And more recent experiments with new forms of work organization and forms of industrial democracy all point to the inadequacies of our present insights.

Such problems themselves serve to highlight the importance of procedures for establishing and reinforcing patterns of accountability and control within enterprises. For the conflicts and incompatibilities that have been all too briefly noted arise because of, rather than in spite of, the vital role which management accounting systems play in creating selective visibility in organizations. They represent one vital way in which the management group can strive to embody meanings and purposes within organizations (Batstone 1978; Pettigrew 1977), seeking thereby to influence the consciousness and actions of organizational participants.

Because of both the importance of the roles served by management accounting systems in enterprises and the limitations of our present knowledge it is important that more explicit consideration should be given to the ways in which it might respond to the emerging pressures for new forms of enterprise accountability and control.

SOCIAL INFLUENCES ON THE DEVELOPMENT OF MANAGEMENT ACCOUNTING

However before going on to consider the current, and indeed future, pressures on management accounting, it is important that we should briefly consider the broader social as distinct from the purely organizational nature of existing modes of management accounting for such aspects of the subject have been ignored in most of the discussions to date. For this purpose we focus on three broad but important influences on the development of management accounting: external environmental pressures and threats; prevailing conceptions or organizational rationality and the distribution of power; and the increasing concern of the State with the specifics of management practices and actions.

Management Accounting as a Response to Environmental Pressures and Threats

Historically management accounting procedures would appear to have developed first in enterprises newly facing market competition (Pollard 1965). In the early days of the industrial revolution, and indeed before for that matter, so many of the emergent industrial enterprises could shelter behind the protective barriers afforded by monopolistic or quasi-monopolistic control. There were, as a consequence, few incentives for internal economising. However with the emergence of competition the achievement of economic surplus became more dependent on establishing greater internal efficiency. Early approaches to costing and the identification of economic inefficiency started to be developed and as insights were gained such preliminary

forms of management accounting themselves started to become an element in the com
petitive struggle for economic power and financial gain.

Contemporary studies show that the very same pressures are still evident. Enterprises facing competitive market environments are much more likely to have highly
developed financial control systems than those enjoying the protection of monopolistic power (Khandwalla 1972). And other studies show how the 'newly poor' enter
prise initially strives to achieve greater internal efficiency by extending and
intensifying its financial control systems even though the consequent shift in or
ganizational visibility towards internal rather than external phenomena may well
jeopardise its chances of survival in the longer term (Olofson and Svalander 1975

Indeed more recent evidence demonstrates how the development of management accoun
ing insights continues to respond to the changing nature of environmental pressur
For whilst to date most of our evidence has focused on the establishment of economic visibility, the emerging interest in energy accounting and forms of internal social reporting, particularly those variants of human resource accounting
(Flamholtz 1974) which have sought to link the domains of social and economic actions, points to the more general nature of the relationship between environmenta
pressure and the establishment of new patterns of organizational visibility.

Management Accounting and the Establishment of Organizational Rationality and Powe

So far the procedures of management accounting have played a vital role in establishing patterns of organizational consciousness that emphasise the desirability
of rather particular economic ends (Batstone 1978). Within enterprises there are
many competing rationalities or ways of conceiving, understanding and steering
organizational action. Different occupational groups bring their own conceptions
into the enterprise and the variety of tasks and positions within the enterprise
itself stimulates a divergence of orientations and interests. The achievement of
a particular order and, in consequence, the establishment of power, is therefore
dependent upon means for both linking divergent rationalities and, be they internal or external to the enterprise, establishing the dominance of particular interests. The mechanisms of planning and budgeting, the procedures and criteria for
resource allocation and the routine methods of establishing organizational visibility which constitute the core of any management accounting system play an important, albeit far from unique, role in such a process.

Moreover in trying to establish the dominance of a particular mode of organizational rationality, management accounting systems are capable of influencing the conceptions and actions of organizational participants in many other important respects. The ways in which they establish organizational segments and intra-organi-
zational boundaries can influence participants' maps of the organizational world,
the way in which tasks are conceived and performed, and the potentiality for organizational co-operation and conflict. And the conceptions of socio-economic rationality and efficiency that might be implicit within the procedures of an accounting system can have a vital influence on the organization of the labour process and managerial attitudes towards the segmentation of tasks, the relevance of
particular skills and the role that might be played by particular forms of incentive.

When viewed in such a way, the role played by management accounting systems cannot
be considered in isolation. It is but an aspect of the way in which particular
forms of control are established in organizations and society at large. At the
very least such a perspective points to the relevance of the broader socio-economic influences on the development of management accounting and the importance which
it assumes in particular enterprises.

Management Accounting and the Evolving Role of the State

A discussion of the influence of the State on the development of management accounting practice is a speculative endeavour at this stage and one that is easily

and perhaps inevitably influenced by the particular circumstances and institutional arrangements of one's own country. However increasingly we have come to recognise the vital role which might have been played directly and indirectly by the
State in this area and these impressions have been confirmed by discussions which
we have had with industrialists.

The rather direct influences of taxation practices are, of course, familiar to all,
although perhaps we have still to gain a realistic understanding of the way in
which taxation policies have stimulated the development of mechanisms for economic
calculation within enterprises. By now we are also familiar with the role played
by the State in the development of management practices, including approaches to
national economic accounting and organizational planning, control and regulation
as well as many of our current procedures for personnel management and assessment,
during conditions of war (including, for this purpose, the organization of the
space race during the so-called 'cold war' period) and the subsequent dissemination of these to industrial and commercial enterprises.

However we are much less familiar with the ways in which the evolving economic interests of the State have become increasingly concerned with the specifics of management practices in enterprises thereby either directly or indirectly influencing
the development of forms of economic calculation and management accounting. Yet
during periods of economic crisis, including times of national recovery following
wars, the quest for more favourable patterns of economic performance has resulted
in an enormous proliferation of both economic and informational linkages between
enterprises and the State and a consequent elaboration of the procedures for economic calculation and regulation at the enterprise level.

Government involvement in the encouragement of industrial investment and in the
support of declining industrial sectors have clearly had such an effect. So have
policies of price control and regulation, with these often resulting in an enormous development of the necessary justificatory financial information. And, in
the United Kingdom at least, so have many of the postwar incomes policies. By
often striving to link wage increases with demonstratable productivity gains, such
policies have themselves stimulated the development of productivity accounting and
the integration of incentive schemes with procedures for financial reporting and
control.

Such ramifications of the evolving economic role of the State are worthy of much
more detailed investigation. However in the context of the present discussion the
all too brief overview is perhaps sufficient to demonstrate how broad questions
of national economic and social policy are influencing the forms and roles of procedures for economic calculation and management accounting within the enterprise.

Therefore, whilst reflecting organizational factors and those needs for information
which any organization has in order to manage its own financial resources, management accounting systems are also a reflection of the wider environment in which
the enterprise operates. As at least some elements of that environment have changed,
so the forms of management accounting has also tended to change so as to more adequately relate to new patterns of economic control, emerging competitive pressures,
prevailing views of the management function and changing institutional and national concerns. More importantly within the context of the present discussion, as
the wider environment continues to change, so there is no reason for not expecting
that there will be renewed pressures on management accounting to adapt and a consequent need for new insights and understandings. Indeed, as we have already noted,
there is evidence today of precisely such pressures and needs.

ORGANIZATIONAL CHANGE, INFORMATION PROCESSING AND THE EMERGENCE OF ACCOUNTING ALTERNATIVES

At the level of the enterprise the demand for and roles served by information are,
in part at least, a refelction of prevailing modes of exerting social control over

the activities of and within the business enterprise. As was illustrated in Fig. 1 different social control alternatives can make different demands on the social processing of information and, in addition, the management of information is itself a mechanism for establishing and reinforcing particular approaches to the control of the enterprise.

However pressures for greater information can be met in various ways, only some of which involve the further development of mechanisms for reporting, disclosure and accounting. As is illustrated in Fig. 2, there are two broad alternative approaches to the social processing of information. The first of these involves a reduction of the constraints on the dissemination and use of existing sources of information rather than the production of new information. For societies and organizations invest in many ways of constraining the use of information and there are, in fact, wide differences between nations and organizations in the extent of constraining mechanisms. At the societal level laws of libel, slander, copyright, patent, contemp and official secrets legislation all strive to constrain the use of what is already known and individual organizations have similar, albeit less formal, mechanisms for maintaining secrecy and limiting access to information.

SOCIAL INFORMATION PROCESSING
ALTERNATIVES

1.   REDUCE CONSTRAINTS ON EXISTING SOURCES OF INFORMATION

    i) Macro-legal constraints and organizational rules
      of secrecy
   ii) Access to information.

2.   PROVISION OF 'NEW' INFORMATION

    i) Reporting and disclosure of information
   ii) Creation of 'information intermediaries'.

Figure 2.

Alternative approaches to the Social Processing of
Information on Enterprise Activities.

So one way of increasing the supply of information on the activities of enterprises is to reduce the extent of such constraints either by directly changing the legal or administrative provisions or by granting rights of access to information. And there have been many such changes in the last few decades ranging from the enactment of the Freedom of Information Act in the USA, and the debates that this had encouraged in numerous other countries, throught the access provisions contained in the recent legislation on health and safety at work and the management of the environment that has been enacted in many countries, through to the more radical rights of access granted to employees and trade unions in recent Swedish legislation. It should be stated, however, that the removal of such constraints on the dissemination and use of existing sources of information is far from being an unproblematic way of responding to the basic pressures for more information. For without adequate safeguards, the granting of access to information can increase rather than reduce information inequalities in organizations and societies at large as those already having some access to information have a better basis for exploiting the new provisions.

An alternative way of processing information is to invest in the production of 'new' or different types of information. And again this can be done in different ways. The direct reporting or disclosure of additional information, including accounting information, readily comes to mind. An alternative approach, however, is to invest in the creation (and control) of agencies for the processing of information that can act as intermediaries between the suppliers and users of information. Yet again there have been numerous examples of the development of both of these approaches in the last few decades. The enormous increase in disclosure provisions within and outside the enterprise is well known to all and has, in fact, been supplemented by possibly an even greater increase in voluntary disclosures as enterprises have sought to respond to emerging environmental pressures, often looking at the role which information can play in the establishment of a new legitimacy and image. Recent years have also witnessed an equally great expansion in the number and activities of information intermediaries dealing with the corporate sector ranging from the media, through independent consumer organizations preparing regular consumer orientated audits of enterprise products and services, to the emerging activities of alternative pressure and interest groups.

It is important to have an appreciation of the full range of ways in which information on enterprise activities can be processed for demands for greater accountability information can be, and are being, satisfied by the development of 'accounting alternatives' rather than necessarily by the development of accounting itself. But the further development of modes of accounting, both within and outside the enterprise, remains a vital aspect of such patterns of organizational and social change because accounting systems have an important role to play in crystallizing and propagating broad conceptions of the rationale for an enterprise.

However just as there are alternative ways of socially processing information on enterprise activities so there are alternative ways of accounting for their performance. Accounting can be seen as being posited on a series of assumptions about the nature of the enterprise and its relationship to the wider environment. For the purpose of this discussion I emphasise two key assumptions underlying the delineation and construction of an accounting system, namely those concerning the management of conflict within the enterprise and the nature of the relationship between the enterprise and the wider social environment in which it operates.

Concerning the management of conflict within the enterprise let us simplify our discussion by distinguishing between an assumption of either a unitary or dominated organization and one which is characterised by a pluralistic or even conflictful mode of operation. Whilst unitary and dominated organizations clearly differ, for the purposes of accounting there are similarities since both demand an accounting for a single interest, be that interest shared or imposed. Similarly the obvious differences bewteen the presumption of a pluralistic organization and that of a conflictful one may be less relevant in accounting terms since both call for an accounting for multiple interests. Concerning the other underlying assumption on the relationship between the enterprise and its wider environment, an equally simple distinction is made between an accounting for an enterprise that is seeen as operating in isolation of its social environment and an accounting for an enterprise seen in its wider social context.

The varieties of accountings which stem from a consideration of these two underlying sets of assumptions are illustrated in Fig. 3. An accounting which is posited on an assumption of a unitary or dominated organization that is operating in isolation of its wider social environment is the present technology of profit and loss accounting and its internal management accounting manifestations. And whilst some economists have provided a means for considering, analysing and calculating the relationship of the enterprise to its wider social environment, present modes of social cost-benefit analysis, which are indeed forms of accounting, are still based on the social assumptions which are implicit in neo-classical economics. Alternative accountings based on more pluralistic assumptions of the enterprise do exist however. Such calculations of enterprise performance as value added (Burchell, Clubb and Hopwood 1978; Grojer and Stark 1977) which can allow for wider conceptions of enterprise interests might be included in this category together with the emerging interests in and approaches to the design of self management information systems (Magnusson 1974) information and accounting systems that facilitate rather than constrain the operation of autonomous working groups and (den Hertog 1978) the development of lateral rather than vertical relationships in enterprises, and those multi-dimensional forms of internal accounting which provide accountings rather than an accounting of enterprise activities (Hedberg and Jönsson 1978). Fi nally the independent social audits conducted in several European countries, part cularly in the United Kingdom (Medawar 1976), illustrate the potential for the de sign of pluralistic accounting systems that explicitly consider the enterprises relationship to its wider social environment.

MANAGEMENT OF CONFLICT

	Unitary or Dominance	Pluralistic or Conflict
Enterprise in Isolation	e.g. Profit & Loss Accounting, Management Accounting Systems	e.g. Multiple or Flexible Definitions of Surplus, Self Management Information Systems
Enterprise in Society	e.g. Social Cost-Benefit Analysis	e.g. Social Audit

RELATIONSHIP TO WIDER SOCIETY

Figure 3.

Alternative Modes of Accounting Practice

However these categories of accounting possibilities do not provide a basis for con sidering a number of quite interesting recent developments in the accounting domain For many of the more recent innovations have reflected managerial uncertainties rather than certainties of the social position of the enterprise. Rather than immediately striving to develop more pluralistic and social approaches to accounting, management has tried to elaborate and adapt existing accounting technologies in response to the questioning of existing forms of organizational legitimacy and control. So, as is illustrated in Fig. 4, a set of intermediary technologies has been created by the elaboration of existing mode of accounting practice. The technology of profit and loss accounting has been extended so as to provide an accounting for the human resource (Flamholtz 1974); accounting, economic and psychological understandings have been drawn upon in the construction of new forms of 'social calculation'; and at least the concepts of social cost-benefit analysis, if not in most cases the procedures, have provided a basis for experiments in corporate social accounting and reporting (Bauer and Dierkes 1973).

Admittedly the above framework for considering the social bases of accounting is simplistic and preliminary. And I want to emphasise that. However be that as it may, I think that it is nevertheless useful because it enables us to see that there are broad alternative frameworks for accounting, that forms of accounting can and do reflect prevailing conceptions of organizational and social life, and perhaps most importantly, that at least some of the preconditions for accounting change are social in nature. Whilst social uncertainty might stimulate the adaptation and elaboration of existing modes of accounting practice, newer and different forms of accounting must seemingly be grounded in the reality of, rather than the fear of, social change.

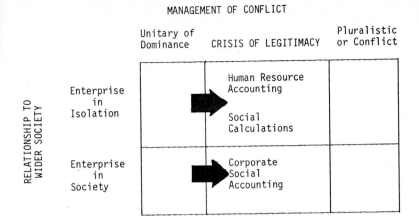

Figure 4.
Social Uncertainty and Alternative Modes
of Accounting Practice

TOWARDS ALTERNATIVE MANAGEMENT ACCOUNTING SYSTEMS

So what are the implications of the above analysis for the design of alternative management accounting systems in enterprises? The first is that the pressures for new information and different modes of information processing which might stem from organizational change and new conceptions of enterprise accountability do not necessarily have to directly result in the development of accounting practice. For there are, as we have seen, organizational alternatives to accounting. If, however, there are pressures for accounting itself to respond to the patterns of change, the analysis would lead us to expect that much greater emphasis is going to be placed on the development of both forms of accounting that can stimulate and facilitate self management and regulation within the enterprise and multiple dimensional approaches to accounting, with the integration of the different approaches being seen as a political rather than a calculative task. In other words we need to think in terms of competing accountings rather than the elaboration of any dominant Accounting.

In fact such implications are not incompatible with many emerging aspects of information system and management accounting practice. The development of forms of organizational structure, such as the management matrix, that seek to integrate lateral and vertical dimensions of organizational life has resulted in an increased awareness of the variety of ways in which enterprises seek to process information (Galbraith 1973; Knight 1977). Whilst the production of routine information flows remain vital in such contexts, they complement rather than replace more structural and personal approaches to information processing. And in the context of these and other experiments, consideration already has been given to the potentiality of multi-dimensional and even conflicting (or at least 'semi-confusing') flows of information (Hedberg and Jönsson 1978).

However there is a real danger that such directions of development might clash with the dominant conceptions which some accountants and information system designers hold of the nature and organizational roles of their systems and the reality of information use in organizations. So often almost exclusive emphasis is put on the need for formal, 'tidy minded' and tightly integrated information systems, forgetting, in the process, the vital roles played by the wide variety of competing, overlapping and reinforcing flows of information that already exist in enterprises

and thereby the variety of possible approaches to the information management task.
For, as is illustrated in Fig. 5, the official, routine information systems of the
accountant and the information system specialist are complemented by the private,
unofficial systems that are developed by managers and employees themselves, the
multiple and interlocking grapevines which permeate organizational life and those
official provisions for the ad hoc and structural processing of information. In
their search for organizational formality and certainty, information experts so
often have adopted a partial and unnecessarily constraining view of the way in
which information and intelligence is processed in organizations and the possibili
ties for action and change. The fact that at present so many aspects of organizational reality do not influence or enter into legitimate professional discourse in
the information and accounting areas might well be a major constraint on the possibilities for adaptation and change.

	Routine	Non Routine
Official	e.g. Management Accounting Systems, MIS	e.g. Ad hoc Information Processing, Access Capabilities, Structural Approaches to Information Processing
Unofficial	e.g. Black Books, Just-in-Case Files	e.g. Grape-Vine

Figure 5.
Varieties of Information Processing in Organizations

Similarly information specialists have tended to ignore the ways in which organizational participants ignore, adapt and extend features of standardized management
information and accounting systems so that they relate to the needs and requirements of specific yet varying organizational circumstances. In this way the standardized approaches often provide a basis for the construction of local information systems. And the way in which the standardized systems so frequently ignore
the provision of information which facilitates organizational integration often
stimulates, as illustrated in Fig. 6, the search for and development of information
organizational coupling and the provision of a broader contextual perspective. However the informal development and potentiality of such local, coupling and contextual information systems has as yet hardly influenced either the conceptual frameworks or designs which underlie the official, routine approaches to management
accounting and information systems. Yet such a framework, grounded as it sometimes
is in the reality of present organizational practice, might provide the outlines
of an approach to the design of management accounting and information systems that
complement the policies of enterprises that are trying to move towards more decentralized modes of operation.

When seen in such terms the paradox of the challenge offered by the need to design management accounting systems that complement rather than constrain new forms
of enterprise management and accountability is that it might stimulate not only a
search for the novel and the new in system design but also a greater recognition
of the present realities of information provision and use in enterprises. For
often beneath the austere surface of present system strategies and professional

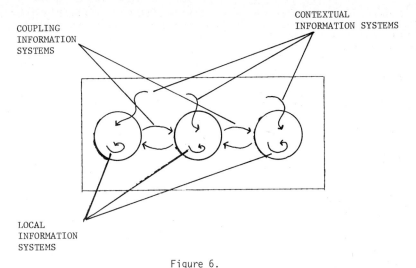

Figure 6.

Organizational Segmentation and Alternative Modes
of Information Processing.

discourse are a mass of informal adaptations that provide fascinating and important insights into organizational functioning. If, as seems likely, emerging system
designs must call and build upon elements of such an organizational underworld,
many of the 'new' approaches that will be created and formally sanctioned might
not be at variance with organizational practice even if they differ radically from
the conventional wisdom of the accountant's art.

CONCLUSION

It only has been possible to provide an all too brief overview of the challenges
created by emerging pressures to design management accounting (and information)
systems that support new concepts of enterprise accountability and management.
Hopefully however, the discussion has demonstrated that a search for responses to
such challenges is capable of, and indeed likely to, raise a whole series of fundamentally important questions about the role and design of management accounting
systems in today's enterprises.

There is a particular need to develop a social as distinct from an organizational
appreciation of the management accounting function. What social roles has it served,
what social pressures have stimulated management accounting developments and what
are the potentialities for management accounting adapting to new social circumstances? And at the organizational level the search for such new insights and understandings will provide a new urgency for our need to understand the functioning
and use of management accounting and the actual as distinct from professional body
of experience and knowledge.

However our analysis has also introduced an element of caution into the discussion.
Not only are the challenges for new understandings real and difficult, but we have
also pointed to the distinction between those innovations which might seek to
conserve present structures and approaches in times of social turmoil and those
that more genuinely seek to facilitate the development of new bases for enterprise
management and accountability. Whilst it is inevitalby tempting for those currently

in positions of organizational power to emphasise the development of the former, neither practitioners nor scholars should be confused by them and hopefully some at least will strive to respond more positively and directly to the underlying patterns of social development.

REFERENCES

Accounting, Organizations and Society (1978). Towards a Bibliography of the French Social Accounting Literature. October.

Batstone, E. (1978). Management and Industrial Democracy in Industrial Democracy: International Views. SSRC Industrial Relations Research Unit, University of Warwick.

Bauer, R. and M. Dierkes (1973). Corporate Social Accounting. Praeger, New York.

Briefs, U. (1975). The Role of Information Systems in Employee Participation in Management Decision-Making in E. Mumford and H. Sackman (eds.), Human Choice and Computers. North-Holland, Amsterdam.

Burchell, S., C. Clubb and A.G. Hopwood (1978). Accounting in Its Social Context: A Preliminary Social History of Value Added. Paper presented at the Workshop on Accounting in a Changing Social and Political Environment, London, June.

Chandler, A. (1962). Strategy and Structure. MIT Press, Mass.

Dekker, H.C. and Th.P. Van Hoorn (1976). From Social Reporting to Societal Accounting in the Netherlands. Research Memorandum 7709, Department of Economics, University of Amsterdam.

den Hertog, F. (1978). The Role of Information and Control Systems in the Process of Organizational Renewal: Roadblock or Road Bridge? Accounting, Organizations and Society, Oxford. Vol. 3, No. 1, pp. 29-46.

Dierkes, M. (1974). Die Sozialbilanz. Herder and Herder, Frankfurt.

Flamholtz, E.G. (1974). Human Research Accounting. Dickenson Publishing, London.

Galbraith, J. (1973). Designing Complex Organizations. Addison-Wesley, New York.

Grinyer, P.H. and D. Norburn (1975). Planning for Existing Markets. Journal of the Royal Statistical Society, Series A, pp. 70-97.

Grojer, J.E. and A. Stark (1977). Social Accounting: A Swedish Attempt. Accounting, Organizations and Society, Oxford. Vol. 2, No. 4, pp. 349-385.

Hedberg, B., P.C. Nystrom and W.H. Starbuck (1976). Camping on Seesaws: Prescriptions for Self-Designing Organizations. Administrative Science Quarterly, March, Vol. 21, No. 1, pp. 41-65.

Hedberg, B. and S. Jönsson (1978). Designing Semi-Confusing Information Systems for Organizations in Changing Environments. Accounting, Organizations and Society, Oxford. Vol. 3, No. 1, pp. 47-64.

Hopwood, A.G. (1977). The Design of Information Systems for Matrix Organisations, in K. Knight (ed.), Matrix Management, Gower Press, Epping, U.K.

Khandwalla, P.N. (1972). The Effect of Different Types of Competition on the Use of Management Controls. Journal of Accounting Research, Vol. 1o, Autumn, pp. 275-285.

Knight, K. (1977). Matrix Management. Gower Press, Epping, U.K.

Magnusson, A. (1974). Participation and the Company's Information and Decision Systems. Working Paper 6022, Stockholm School of Economics.

Medawar, C. (1976). The Social Audit: A Political View. Accounting, Organizations and Society, Oxford, pp. 389-394.

Moore, R. (1977). The Acquisition and Use of Company Information by Trade Unions. Trade Union Research Unit, Ruskin College, Oxford.

Mumford, E. and D. Henshall (1978). Participative Work Design in the Office. Associated Business Press, London.

Olofson, C. and P.A. Svalander (1975). The Medical Services Change Over to a Poor Environment - New Poor Behaviour. Working Paper, Linköping University, Sweden.

Pettigrew, A.M. (1977). The Creation of Organizational Cultures. European Institute for Advanced Studies in Management, Brussels, Working Paper 77-11.

Polland, S. (1965). The Genesis of Modern Management. Arnold, London.

Sandberg, A. (1976). The Limits to Democratic Planning: Knowledge, Power and Methods in the Struggle for the Future. Liber Publishing Company, Stockholm.

Ullman, A. (1978). Corporate Social Reporting: Political Interests and Conflicts in Germany. Paper presented at the 3rd Workshop on Accounting in a Changing Social and Political Environment, London, June.

DISCUSSION AND COMMENTS ON PAPER PRESENTED BY ANTHONY HOPWOOD

JAN BENDIX

The paper points to new areas for the management accountant. He will have to adju
his role to fulfil the new demands of social accountability, and here I see a parallel situation to that of the system designer. He too has to look at his job in
a broader perspective and revise his methodologies to meet new demands. If management accountants have the same problem of adjusting their behaviour as systems spe
cialists in my experience, they are going to get into trouble.

In the paper I missed practical examples of accounting systems functioning along
the lines suggested by Hopwood. I might even suggest areas where we need other way
of looking at companies besides the efficiency area. Hopwood mentioned the social
accountability area, but as a practitioner, I would also be looking for figures in
areas of market standing, not the traditional accounting figures, but figures that
would give me a better assessment of the intrinsic character of the position of
a company in the market. I would also like some accounts of innovation capabilitie
How is it for example possible to assess whether a company is good in adapting to
and even shaping its environment by bringing in new thinking (products, organization, methods, etc.). Furthermore, I should like to have an accounting system
giving me some assessment of the degree to which I meet customer/client requirements. To some extent I can get a long-term assessment of it today in my profit
and loss statement but I am not quite sure. And again, the client requirement
should be measured in other terms than the traditional ones derived from the official book-keeping.

In the paper Hopwood mentions an energy accounting system, and closely related to
this would be all kinds of resource utilization systems. To this I might add
the possibility of having an account of employee motivation. We have a large variety of attitude scales whose value is often difficult to assess, but perhaps we
could find better ways of accounting for employee motivation which is extremely
crucial.

These are areas where it seems important to me to identify yardsticks and carry
out measurements in order to plan and control development. I should appreciate it
very much if the accounting research and the accountant function could help us in
this respect in the near future.

PREBEN MELANDER

When I was reading Hopwood's paper for the first time I found it quite interesting.
When reading it again and not being an expert in social accountability, I was a
little confused because of the many problems raised. I am still confused, but hopefully at a higher level. Perhaps we might test that.

I think I disagree with Hopwood about the basic premises, and I should like to have
that verified. And as the need for alternatives is stressed in the paper, I should
like to present my views as an alternative to his presentation.

Hopwood claims that the enterprise is controlled by different groups. I agree about
that. But accepting that and accepting that those groups have different objectives,
I feel the importance of information and social aspects are overemphasized. Social
needs have to be balanced against other (economic) needs in the organization, and
formal information systems are only limited by the means available to attempt to
solve organizational problems.

Hopwood proposes that we must use accounting alternatives. Before we reach that stage, I think we must consider the needs of the participants, and then perhaps determine whether there is a need for information at all.

Here it is important to stress that in my opinion formal information systems play only a secondary role and must be compared with other means that will meet the same needs.

A rough outline of the main items in an 'alternative' strategy is outlined in the figure below.

Strategies for Change of Accounting Function

	Hopwood	'An alternative'
Premise:	Greater emphasis on social aspects in the debate.	Enterprise must balance the needs - social as well as economic.
Strategy:	We should choose among accounting alternatives or accountings.	We should identify the participants and provide the basic conditions for participation.
	We should alter the role of the accountant.	We should then determine the needs for information.
	We should enlarge the information base to include social aspects.	We should determine the degree to which formal information systems might satisfy these.
		We should then create consistent information systems for the different groups.
		We should define the role of management and determine the extent to which they should create, control, and distribute information.
		We should modify the role of the management accountant to meet the demands associated with this strategy.

On the basis of this I should like to put the following questions to Hopwood:

1. What is the role of formal information compared with other means of satisfying the needs of stakeholders?

2. What is the future role of management? Are they for instance to control the information, and how can we make management release more information to external groups beyond what is statutory, or aimed at improving the image of the firm?

3. Are we able to create a consistent accounting language which can provide social information?

ANTHONY HOPWOOD

The discussants have raised an enormous number of issues. I find myself agreeing with many of the points which they raise, although I do disagree with some. My remarks therefore will tend to focus on the latter.

Bendix asked for more practical examples of the issues which I have raised, providing many areas of managerial significance where he sees a potential for the extension of the accounting craft. Although I had attempted to provide at best an overview of current pressures for and patterns of change, I nevertheless can appreciate his search for the specific. I would like, however, to point to some problems which might be inherent in his immediate concern with the practical.

First I think that there are real problems with people inventing new accountings at a distance from the organizational and social realities in which they are to function. A specific organization need be able to utilise a specific new development, but many problems of practice have emanated from the endeavours of those who have attempted to legislate at a distance for the developments which might be (or 'surely are') required by organizations in general. I therefore adopted a cautious stance. Second, in response to Bendix's plea for an array of new accountings, I would like to emphasize the sheer variety of alternative accountings which already existed in organizations. Constructed and used by specialist groups, they already make an enormous contribution to organizational functioning and effectiveness, although only one of them is generally designated as the Accounting - the dominant form of economic calculative practice in organizations today. I am convinced that before anyone starts to explicate the need for ever more accountings and flows of information that he or she should first seek to appreciate the richness of existing practices, however informal and tentative some of them may be. And that leads me on to my third point in response to Bendix. At this stage I remain critical of the attitude which requests information on virtually everything of organizational significance. Such 'shopping basket' approaches can quickly result in enormous increases in the amounts of formalised, standardized and bureaucratised information, the wider organizational consequences of which might be equivocal at best. The approach which was at least implicit in my paper was one of appreciating the diversity of means by which organizations can seek to process information.

We do not necessarily have to extend accounting systems; we do not even need new information systems. Whilst it may be tempting and easy to adopt such strategies, the other approaches which were mentioned in the paper should at the very least be considered beforehand. For by now I think that we have reason to be a little more questioning of the routes which have brought us to there we are.

From what I have said so far it should be obvious that I agree with many of the points raised by Melander, even though they were seemingly voiced as criticisms of my papers. All too obviously too much remained implicit within it! Certainly I hope that I did not overemphasize the roles that are and can be played by formal information and accounting systems. I for one recognize that there are many non-information approaches to control problems and that there are also non-accounting approaches to information problems. Equally, changes in social circumstances do not always result in accounting changes. Accounting systems of any variety are means to an end, but invariably there are other means to the same end.

However, having said that, I nevertheless would like to question at least some of the presumptions which are inherent in Melander's comments. For underlying his 'alternative strategy' for the change of the accounting function is a rather rational, normative and organizationally bounded view of the operation of management practices such as accounting and information systems. Melander, for instance, seeks to articulate the stages of a rational system design process.

Although having previously recognized the existence of conflicting interests in organizations, he nonetheless feels able to presume that 'we should determine the needs for information', that 'we should determine the degree to which ...', that 'we should then create consistent information systems ....', etc. The desire for consistency is particularly interesting in this connection. Is it possible to create 'consistent information systems for the different groups' when those groups are in conflict? And how can the designer strive towards concepts of consistency when in the last resort those concepts are defined by the interpretations and actions of the users of the information rather than the providers? Certainly I would neither expect nor hope to see the construction of any such consistent accounting language or flows of information. To the extent that consistency might be possible, I would prefer to see as being socially and politically constructed within the context of an organization rather than being calculatively determined within the confines of an information or an accounting system. Moreover by adopting an organizationally bounded view of accounting and information, Melander emphasized the possibilities for choice within the organization and the location of the ability of that choice. Whilst acknowledging that such choices exist, I nevertheless sought to emphasize the social as well as organizational construction of accounting practice, and thereby the inherently more complex processes of accounting change.

Ian Mitroff's from Pittsburgh in Pa,
We're delighted he's travelled so far.
His phenomenological stance
Is no positivist chance.
Now we'll learn what he's up to, and wha!

TOWARDS A LOGIC AND METHODOLOGY FOR
'REAL-WORLD' PROBLEMS

Ian Mitroff

Graduate School of Business
University of Pittsburgh, USA

Real-world problems are what have been
termed ill-structured. As such, they require a different methodology for their
formulation, let alone solution. This
paper presents the outline of such a methodology within the context of management
information systems. It argues that the
ability to inspect, challenge, and store
assumptions over time is critical to the
treatment of real-world problems.

The Human Side of Information Processing
N. Bjørn-Andersen, editor
© IAG
North-Holland Publishing Company, 1980

1. METHODOLOGY OF SCIENCE

I would like to present to you some developments which promise to lead us closer to a methodology for strategic problem solving. I have deliberately put the term 'real-world' in my title because I have a rather dim view of most academic researc Most research is rather pedestrian; it is not very interesting nor relevant to the world of action. For the most part this is because the academy largely still has a mythic conception of science. A good part of what I do is concerned with the sociology of science. As such I have been trying to study how science actually gets done (Mitroff 1974).

I am afraid that for the most part universities have perpetuated what I call a storybook version of science, the notion of the disinterested, unbiased, objective researcher (Mitroff 1974). In many ways, the social sciences have tried to act out a mythic concept of science that the physical sciences have long since abandoned. However, there are things occurring which threaten to drive a crack in this mythic image, and, I think, bring us back not just to the real world but perhaps to a methodology of science which is more appropriate to a professional school of management.

I personally like to get out to the real world because the things that are often studied in universities, namely rats, sophmores, and MBA's are not what I regard as 'real people'. I happen to like real decision makers and the problems they face. I would like to talk about an emerging methodology which is trying to attack a class of problems that managers continually face. The kind of problems that we have researched in the universities do not have much of a resemblance to actual problems. Indeed, the first point I want to make is that these new developments are quite radical. For example I really do not think we can capture the thought processes of managers, if we stick to formal logics which are founded on consistency, for the basic fact is that people are under no obligation to think consistently, and in fact they do not (Rescher and Manor 1970).

The main thing the manager needs is a system that helps him to locate his inconsistencies, and to take positive advantages of them because all real data sets I know of have deep inconsistencies in them. I do not think this is because we are perverse or anything like that but because I think this is the nature of real world data. The world is just not consistent. If you take out the inconsistencies, you may be removing some of the most valuable items in the data set. There are developments occuring in formal logic which help us to focus on the inconsistencies explicitly rather than taking them out and have a planner attend to those inconsistencies (Rescher and Manor 1970).

2. ILL-STRUCTURED PROBLEMS

The next point I want to make is that I am mostly concerned with what I and others call ill-structured problems (Mitroff and Emshoff 1979). Ill-structured problems are problems for which the definition of the problem is not clear or 'given' beforehand. This is because the problem is either hard to define or because the problem is not contained within any single point of view. Any single discipline will fail to capture the nature of the problem because it will only focus on certain aspects of it. Real-world problems are not strictly problems of accounting, finance, sociology, psychology. They are mixtures of all those things and God knows what. Furthermore, different experts will have a different view on the problem not because they are not people of good will but because they see it differently and in fact these differences in view are vital. One of the prime contentions I wish to lay before you is that most of the information systems currently in existance have been designe under the presumption of well-structured problems, i.e. assuming we already know what the problem is. For these kinds of problems there exist single answers, perhaps even optimal solutions. I really do not think that is what the manager really needs although he may often ask for it. He may do this partly because he is trained to think of the world in terms of well-structured questions and answers, but this may be due more to his need to avoid insecurity and anxiety than to solve the problems of the real-world.

We have done rather well in building information systems for well-structured problems. The challenge then is to build information systems for ill-structured problems. For ill-structured problems, problem formulation and problem defining are absolutely critical. This is because ill-structured problems bring into focus an even more basic statistical error which I would call the type three error as opposed to the traditional type one and type two errors of classical statistical decision theory.

The type three error is the probability of solving the wrong problem when you should have solved the right problem. Most of us commit type three errors. We solve the wrong problem precisely, which is really nonsense. Precision by itself has no value. In fact, some people have said far better an approximate solution to the right problem than an exact solution to the wrong one.

This raises the thorny question as to how do you know whether you are working on the 'right' or the 'wrong' problem, particularly when problems are dynamic; they change over time. There is no 'exact' answer to this question. If there were, we would be back to the realm of well-structured problem but by hypothesis this is the realm from which we have excluded ourselves.

3. ASSUMPTIONAL ANALYSIS

However, there is a way to get handle on this issue. More and more we have come to understand the critical, key role that assumptions play in the policy-making and problem-solving process. In fact, I would say that the empiricists and the rationalists erred in their location of the basic units of reality. For me, the basic units are assumptions, for the reason that there are no 'simple' facts or propositions.

Assumptions are not necessarily the smallest self-contained units of reality but the core. The more you began to delve into the nature of ill-structured problems you begin to see that what you assume about the nature of a problem is very critical. Different people hold different assumptions, and that leads to the question: how can you get at the assumptions? You cannot, I assure you, go up to a decision maker and say, Now tell me what your assumptions are? That is a pretty difficult question to respond to. But I do think that there are some techniques that you may use to raise assumptions to the surface and inspect the role that they play and challenge them with other assumptions (Mitroff and Emshoff 1979).

Assumptions are really critical because most information systems are really obsessed with one component, the data sector. We have found it important to work back to a much more basic level of reality, namely what an information system would look like that would store assumptions, categorize them, and revise them when they are no longer appropriate. This is necessary because assumptions decay over time. They are not constant; they are not fixed. I do not know whether they have a 'half-life', but they have something of this nature. The assumptions which we have been examining in a number of business situations, particularly their properties, are properties of stakeholders, of teleological entities (Churchman 1968, 1971).

One of the ways we have used to get at the assumptions that are critical in policies is something called <u>stakeholder analysis</u> (Mitroff and Emshoff 1979). This is a technique that people at Tavistock have used for years. I can briefly talk about it in the context of a real case with a major drug company. There were three groups of managers within this company each of which had a different version of responding to an attack on one of their major products. It was a major product that the market was threatening to wipe out or severely undermine. In the United States there is the notion of 'generic brand substitution'. If a patient goes to a pharmacist, the

Figure 1.
FUNCTIONAL STAKEHOLDER ANALYSIS FOR A PHARMACEUTICAL COMPANY

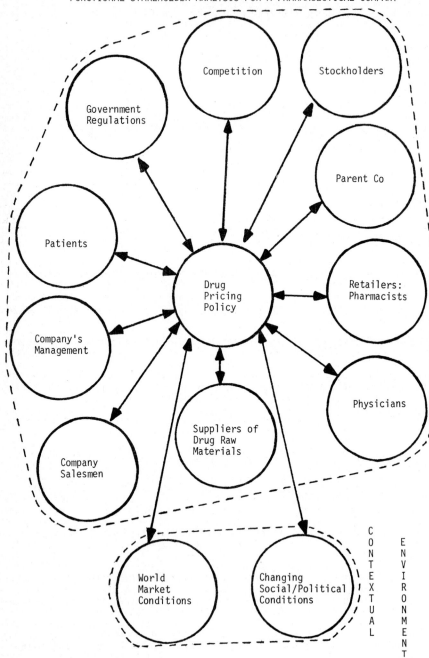

pharmacist can say "Instead of giving you a brand prescription, I can give you generic product at a much cheaper cost". That was the initial definition of the problem and there were three groups of executives all of which were pretty much equal in power, status, and authority, and they had three different policies, three different ways of responding to the problem.

The typical response to this threat is lower the price of the drug; another group wanted to keep the price constant; and the last group, paradoxically at first blush, wanted to raise the price to indicate they had greater confidence in the quality of the drug. Now, what do you do in this case? You cannot turn the data to say "now let me pick out the data which will resolve this situation" because that is really naive. Everyone of the group had data, and lots of it because they started from different assumptions and those assumptions dictated them to go out into the world and collect different data. And in fact all the data were good; but the critical point is that we could not resolve the disagreement between them at the level of the final resultant policies or at the level of the data. The basic dispute was really much further back at the level of the critical assumptions that they were all making, many of which were unconscious to them, that dictated the data that they collected which were then used incestiously to support the policies.

Stakeholder Analysis was used to identify the assumptions of each group. In contrast to stockholder analysis, stakeholder analysis asks a manager to consider all the parties who will be affected by or who affect an important decision. It asks the manager to list as many parties or interest groups as he or she can who have a stake in the policy under consideration (see Fig. 1). This list of parties is typically much broader than the single category 'stockholders'. While important to be sure, the stockholders are only one out of many contending groups which have an impact on and a stake in a corporation. They are neither the only group nor always the single most important group. For the most part the categories are generic and hence, with little modification, apply to most business situations. For example, in the present case, the retailers are pharmacists, although it turned out it was important to differentiate between large-scale, chain retailers and small-scale, singly-owned pharmaceutical outlets.

It can easily be seen from Fig. 1 that depending upon what is assumed about each of the stakeholder categories, the resultant pricing policy is greatly affected. For instance, it is difficult to derive a policy of raising the price of the drug if it is assumed that the physician is price-sensitive to the needs of his patients. In fact, the whole point of getting managers to identify who are the important stakeholder in their situation is to help them confront the important question: "What is it that you have been assuming about the stakeholders or that you have had to assume about them so that starting from these assumptions you are able to derive your policy?" To repeat: stakeholder analysis asks a manager to work backwards. Instead of regarding the problem at the level of the resultant policy, it asks the manager to focus on the underlying assumptions and to regard the real problem as being at this level. What assumptions has he been making and why? What is the effect of making other assumptions? Can his policy stand up to other assumptions, i.e. can it tolerate them? Is it compatible with them? Is the current set of assumptions internally consistent with other assumptions? We have found that the technique of stakeholder analysis is an operationally viable way of ferreting out assumptions.

The important, uncertain quadrant contains the assumptions that are most critical. They are most important to the ultimate deriviation of policy and yet you're uncertain about their status. For example, take the physician. If you're the group that believes you want to raise the price of the drug, you can only do that if you assume that the physician is price insensitive; that the physician is primarily oriented by the desire to deliver high quality medical care to the patient and he is really not concerned with the cost of the drug. But if you are in the low price group, you must assume that the physician is becoming more and more price sensitive.

It is unfortunately beyond the scope of this paper to show in detail how a consensus set of assumptions is developed. For our purposes here, it suffices to mention that a key to this is the prioritization or ranking of the assumptions with respect to two criteria: (1) the relative importance of assumptions; and (2) their relative certainty. A powerful technique which can be used for prioritizing assumptions has been invented by Saaty (Saaty and Rogers 1976). Essentially the technique allows a decision-maker to derive a ration scale weighting (w_i) of the importance of an entire set of objectives, goals, means, assumptions, objects, etc., from a pair-wise ordinal comparison of each element of the set. Starting with the ratios of relative importance w_i/w_j, of two assumptions A_i and A_j to one another, it can be shown that the determination of the w_i reduces to an eigenvalue-eigenvector problem (Mitroff and Emshoff 1979).

The significance of this procedure lies in more than the ultimate set of numbers w_i which it produces. Its true significance is illustrated in Fig. 2. It is not only instructive, but vital to have a group go through the Belief Assessment procedure (Saaty 1976) with regard to two basic questions: (1) with respect to the set of assumptions underlying the support of a policy or plan which assumptions are seen as more <u>important</u> to the plan than others? and (2) which assumptions does the group feel <u>most certain</u> about in the sense of their validity, their confidence in them, etc.?

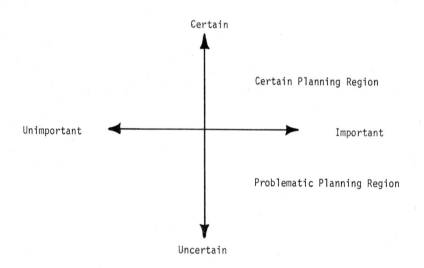

Figure 2.

Belief Assessment of the Importance
Versus the Certainty of Critical Assumptions

Going through the assumption ranking procedure twice, i.e. rating the assumptions on both these questions, allows one to determine which assumptions fall into which quadrant of Fig. 2. Because of their lack of importance, those assumptions falling in the extreme left-hand half of Fig. 2 are of little importance to effective problem solving. Even stronger, while the assumptions falling in the upper right-hand quadrant are the most critical. They are precisely the kind of assumptions one looks to the process, and the methodology as a whole, to identify. Because the assumptions in the lower right-hand quadrant are important and yet because decision-makers are uncertain of their plausibility, truth, reasonableness, etc., they deserve the most intensive discussion with regard to what if anything could be done to make their occurrence or their validation more certain. In fact, the identification and verification of these kinds of assumptions are at the heart of strategic planning.

We have found that individual policies not only differ with regard to the detailed assumptions they make regarding stakeholders but that typically they assume very different stakeholder categories altogether. What one group or policy sees as an important or potentially important party another sees as relatively unimportant.

Two of the major characteristics of the decision-making process I have been describing are: (1) it is dialectical and (2) it is adversarial. This is because if we are going to get a handle on the type three error we do not want to go into an organisation and just look at the assumptions of one group. If we can only see the assumptions of one group, then we have no way to assess their validity. We have found it necessary to go out of our way to either create, or note the existence of, groups which are in opposition one another. In this way, I come back to the issues of participation. For me (3) participative decision-making is any thing but a luxury. It may be expensive but it is not a luxury, because first of all, the assumptions I am talking about are not my assumptions, they are the assumptions of the managers; it is their corporation; the type three error is not for my benefit, it is for theirs; they have to have some way of participating in the policy formation process. I could do a poem on "let me count the number of ways to sabotage the best laid plans". I think most plans probably should be sabotaged if somebody has not participated in their formation. That is not just a cynical comment but I think it is a realistic one. So participation is essential in this if we are to get different groups that can challenge one another bacause I am not sure that a single group by itself can challenge its own assumptions. What we want is a situation where what one group takes as a warranted assumption about the world, another does not. For me a fact is an assumption you are relatively certain about. What one group takes as a fact another group often takes as highly dubious and problematic assertion.

Another thing one would like to do is to track assumptions over time. One of the things we have been trying to ask is "what would an information system do and look like - and I'm not sure I know the answer to that - that would not only store assumptions but would also chart their movement over time?" I think assumptions need to be tracked and I do not know of systems currently in existence which do that. I have a strong suspicion that this might be of help to a decision-maker.

Another thing we would like to do is see whether there is a (5) synthetic policy, or a set of policies which could synthesise the different assumptions.

4. ANALYSING THE STRUCTURE OF ARGUMENTS

In the remaining part of the paper I would like to illustrate what follows from the preceeding. Richard O. Mason and I have been working on a system for tracing the linkage between background assumptions and the policy which can be concluded from them. We have gone out to literally almost any field we could find to give us a handle on this problem of linkage, and one of the things we have come across is a framework for analysing the structure of a policy argument; it comes from logic. A British philosopher, Stephen Toulmin, who has been replanted in the United States, wrote a book entitled The Uses of Argument (1958). In this book he lays out a different way than the traditional syllogism of trying to capture the structure of arguments because the syllogism is too limited in capturing the flavour of real arguments. Real arguments are much more open and loose that that of structured deductive logic.

The frameworks of Toulmin is essentially this:

R $\longrightarrow$ B $\longrightarrow$ W $\longrightarrow$ D $\longrightarrow$ C

The W stands for Warrant rather than calling it a major premise
The D stands for Data
The C stands for Claim.

If you had a deductive system and you had a tight W then by deduction you would ge
from the W to the data to the claim and you would deduce the claim. Toulmin says
that when you look at real arguments there are other elements which come into play
One is something he calls the B or the Backing; if the Warrant is not convincing
to you on its face merits, the backing is brought in to give you additional suppor
for the claim. In addition Toulmin says that if you look at a real argument there
is always another element which is present and that is the R or what he calls the
Rebuttal. The Rebuttal is either a face-saving device so that it says that in
general the W holds except in special cases or the Rebuttal can be an explicit
attack on the Warrant by a counter-policy.

Now when we get to this point, we can see that the Rebuttal explicitly introduces
contradictions into the policy process because the Rebuttal is designed to attack
all the basic assumptions that a decision-maker is making from his single point of
view. Furthermore, there can be contradictions, explicitly or implicitly, present
in any one of the elements. In fact one of the things I have been working with is
a simple scheme to try and capture this. In fact, I am currently working with a ma
jor U.S. Corporation to try to build a system to do precisely this. They have a
large data bank for market research information. You come into this data bank and
you would like to derive some Claims but you do not always come into it with a
Warrant explicitly in mind, and, if anything the question is, Can you work backwards to help the decision-maker be more aware of the Warrants they have been pre-
supposing. In addition, every policy I have ever seen has attacks on it. A simple
way to capture the attacks on a policy is through the following: If I am a propo-
nent of an argument, I am trying to argue that from the data I can legitimately
conclude a specific claim say C_1. But if I am an opponent of the policy, one of
the strongest ways of being an opponent of the policy is to grant you the data but
say that from the data, you do not get to the claim C_1, but that you get to a
counter-claim, say C_2, and you do not get to the Warrant, you get to a counter-
warrant, W. Well, when you put all these elements together in a single set, the
complexity of policy-making becomes very obvious and the ill-structured nature of
policy becomes even more apparent because when you conjoin all this together, look
what you get. You get a full set of propositions which are internally inconsistent,
viz. $(D \longrightarrow C, D \longrightarrow \sim C, D, W, \sim W)$.

How does the manager or the decision-maker sort through this? What can you legitimately conclude from an inconsistent set of propositions? Traditional logic does
not help you here. The machinery of traditional logic comes to crashing halt or
some would say it suffers a massive cerebral hermorrhage. This is where some non-
traditional machinery that logicians have been developing comes into play.

Logicians like Nicholas Rescher (Rescher and Manor 1970) have been developing
schemes, which in effect allow the decision-maker to take a set of inconsistent
propositions, sort it into sub-sets which are consistent but in such a way that
the inconsistencies between sets are in maximal tension. This forces the decision-
maker to consider which of the valid inferences that can be concluded from the
separate sets, he indeed wishes to conclude.

5. CONCLUDING REMARKS

To try and summarize, let me emphasize again, I am more concerned with problem
formulation than I am with problem solving. I really do not know how to differentiate the two but if I were forced to place my emphasis, it would be with problem

formulation. I think that it is really the much more important of the two. I think we have neglected it, not only in management but we have neglected it in natural science. Somehow the myth is that problems are just 'out' there and that everybody can agree on them and that all we have to do is to get consensus on what the problems are and that we can solve them. If anything, one of the things we have found is that one of the biggest places where organisation development is needed is to train managers to disagree. It is not that they do not disagree but they do not know how to do so constructively, i.e. in order to surface their assumptions.

I am currently engaged in studying to what extent what I have been discussing can be computer assisted, and I hope in the right sense, because if not, I know that it will be computer resisted. I am not just making a play on words I know it will be computer resisted if the manager is not deeply involved in his making sense out of his precarious world. We must help the manager to help him study himself. I hope the manager is willing to return the favour. We may need him more than he needs us. In reality, both of us need one another to study and to criticize our respective assumptions.

REFERENCES

Ackoff, R.L. (1967). Management Misinformation Systems. Management Science, Vol. 14 B-147 - B-156.

Churchman, C.W. (1971). The Design of Inquiring Systems. Basic Books, New York.

Churchman, C.W. (1968). The Systems Approach. Delacorte, New York.

Mason, R.O. (1969). A Dialectical Approach to Strategic Planning. Management Science, Vol. 15, B-403 - B-414.

Mintzberg, H., D. Raisingham and A. Theoret (1976). The Structure of 'Unstructured' Decision Processes. Administration Science Quarterly, Vol. 21, pp. 246-275.

Mitroff, I.I. and J.R. Emshoff (1979). On Strategic Assumption-Making: A Dialectical Approach to Policy and Planning. Academy of Management Review, in press.

Mitroff, I.I. and R.H. Kilmann (1978). On Integrating Behavioral and Philosophical Systems: Towards a Unified Theory of Problem Solving. Annual Series in the Sociology, Vol. 1, in press.

Mitroff, I.I. (1974). The Subjective Side of Science. Elsevier, Amsterdam.

Pounds, W.F. (1971). The Process of Problem Finding. Industrial Management Review, Vol. 11, pp. 1-19.

Rescher, N. and R. Manor (1970). On Inference from Inconsistent Premises, Theory and Decision, Vol. 1, pp. 179-217.

Rittel, H. (1971). Some Principles for the Design of an Educational System for Design. Journal of Architectural Education, Vol. 26, pp. 16-27.

Saaty, T.L. and P.C. Rogers (1976). Higher Education in the United States (1985-2000), Scenario Construction Using a Hierarchical Framework with Eigenvector Weighting, Socio-Economic Planning, Vol. 10.

Toulmin, S. (1958). The Uses of Argument. Cambridge University Press, Cambridge.

DISCUSSION AND COMMENTS ON PAPER PRESENTED BY IAN MITROFF

AAGE MELBYE

The above paper by Ian Mitroff deviates in its published form significantly from the paper submitted by the programme committee to me as an invited opponent at the conference. Therefore the editor has offered me the opportunity to revise the comments I made at the conference.

The core of my oral comments was a critique of the fact that a paper like Mitroff' was presented at a conference on computer impact. To me the content of Mitroff's paper was - to say it mildly - rather distant from the main theme of the conferenc as stated in the announcement. Having read the new version of the paper this proposition still seems to be valid. I consider this a most regrettable point for the programme committee, the audience at the conference as well as the readers of the proceedings.

I do not want to waste more of my own or anyone's time in making further comments on this paper.

LEIF BLOCH RASMUSSEN

The original paper by Ian Mitroff submitted to me as an invited discussant was entitled "Management Myth-Information Systems: A Second Look". It contained a section on myths and their significance for the design of information systems. Unfortunately, this section was not included in Mitroff's presentation at the conference which I feel sorry about. Instead I found a section on "Basic Assumptions" which is something quite different, devoted to man as an organizational entity.

Myths on the other hand are much wider. They represent our collective unconsciousness, guiding our experience and reflection. They can also be taken to represent the trends in our efforts to design computer systems. Through the analysis of myths it may be possible to investigate the history of the design of computer systems, the reasons for our failures and possible future actions. They are not necessarily based on cold logic, as in Hedberg's paper, but on inspiration and imagination. Therefore to me it seems necessary to stress and illustrate the importance of myths

The myth-story of the design of computer and information systems then goes like this:

Epimetheus (the symbol of 'thinking afterwards') was the first god of the designers and practitioners. We designed computer systems because it was exciting and had some short-term economic spinoffs. But as indicated by the theme of this conference and the papers presented, we ran into heavy difficulties as we must according to the Pandora myth. Pandora, a woman possessing all gifts, was offered to Epimetheus. Even though Prometheus, the brother of Epimetheus, had warned him not to accept any gift from the gods, he married Pandora. She was then sent to earth, but Hermes implanted trickery in her and she traced the jar in which a well-meaning god had hidden all man's plagues. She opened the lid and all the plagues were let out. Only hope was left for mankind.

Current practitioners find hope with Prometheus (the symbol of 'thinking ahead'). Scientific method especially within the natural sciences is expected to enable us to take all possible impacts into account by developing a scientific design process using logic and forecasts. The problem is of course that the researchers or the practitioners who try to follow these scientific guidelines are prevented from acting.

The basic conflict between thinking without acting and acting without thinking must be confronted with other (new) possibilities. One of the most evident possibilities is Apollo (god of medicine and music). Curing the negative psychological and sociological impacts of computer systems by ergonomics, and extended into socio-technical design, seems to be an Apollonian response to the challenges we face. But in order to evaluate this approach one must bear in mind that the god of medicine is also a pittiless archer who may inflict rapid death. He is also the god of epidemics.

More promising approaches may, however, be expected from following Athena (the god of war and wisdom) and Dionysus (the god of wine and poetry). Athena suggests both a political and an epistemological approach. This means that dialectics, whether materialistic or idealistic, must play a central role in future design. The involvement of the unions in the design process must probably be seen in this perspective.

Also Dionysus is a possibility yet untried on a conscious level. Contrary to thinking and sensation, feelings and intuition must be brought out in the open and given a central role in systems design. This does not mean a return to Epimetheus who is blundering and looking through the rear-view mirror. Dionysus is not the conquerer of others, instead he is able to create the creator. Here the conflicts are deepest. Will computer systems help in creating the creator or will they forever distort human feelings and human creativity?

IAN MITROFF

The three groups in the drug company example I referred to in my talk constituted a dialectic; there was a real contest of wills. When the assumptions were surfaced it was plain that it was a case of night and day; it was like trying to synthesize poetry and wine. It was not possible in this case. Each group would not give up its pet policy even though they eventually had to pick one policy. I do not have time to explain here how we did this.

I do not make the assumption that MIS currently exist. If anything, I have been working collaboratively with managers to help design such a system. I do not think that this goal is unrealizeable. The fallacy may in fact be that of thinking that it is going to be horribly complex. On the contrary, it shall be horribly simplified before somebody uses it.

ROLF HØYER

I very much enjoyed Mitroff's paper and agree with his main propositions. From my own working with companies I have seen that it has frequently not been permitted to discuss the basic assumptions, - one has only been occupied with analysis of symptoms. Basic assumptions has been a taboo area. But an external consultant could legitimately bring up these issues which might be impossible to discuss and handle internally.

NIELS BJØRN-ANDERSEN

What are really facts and what are really assumptions? In many instances one is not aware which is which. One builds up a hierarchy of assumptions which at some point in time one felt was at least substantiated by data. They grow and become part of one's value system. So it is only for a brief period in time that things are assumptions. They tend to become integrated into one's basic values. It seems difficult to differentiate between the facts and assumptions.

IAN MITROFF

People need to be trained to discuss basic assumptions. They cannot do it on their own. They do not know how.

In the drug company we worked with the managers to obtain a common agreement about what was a fact and what was an assumption. You may argue that we merely transform the uncertainty from the individual level to the group level, but that is OK. In this way they were more certain about the uncertainty. I am not tuned to consistency and consensus. I believe in enlightened debate.

A.W. ZIJLKER

Would you not expect that the next time you played the same game with the same people on a similar subject, people will have learned the game and will begin to play round and say, well last time I called something an assumption instead of a fact and it weakened my position? So next time I will call something uncertain something certain instead. In this way the insight will be self-defeating.

IAN MITROFF

Of course, people learn; they have to. But we have to put our faith in conflicts and that other groups will always challenge the classification of facts and assumptions. It has to be the groups that keep the game honest, not me, for it is <u>their</u> game.

There is something very critical in doing the stakeholder analysis. We always tell people to look for the snaildarter. This refers to a US-case in which a billion dollar dam project was threathened with a delay, if not the project killed all together, because the planners of the dam completely neglected one of the most important stakeholders in the game. The snaildarter is a small fish; and because the planners had not taken the possible extinction of it into account, the environmentalists literally came out of the waters and said that they would not let the building go ahead. So if the planners do not raise the issue of assumptions, some one else will. And the opponent will just love to have the planners do all the safe rational calculations and then raise assumptions about the snaildarter, the tiny fish that will bite a hole in the best laid out plan of mice and men!

Gröholt is a grass-roots prophet,
Who knows that the user can make it.
Industrial democracy
Will defeat the bureaucracy,
In the future where the user will profit.

SOCIAL DEVELOPMENT AND ACCOUNTABILITY,
PROFESSIONALISM
AND THE FUTURE ROLE OF SYSTEMS DESIGNERS

Per Gröholt

Standard Telefon og Kabelfabrik A/S
Økern, Oslo

Most of the so-called 'professionals' in
this field will disappear during the nineteen eighties. A few of them will remain
and become real professionals - that is
to say hardware/software experts with academic backgrounds. In an intermediate period the role of the qualified system designer will be broadened to include social
design and organisational development (OD);
later this will gradually change. The system and OD designer will no longer be assisted by the user but will himself assist
the user. Finally the user will become his
own system and OD designer.

The Human Side of Information Processing
N. Bjørn-Andersen, editor
© IAG
North-Holland Publishing Company, 1980

SOCIAL RESPONSIBILITY, DEVELOPMENT AND ACCOUNTABILITY

In order to survive every company has to be profitable and socially responsible.
Today, however, there exists a marked imbalance between economical (technical) insight and social insight.

I shall describe six strategies, the use of which may help to overcome this imbalance:

   1.   Decision strategy.
   2.   Project strategy.
   3.   Check-list strategy.
   4.   Goal strategy.
   5.   Social accounting strategy.
   6.   Organisational strategy.

These strategies are of great importance in social design - an area of future responsibility for any systems designer.

Our choice of strategy depends on the conditions prevailing in each individual com
pany. Very often a combination of strategies will be advantageous. As for the
social accounting strategy, a gradual development through the strategies 1-4 and
not vice versa is normally to be preferred. A 5-10 years process in this field
may result in a social information system.

To a certain degree, social responsibility is practised by all companies. It is
therefore not a question of implementing new ideas, but rather of systematizing
and developing further something which already exists. Our goal is to raise social
consciousness and the quality of evaluation to the level of technical and economic
insight. As it is now, decisions are based far too much upon technical/economic
concepts and objectives.

In the following I shall give a brief description of each strategy followed by
some practical examples, mainly from the EDP system area in Norwegian companies.
Available experiences are limited in number and reflect the fact that we are only
at the beginning of a development towards a more systematic way of practising social responsibility within companies.

Decision Strategy

Analyses and evaluations are frequently undertaken to serve as a basis for decisions. Generally these relate to technical and economic matters, while the social
consequences are treated superficially. This is particularly the case for decisions
concerning new investments in buildings, machinery and equipment as well as for
changes in existing routines and systems. Accordingly, sufficient consideration
for the human and organisational consequences is not shown when electronic data
processing (EDP) is introduced. Frequently this results in partly unprofitable
and inadequate systems. The same could be said of all changes within the firm.

The social aspects must be analysed and evaluated as thoroughly as the technical
and economic ones. Top management should not make decisions until social information has been submitted and considered along with their technical and economic
counterparts. However, it would be unwise to demand that this be done for all decisions. Social consciousness must expand gradually. But nothing would be better
than to have this learning process in each individual decision on the operational
level while the employees at the same time are given a realistic understanding of
the possibilities and problems that may arise.

A Norwegian manufacturing firm has implemented social decision criteria to be
taken into account when new EDP projects are evaluated. These criteria come in
addition to the technical and economic criteria (later described more fully). No

feasibility study in this field is accepted unless it contains an analysis of the social consequences and possibilities of the EDP project.

Project Strategy

The first implementation strategy involves the inclusion of social information as an input for decisions. The second strategy involves establishing specific projects within the area of social responsibility. Such projects may include working environment, resource consumption, pollution, product safety, the local community, etc. Several of these projects may include the use of computers and terminals.

The new legislation in Norway on the working environment will give an impetus to a lot of projects and enable better systemization and further development of social responsibility within the firm. For most firms strategy 2 will be a good start.

Check-List Strategy

This method is particularly well known through 'operation grid' programmes and is also suitable within the area of social responsibility. An extensive questionnaire has been developed by Humble (1974). The booklet contains close to a hundred questions partly supplemented by practical examples on social responsibility.

The method is simple but requires serious and thorough work with each of the questions and that the replies are used as a basis for the development of a definite action programme.

The Norwegian company, Borregaard, has developed a special questionnaire to cover the area of systems and social responsibility.

Strategy for Goal Setting

Instead of making use of a check-list, one may start with the firm's goal or objective - if such exists. If the firm has not formulated any objective or if this does not include definite social objectives, an intensive time-consuming effort will be necessary. The development of objectives with social content presupposes that the firm is sufficiently mature to undertake such a process. On the basis of the general objectives one must further formulate secondary objectives, which in turn may serve as a basis for the development of concrete action programmes.

The Norwegian industrial firm, Standard Telefon og Kabelfabrik (STK), has for some time cooperated with the employees and their unions in developing the firm's objectives. Broad participation and plenty of time were important factors in the educational process. The objectives were published in the spring of 1975 and are shown in appendix A. These objectives have been developed further into specific objectives for computer based systems within STK.

Social Accounting Strategy

The social accounting statements are meant to be systematic social information system within the firm. Such an information system may become necessary as social responsibility becomes more clearly expressed in the firm's objectives and actions. At the present the social accounting statements are only an idea and must be discussed as such. They have not yet been given a definite and final form. In the long run the social accounting statements may become more important than the financial and managerial accounting statements. There is, however, still a long way to go. Even though a few firms in the United States and Europe have tried to set up social accounting statements, it is not recommended to begin with this strategy.

As the level of information and consciousness concerning social aspects is raised within the firm, one may gradually try out a continuously running social information system. The Norwegian aluminiumcompany, ÅSV, has a separate section in its monthly managerial report, that covers several physical environmental factors such as fluoride emissions, dust emissions, and sulphur emissions. The figures reported represent the present month along with the recent six months, and they show planned and achieved results as well as deviations. The Board of Directors and the union management committee discuss these reports during their monthly meetings.

Organisational Strategy

This strategy involves the kind of reorganisation that is necessary in order to work out a plan for social responsibility in the firm. Social responsibility should normally not involve changes in the firm's organisation. If large changes are necessary it is doubtful whether such a policy ought to be carried through. Different evaluations of social responsibility may prevail in a firm. It is therefore very important that a long-term strategy is planned, which, if necessary, includes changes in the firm's organisation and personnel resources.

One top executive in a Norwegian firm regards it as a necessity for the firm to act with greater social responsibility in order to survive in the long run.

Some key personnel in the top management are against this. At the same time the top executive depends upon these people. The result is that the new policy can only partly be carried through. Taking a long-term view, the top executive has worked out a plan for the transfer or replacement of the key personnel who today prevent the realization of greater social responsibility.

EDP may be used as a reorganisation tool and this may include strategies for the development of social responsibility.

Conclusion

As mentioned in the introduction, a combination of two or more strategies will probably be the most functional solution. If the firm is facing great problems, either technical, financial or administrative, one ought to be careful in adopting social responsibility on a large scale. However, a preliminary preparation may be started. Social repsonsibility may,on the other hand, be a tool for the survival of the firm in the long run, depending on the developments taking place in our society. By practising social responsibility, the firm may even come to participate in determining these developments. From the point of view of the business community in general as well as of the individual firm, it is to be preferred that such developments be steered from within the organisation rather than from the outside.

SYSTEMS, ORGANISATIONS AND USERS

Impact of EDP Systems

Systems have become a major factor in the development of organisations. Research reports as well as my own experiences have convinced me that systems have great social impact on human beings, organisations and society.

In 1975 in my company (STK, Oslo, a manufacturing organisation with 3,5oo employees) we made a rather thorough analysis of possible human and organisational effects of EDP systems implemented during 1968-74. The analysis covered three major projects: production planning and costing in the cable factory, material planning and costing in the switching factory and an integrated purchasing system. The total cost of these three projects was 3 million dollars and system design work amounted to 100 man years.

The findings may be summarized by the following main points:

1. Work Content

    EDP solves problems which cannot be solved manually -
    thus leading to increased job satisfaction.

    EDP may cause increased alienation.

2. Quantity of Work

    EDP eliminates routine work to a far greater extent
    than is created by EDP.

    EDP causes human problems due to job insecurity among
    the employees.

3. Management Problems During Project Work

    EDP reveals management problems.

    EDP encounters rather strong resistance especially
    from middle management. Successful implementation is
    dependent on active participation from the same group.

4. Changes in Management Position Due to EDP

    EDP changes the role of the manager from that of making
    decisions in each single case to that of making system
    decisions (designing decision rules).

    EDP may cause increased centralization or decentrali-
    zation - depending on management style.

5. Behavioral Requirements (Built-in)

    EDP has built-in requirements for formalization and
    structuring.

    EDP assumes stronger integration of information/
    routines and this may cause human and organisational
    problems.

6. Behavioural Aspects of the System Designer

    EDP may cause human problems due to the lack of human and
    organisational knowledge of the designers.

    EDP systems are easier to implement when the desingers
    have long experience of the user area.

On the basis of these findings we have concluded that increased insight into social
and organisational problems due to EDP will reduce, but not eliminate, human problems, and may simultaneously give increased profitability to EDP projects. Effective application of EDP assumes simultaneous development of human beings, organisation and society.

These conclusions have caused changes in our corporate design strategy and the
following objectives have been included in our EDP five year plan:

    'EDP may create social problems, but it may also open up new
    possibilities for meaningful work situations. Future use of
    EDP should be viewed as a contribution to the realization of
    the firm's goal.

    In addition to the improvement of the firm's ability to compete
    EDP should also contribute to a better work environment, increased
    decentralization and further democratization.

In order to improve the work environment it seems natural
to build upon the firm's existing work environment profile
which specifies a total of 19 work environment factors,
of which 10 psychological factors are of primary importance
in connection with EDP. What we want is to make changes
caused by EDP contribute to the improvement of the physical
and psychological environmental factors from the point of
view of each individual employee's work situation.

EDP may result in increased centralization as well as increased
decentralization. If we are not aware of both possibilities
the implementation of EDP based information systems may easily
result in increased centralization due to top management's
direct access to most data. But EDP also increases the possibilities for decentralization, especially when terminals are
being used. EDP projects ought not to be implemented until the
possibilities of increased decentralization have been evaluated.

Democratization here means full participation (co-determination) by the employees and their representatives in
developing and implementing EDP systems which affect the
employees.

In the future a pilot project ought not to be accepted for
implementation unless the above mentioned social factors
have been considered'.

In order to implement these objectives we have started a two year training programme for all our system designers in the field of psychology, group dynamics
and organisation development.

Gradually, but slowly our system designers are developing into OD (organisation
development) agents. In my concluding remarks I shall come back to the future
consequences of this development.

Relationship Between Designer and User

Before going deeper into the future, I should like to say something about the
relation between designer and user. The task of today's designer is to produce
systems; to deliver a definite product by a fixed date. The product requirements
are mainly technical and economical.

In this process the designer is 'assisted' by the user. Various degrees of user-
involvement have been tried out without fundamentally changing the designers role
as a producer of systems - a 'professional'. Several technical, economic, organisational and human reasons have been put forward to explain this state of affairs.

In 1976 we participated in a research project 'Systems and User' supported by
The Federation of Employers (NAF), The Trade Unions (LO) and The Norwegian Productivity Institute (NPI). An inventory on-line project in our cable division was
one of the key action-oriented cases to be studied from its very beginning to its
final implementation. The researcher participated in all phases of the project
from the beginning of the pre-study and onwards. Heavy user involvement was a
main strategy (See Fjalestad 1976).

During a two year period I was closely involved in the project, partly as a member
of the Advisory Research Board, partly as a working member of the cable project
steering committee and finally as a coordinator for all systems activities in our
company. My own experiences from the project can be summarized in the following
points:

1. We did not succeed in heavy user involvement due to a
    series of human, technical and organisational problems
    and limitations.

2. The system designers were unable to function with heavy
    user involvement due to the same factors as mentioned above (1).
    (The report contains the same conclusion, but it is not
    so explicit.

Although we are familiar with the explanations we are almost unable to change our
approach. I feel that we basically encounter at least two major problems which
prevent possible solutions. The first is a lack of understanding as to how learning
processes take place, the second is our notion of user assistance (the user shall
assist the systems designer).

Due to the time-pressure and constraints of a technical and economical nature the
prerequisites for human organisational learning processes do not exist.

Secondly, the 'professional' designers are brought into an almost impossible situation due to the user assistance myth. This is especially the case with projects of
some degree of complexity. To change the attitude of the professional systems designers towards assisting the users instead of the users assisting the designers
is very difficult, if not impossible, especially since their future existence as
designers is at stake.

In the meantime, external factors such as governmental legislation, union agreement and general social pressure are now entering the scene and more or less force
changes in system design approach. This is especially so in the Scandinavian countries.

The joint agreement in Norway on data based systems requires that all EDP plans
and projects contain both technical, economical and social evaluations and that
union representatives are strongly involved.

In my company we have a separate Union Board for data based systems with their own
whole day secretary (paid by the company). All plans and projects are studied by
the secretary before being presented to the Board for consideration and decision.

FUTURE ROLE OF SYSTEMS DESIGNERS

I have tried to cover some aspects of social responsibility, systems, organisations
and users in order to give a picture of some major factors which in my opinion
will strongly influence the future of systems designers. Before drawing up possible
future scenarios, let me present a more integrated viewpoint.

As mentioned earlier in my presentation, systems have great influence on social
values, human beings, organisations and society. A designer who is 'a professional'
and who lacks this understanding of interrelations and wholeness will meet with increasing problems and miss opportunities to develop human beings and organisations.

A simple case may illustrate my point of view. On-line terminals are introduced on
the shop floor. The job contents of the workers and of the foreman change. The position of the foreman is threatened. Information is now directly available to the
workers without having to pass through the foreman. A systems designer who does not
consider these aspects creates problems for the foreman, whereby possibilities for
human and organisational developments are lost.

As a 'professional' the designer may bring in other 'professionals' - a personnel
or an OD specialist. Since OD agents have met with increasing problems in their
work they are 'happy' to assist the systems designers because the latter are
changing the organisations far more than the OD agents could ever have dreamed of.

(Up to now the company personnel and OD function have had little or no understanding of what has been going on in the system areas). A joint venture may give some results.

In our case much more could have been achieved if the designer had also had relevant insight into behavioural aspects. Combined with necessary technical and manufacturing (user) know-how he could gradually have secured the foreman's confidence and avoided problems and created new job content with the foreman. (To involve various professionals in the social network may destroy the inherent potentials and we are often left with various degrees of 'specialist' manipulations).

In our case the designer has become an OD change agent. The fundamental argument for this approach is that human and organisational development must be linked to real changes (physical or procedual) in order to be effective.

However, we cannot stop here, turning the designer into an OD agent (even though this may help). The foreman and the workers themselves should be the change agents asking for necessary assistance from staff (not specialist) when trying to solve their own problem. In the Scandinavian countries the development towards such goals (participation, democratization and equality) is strong and will continue, supported by the computerization of society.

Such may be an ideal picture. However, from long experience we know that today it does not work. The next question follows: what has produced such conditions of inactivity and low creativity? The answers are manifold, the professionals themselves play an important role. They are not aware of the problems their systems are causing, and they might feel: Why should I be concerned about whether people get alienated from their own problems, that must be their responsibility.

But we are a breed of new 'professionals' equipped with new techniques. The development of the hardware and software techniques has simultaneously and to an increasing extent been such as to enable the user himself to take care of his own problems (e.g. microprocessors, digital communication, data bases and high level programming languages).

We are approaching holistic conditions where technical, economical and social aspect will be integrated and where all of us, including foremen and workers are 'professionals' who may mutually exchange their insight on a basis of common understanding of part and wholeness. Due to complexity, wholeness cannot be understood based on technical insight, but on social coordination through principles of self-government and common social objectives, the only way to control and coordinate experts (which we all are becoming).

CONCLUSIONS

On this background the future of the systems designer appears both frightening and encouraging. Most of the so-called 'professionals' in this field will disappear during the nineteen eighties. A few of them will remain and become real professionals, i.e. hardware/software experts with an academic background. During an intermediate period the role of the qualified system designer will be broadened to include social design and OD functions. Later this will gradually change. The system and OD designer will no longer be assisted by the user but will himself assist the user. Finally the user will become his own system and OD designer.

This may be the future outlook for system designers.

At the same time social responsibility will develop and make possible cooperation between experts (professionals) based on common social goals. Thus systems design and social design have become simultaneous processes.

REFERENCES

Fjalestad, J. (1976). Medvirkning i Systemudvikling. Projekt 1034, Report No. 2, Norwegian Productivity Institute, Oslo.

Humble, J. (1974). Social Responsibility Audit. A Management Tool for Survival. Foundation for Business Responsibilities, Room 18, 11 Portland House, London.

Gröholt, P. (1976). Næringslivets Sosiale Ansvar. Bedriftökonomens Forlag, Bergen, Norway.

APPENDIX

Company objectives for Standard Telefon og Kabelfabrik A/S, Oslo, Norway.

Primary Objectives

STK wants to be a competitive firm which, by combining its resources in a manner that is sound, efficient and favourable for society, will ensure:

- the firm's future existence,
- satisfactory compensation to employees and owners,
- stable employment and a satisfactory environment,
- opportunity for personal development and growth

Secondary Objectives

In order to achieve the primary objectives STK has formulated the following secondary objectives: (Abstract containing objectives relevant to social responsibility).

1. Products and Marketing

   a) STK will engage actively in product development and will follow a marketing policy that aims at advising the customers to choose products according to the individual customer's personal needs.

   b) STK will engage in objective advertising and public relations.

2. Resource Utilization

   a) STK will try to keep consumption of scarce and non-reproducible material resources at a minimum.

   b) STK will try to use material resources in such a manner that pollution of the environment is avoided.

3. Employees

   a) STK will cooperate with the employees and their organisations in order to enable the individuals and the firm to reach their respective objectives.

   b) STK will give the employees opportunities for development and growth by arranging for training, further education and expansion of the job content.

   c) STK acknowledges that it has a special responsibility for employees who have a reduced work capacity due to work accidents.

   d) STK will give fair and equal opportunities to men and women.

4. Society and the Community

   a) STK will try to offer steady employment and as far as possible avoid layoffs and dismissals.

   b) STK will contribute to the employment of handicapped persons within the firm to an extent corresponding to its size.

DISCUSSION AND COMMENTS ON PAPER PRESENTED BY PER GRØHOLT

TILO STEINBRINCK

The strategies suggested by Gröholt for designing information systems are to be highly recommended. Especially I should like to emphasize one central point of the objectives included in the five year EDP-plan drawn up for STK that :

"Changes introduced by EDP should contribute to the improvement of the physical and psychological environmental factors from the point of view of each individual employees' work situation"

I very much agree with this positive formulation. This is in accordance with the experiences we have in our service bureau that it is necessary to formulate and work towards positive goals.

In the paper it is mentioned that there are many difficulties in actually carrying out participation. I should like to pass on to you some experiences which we have found useful in our work at Datenzentrale Schleswig-Holstein.

One important lesson is that there is no admission for artists. The task of doing systems design is not an artistic one carried out by individual geniuses. All design must take place in groups, so techniques for handling group processes and participation are important.

Another important factor is the need for a systematic approach to programming and systems design. In Germany we say that design must be carried out in the engineering way which is a factory approach with a high degree of specialization and coordination.

Furthermore I should like to argue against doing experiments. 95% of all designers will not be allowed to carry out any experiments. They have to fit their systems and programs exactly into the organization. This creates the possibility for the highest degree of participation.

Participation, however, must be planned and carried out systematically. In our computing center we have approximately 400 projects at any point in time with more than 400 clients with different projects using our services. Our model for participation relies upon the existence of automation committees for the land and municipalities of Schleswig-Holstein.

Within the land every ministry and authority has an automation referent who is responsible for all communication to the service bureau regarding development and production. Furthermore, they have sub-committees for special items.

Within the municipalities we have committees specialized by subject, i.e. finance committees, hospital committees, urban planning committees, etc. In all committees, most importantly, there is a predominance of users, not data processing specialists. We see ourselves only as a service bureau which has to provide service to the users.

This participation requires a very exact and strict planning. The project organization consists always of a project steering committee and a project team. The steering committee is independent and has participants from users, management, workers' councils, etc.

Finally, we have a set of guidelines for developing systems, i.e. consultation and execution of all parts of the project. It is worth noting that the group of participants changes according to the phase in the development of the system. This is a very systematic approach with which you can create genuine participation.

PER GRØHOLT

I agree with Steinbrinck that we must formulate positive individual goals, but people have to be helped in defining their own goals. They have to define what they mean by a good job content, what they understand by decentralization and what they understand by participation. We have facilitated this process for the users at STK with very good results in the form of precise objectives.

As to the engineering approach, I agree that we shall be professionals as systems designers. But I totally and fundamentally disagree with Steinbrinck when he claims that we shall only carry out programs that fit into the existing organization. In that way we do not contribute substantially to the achievement of organizational goals.

Finally, Steinbrinck talks about participation, but I think that his approach is far too complex. The committee and project groups open up the possibilities of manipulation and they are very poorly suited to providing real influence for the end-users. I also have a suspicion that the users in Steinbrinck's model are represented by very high-level-managers with little understanding of the administrative clerks who in practise have to work with the computer system. I feel that the method proposed by Mumford provides far better possibilities for genuine user participation.

A.W. ZIJLKER

I should like to play a devil's advocate. Especially, I should like to use some of the things I learned from the presentation by Mitroff, or in other words, I should like to do some assumptional analyses on the paper.

The first and very essential assumption made by Gröholt is that there is a marked imbalance between the technical-economic insights on one hand and on the other hand the social insights. - Using the certainty/importance classification by Mitroff I might classify Gröholt and myself as shown in the figure below.

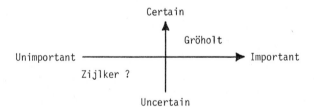

While Gröholt is obviously placed on the top right corner I place myself with a questionmark (as I am not too positive about this) in the bottom left corner. As a matter of fact in my opinion we do not know so much about economics. We listen and read about inflation, stagflation etc., but it is quite apparent that it is difficult to be sure about economics.

As regards the technique - which is something I have studied - we found out that the more we know the more we become aware of the things we do not know about.

On the other hand, I have been very impressed by the fantastic social insight provided eg. by Mumford. I am very impressed by people like McGregor etc. So I have a feeling that the balance is not so bad after all. If the balance was so bad a conference like this one would not have taken place.

Gröholt makes the second assumption that the implementation of social strategies etc. is a major area in future systems design. Of course social strategies are important, but whether they belong in future systems design I do not know. Anyway, based on that assumption Gröholt draws two conclusions:

1. If in doubt (about social implications) don't.

2. Systems designers need behavioural insight (the "holistic" approach).

Both of these conclusions I should like to question but before I do, let me just go briefly into the stakeholder analysis and analyse for each stakeholder their assumptions about whether social responsibility is a major area in systems analysis in the future.

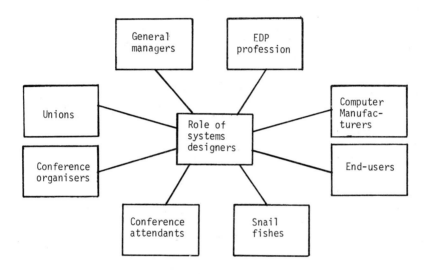

Stakeholders

I suspect that the edp-profession is very certain that it is very important. The computer manufacturers who invented the edp-profession are also very certain that it is very important, and representatives for unions have demonstrated to us that they are certain about this too.

The conference organisers of course find it important, but it is also important to them that it remains uncertain, but that holds for all conference goers as a matter of fact.

The general managers are probably more in doubt. Most managers I have met say "is it really so important" and "are you really certain that it is your task", so he is in the uncertain area. And finally the end-users. It is important to them that their own working environment is nice and attractive, but I doubt that they are interested in social strategies.

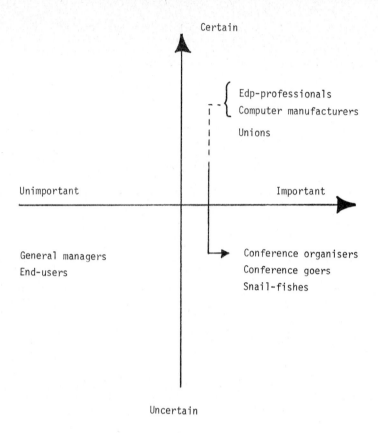

Stakeholder assumptions about whether social
responsibility is a major area within systems analysis

Then we have also been told that we must track the development of attitudes over
time. Here I suspect that the computer profession will learn after a while that it
is not their cup of tea to be socially apt so they will move over to the uncertain
area or the computer manufacturers will find out that the computer professionals
become real professionals, and they cannot sell so much to them any more. So the
computer manufacturers will begin to doubt whether it is important to have these
socially conscious people in the computer area. The manufacturers will like the
socially responsible somewhere else where they may remedy the mistakes done in the
computer field, but they would not like to have the socially conscious people involved in the decision processes on new equipment. So they move into the uncertain
area too.

Based on this 'analysis' I come to the conclusion that

   - management can never postpone action until they know everything - they
     are real do'ers, right or wrong

   - systems designers are by nature technique oriented people; that is why they started to go in that direction - so let us try to compensate them and let them work in teams with other disciplines (which is really what we have done over the last twenty years I think).

Finally I should like to draw two other conclusions,

- Gröholt says that self-development is the ideal for solving problems. In principle I agree with him. But the problems arise whether this is true for the realisation of corporate goals. Mumford said that a condition for participation and a good introduction of a system is that everybody gains and nobody loses. - I would like to live in such a world.

- Gröholt also concludes that there will be a new breed of computer professionals. I think we have heard that before. Do you remember twenty years ago, everybody was talking about 'the saints go marching in' - those were the designers of that time. This new breed might develop in the same direction, but I will advise ourselves to become humble toolmakers instead of holy (-istic) system designers.

PER GRÖHOLT

I have attended quite a number of executive meetings in Europe and abroad and if you analyse the assumptions behind what they are saying you will discover that they are not really socially conscious.

As to the question about whether computer professionals will be social designers in the future too, there is a clear answer to that, because my idea will be to eliminate the designers altogether in the future. So the narrow professional Zijlker is talking about has no role in the future.

As to the more fundamental problem of social responsibility, I do not agree about the conclusions drawn by Zijlker. I have written a little book on social responsibility which should give you a number of arguments and analyses of the ideas, but it will take too long to bring these forward now.

Zijlker loved the role of humble toolmakers. I believe in that approach, but I think in the Scandinavian countries at least, we face a reality where we really have to be professional designers. In a way the future has caught up with us and we have to design in a socially responsible way and really be professionals in that sense in order to survive. It is not sufficient to be humble.

JOHN BANBURY

In a hierarchical organization, the end user is obviously not a single individual. He will be a member of different groups which are among other things related by power differentials. It seems to me that this makes participation extremely difficult especially in the design and implementation of systems which have a marked emphasis on control. How would Gröholt cope with that kind of complexity?

PER GRÖHOLT

Due to the complexity I do not recommend using committees and project groups. The systems have to be integrated in the user area. A second comment is that we should be careful in using the concept of user participation. We might even be damaging what we are trying to achieve. The same thing holds true when we are using the concept of a manager-subordinate relationship. Here it is implied that there is a definite approach to decision making and to authority relations. Therefore we ought to give up the term 'user participation' and instead talk about expert participation in systems design.

ROLF HØYER

Listening to Steinbrinck, Zijlker and others at the conference, I get the impression that a number of people share the fundamental belief that participation is just a cost. And costs in most companies are to be defeated. However, participation should also be regarded as a way of attaining business goals, not just a way of attaining self-development for people in an organization. It is a method for developing an organization which does business better and yields better profits and growth. But at the same time it gives a more stimulating and rewarding way of living.

PER GRØHOLT

I have one comment to Hedberg who was stressing very strongly the management power aspect and the value aspect. Really it is important. However, what I missed in his paper was the list of limitations e.g. lack of know-how, lack of understanding, lack of ability to communicate. These limitations should be more strongly brought out and debated, not to discourage participation, but to give everyone a realistic picture and avoid disappointments.

Finally, let me apologize for everything I said. I do not know for certain whether it is correct or not. Only I know that in a way we should all be devils advocates coming up with alternatives and ideas and work together to further continued progress.

There is an analyst named Ackoff,
And on management systems, he took off.
Only the adaptive brain,
Can control computer pain,
And minimise MIS rip-off.

FROM INFORMATION TO CONTROL

Russell L. Ackoff

Wharton School of Finance
University of Pennsylvania

The method normally employed in the design
of computer-based systems is analytical.
It is argued that although a system can be
described using this method, it can only
be explained, hence understood, by use of
synthetic or systems thinking. The two
methodologies are contrasted. Then, to illustrate the main points made, a synthetic
design of a management information system
as a part of a containing management system
is described. Some examples of such a system are provided. Alternative segmenta-
tions of a total-organizational management
system are then considered. Finally, two
suggestions are made that are directed at
humanizing the impact of computerized systems.

INTRODUCTION

This paper is not about a forecast, but about an opportunity. Because I believe that the future depends largely on what we do between now and then, and that what we do is a matter of our choice, I am less interested in predicting what choices you will make than in influencing them. The type of choice on which I will focus is methodological, but I will try to show the relevance of such choices to the theme of this conference: "the sociological and psychological aspects of computerization."

ANALYTIC THINKING

The method normally employed in the design of computer-based systems is analytical. Analysis has been the dominant mode of inquiry in the Western world ever since the Renaissance, our rebirth. It is not surprising that Renaissance man adopted analysis in his search for knowledge and understanding because it is the method that comes naturally to every curious child who tries to grapple with the unknown.

Analysis is a three-step process. First, it involves decomposing or disassembling the thing to be understood into its parts and, if possible, into its ultimate (indivisible) parts, its elements. Second, an explanation is sought of the behavior or properties of each of these parts taken separately. Third, the explanations of the parts are then aggregated by finding the relationships between them into an explanation of the whole.

Around the turn of this century difficulties and dilemmas appeared in each branch of science and each domain of practical endeavor-- difficulties and dilemmas that brought some to question the adequacy of the analytical method. These difficulties and dilemmas arose out of the increasing complexity of systems with which we were dealing and the increasing turbulence of their environments.

Analysis -- and the reductionistic and mechanistic view of the world that it yielded[1] -- had worked well as long as our concerns were with machines, instruments that enable us to do (physical) work, to apply energy to matter so as to change one or more of its properties. Difficulties and dilemmas arose as our focus shifted to biological systems, organisms, and social systems, particularly organizations. Organisms and organizations are purposeful systems that, we discovered, cannot be well understood if they are viewed -- as they were for several centuries -- as machines, even as very complex machines.

Moreover, the three technologies that emerged as the principal instruments for affecting the behavior of organisms and organizations involved "machines" that did no physical work, hence differed from "classical" machines in a fundamental way. These technologies yielded artifacts which

(1) generated symbols that represented the properties of objects and events (data) and, therefore, observed -- for example, the ohmmeter, thermometer, and barometer;

(2) transmitted symbols and, therefore, communicated -- for example the telegraph, telephone, wireless, radio, and television; and

(3) manipulated symbols logically and, therefore, "thought" -- computers.

---

1. For a description of how reductionism and mechanism followed from the commitment to analysis, see Chapter 1 of Redesigning the Future (Ackoff 1974).

These technologies were replacements for the mind of a man rather than his muscle. Such substitution came to be known as automation. The combination of these technologies into servo-mechanisms created a particularly critical dilemma because such devices came to be known as teleological mechanisms, a contradiction in terms.

SYNTHETIC THINKING

By the early 1950s the accumulating dilemmas, difficulties, and technological developments led us to suspect that there was something in the nature of purposeful systems that limits the effectiveness of analyzing them. Our suspicion was confirmed when we came to understand the nature of systems.

A system is a set of two or more elements (1) each of which can have an effect on the behavior of the whole, and (2) are so interconnected that any subsets formed of them are also interdependent -- that is, the effect of any subset of parts on the behavior of the whole, depends on the behavior of at least one other subset. Therefore, a system is a whole that cannot be decomposed into parts that have an independent effect on the whole. From this it can be shown deductively that every system has properties that none of its parts do. For example, a person can run, sing, and read but none of his or her parts can. Finally, it follows that a system is a whole which, when taken apart, loses its essential properties and, therefore, cannot be understood by analysis.

Analysis yields descriptions, not explanations, of systems; it reveals their structure, how they work; hence its product is know-how, knowledge, not understanding. It does not explain why systems work as they do

A method for acquiring understanding of systems was required. Its development began in the 1950s and came to be known as synthetic or systems thinking. Like analyses it involves three steps:

(1) identification of one or more larger systems (suprasystems) that contain the system to be explained,

(2) explanation of the behavior of the suprasystem(s), and

(3) explanation of the system by identifying its role(s) or function(s) in the relevant suprasystem(s).

In synthesis the thing to be explained is taken to be a part of a larger whole rather than, as in analysis, as a whole to be taken apart.

I believe that the failure of many information systems to perform satisfactorily derives from the fact that they were designed analytically -- as an assemblage of parts rather than as a part of a larger whole. Such systems may be efficient, but they are unlikely to be as effective as possible. Synthetic design is required to assure effectiveness. Let me try to support this allegation by looking at Management Information Systems (MIS) synthetically.

The first question to be addressed is: Of what larger system is an MIS a part? The answer is apparent: it is a part of a Management System.

What is management? It is the control of an organization by one or more of its parts. An organization is a purposeful system some of whose parts are purposeful and among these there is a functional division of labor. Therefore, an organization is a purposeful system some of whose parts are purposeful, and which is itself a part of a larger purposeful system. The performance of an organization is affected by the pursuit of purposes at each of these three levels. Therefore, the management of an organization involves taking into account (1) the organization's purposes -- the self-control problem; (2) the purpose of its parts -- the humanization problem; and (3) the purpose of the containing system(s) -- the environmen-

talization problem. Until recently, managers, and those who serve them, have focused almost exclusively on the first of these problems. This is changing because
of increasing pressures from the environments of systems and their parts, and increasing awareness from within of the dependence of the attainment of organizational objectives on the attainment of the objectives of the stakeholders. The theme
of this conference is a reflection of the "appreciative" change that is taking
place.

DESIGN OF A MANAGEMENT SYSTEM

Now, using a very broad brush let me sketch a design of a management system.

Management involves (1) the identification and anticipation of problems and opportunities, (2) decision making -- the solution of problems and the exploitation of
opportunities, (3) the maintenance or improvement of decisions with experience and
under changing conditions, and (4) a supply of information required to carry out
the preceding three functions. A management system, therefore, consists of four
interacting subsystems, one corresponding to each of the functions required. (See
Figure 1. In the description that follows letters and numbers in parentheses refer to this figure).

Management of an organization obviously requires observation of the organization
managed (B) and its environment (A). To observe is to generate data (1). Data consist of symbols that represent properties of objects and events. They are raw material that require processing to convert them into information (2). Information
also consist of symbols that represent the properties of objects and events, but
these differ from data in their usefulness. Data must be processed to convert them
into information: Therefore, data processing is a necessary part of the information subsystem (C).

When a decision maker receives information -- from himself, others, or a computer
-- he does not always find it useful. He may find it incomprehensible or unread-
able, doubt its validity, or question its completeness. On the other hand, he may
accept it but want additional information. For these or other reasons, the receipt
of information often leads decision-makers(D) to make inquiries (3) that either
require additional information or "redoing" the information already received.

Inquiries made by decision-makers require two additional capabilities in the information subsystem (C). It must be able to generate new data -- that is, inquire (4)
into the organization (B) and its environment (A) so that the necessary data (1)
are obtained. It must also have the ability to reuse data that were previously received and, possibly, used. This means that it must be able to store data in such
a way as to be able to retrieve them when necessary. A data -storage facility is,
of course, a file whether in a drawer or a computer. A computerized data-storage
facility is a data bank.

Once the new or old data have been processed to provide the information that constitutes a reply to the inquiry that initiated the process, it is transmitted to
the decision-making subsystem (D). This inquiry-information cycle may continue until the decision-maker has all the information he wants or feels like having, until he has run out of time and must make a decision using whatever information he
has, or until the cost and time of further inquiry is not likely to be justified
by the additional or improved information it would yield.

The output of a decision is also a set of symbols, ones that constitute instructions and, sometimes, motivation (5). An instruction is a communication to others
or oneself that is intended to increase the efficiency of the organization (B).
Motivation is a communication that is intended to affect its values, hence increase its effectiveness. Both are directed at implementation of the decision.

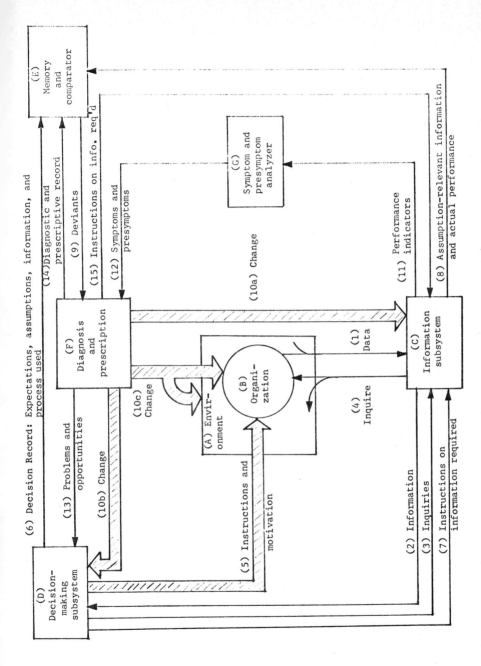

Figure 1. Diagrammatic representation of a management system.

220

Russell L. Ackoff

Now consider what is required to monitor and control a decision. Every decision has one or two purposes: to make something happen that otherwise would not, or to prevent something from happening that otherwise would. In either case there is one or more expected effects and times by which these are expected. To control a decision, these expected effects and times of realization should be made explicit. Additionally, the assumptions on which these expectations are based and the information and decision-making process used in reaching them should also be made explicit. Together these make up the decision record (6) which should be stored in an inactive memory (E). Human memories are generally much too active for this purpose. They have a way of revising earlier expectations in light of current experience.

The decision record should also be used to inform the information subsystem (C) about what information is needed to monitor the decision (7). The assumptions should be checked periodically to see if they still hold, and the actual effects of the solution (8) should be observed and brought together with the decision record. The actual and the assumed conditions and the actual and expected effects should be compared (E).

When assumed and actual conditions, or expected and actual effects, agree, nothing need be done. All that needs to be noted are deviations (9) of actual from assumed conditions and actual from expected effects. Such deviations indicate that something has gone wrong. To determine what has and what should be done about it requires diagnosis (F).

The purpose of diagnosis is to find the causes of deviations and to prescribe (F) corrective action. Although the causes may be difficult to identify, they are only of four types.

1. The information used in making the decision was in error, and therefore the information subsystem (C) requires change (10a) so that it will not repeat that type of error.

2. The decision-making process may have been faulty. In such a case a change (10b) in the decision-making subsystem (D) should be made.

3. The decision may have been correct, but it was not implemented as intended. In such a case changes (10c) are required to improve either communication of instructions and motivation (5) or the organization (B) or its personnel so that they are more likely to carry out instructions as intended in the future.

4. The environment changed in a way that was not anticipated. In such cases a way of better anticipating such changes, decreasing sensitivity to them, or reducing their likelihood should be found. These may require any one or combination of the three types of change already mentioned or efforts to change the environment (A).

The diagnostic and prescriptive function (F) assures both learning (improved efficiency under constant conditions) and adaptation (maintaining or improving efficiency under changing conditions).

Now consider the problem identification and anticipation subsystem (G-F).

We normally use the term "symptom" to mean an indicator of a threat to the health of an organism or an organization. However, it may also be an indicator of an opportunity; that is, it may indicate that something is exceptionally good as well as exceptionally bad. A symptom is one of a range of values of a variable that usually occurs when something is exceptionally right or wrong but seldom when things are normal. Thus a fever is an abnormally high body temperature that is seldom associated with good health but is often associated with bad health.

Variables used as symptoms are properties of the behavior or performance of organizations. Such variables can also be used dynamically as presymptoms or omens: indicators of future opportunities or problems. For example, the range of normal body temperature is about one degree Farenheit. Suppose that in five consecutive readings of a person's temperature taken half an hour apart, normal but rising temperatures are observed. This would indicate that, unless there is an intervention, that person will have a fever in the near future. The same would be true if we observed small but repeated increases in the number of defects coming off a production line.

A presymptom is nonrandom normal behavior. The nonrandomness may take the form of a trend or a cycle, among other things. There are many statistical tests for nonrandomness, but even the naked eye and common sense can identify most of them.

A complete management system regularly obtains information on a number of performance indicators (11) some of whose values are symptoms. In many organizations this is the function of the controller; in a hospital it is a function of the nurses. Controllers and nurses usually obtain and examine a large number of performance indicators in search for symptoms and presymptoms. Therefore, in a complete management system the information subsystem (C) is responsible for obtaining and providing measures of a number of characteristics of performance, performance indicators (11). This subsystem supplies them with symptom and presymptom analysis (G). When symptoms or presymptoms are found, they become an input to the diagnostic process (12 to F). Once a diagnosis is obtained, the problems or opportunities detected (13) are reported to the decision-making subsystem (D) for action.

Finally, a diagnostic and prescriptive record (14) , much like the decision record (6),is issued by the diagnostic and prescriptive subsystem (F). It is sent to the memory (E) where its elements are subsequently compared with the "facts" (8) that are supplied by the information subsystem (C) in response to instructions on information required (15). Deviants (9) are subsequently reported to the diagnostic and prescriptive subsystem (F) where corrective actions should be taken. This assures learning and adaption in this subsystem.

Note that there are three levels of control in the management system. First, the system taken as a whole controls the organization of which it is a part. Second, the diagnostic and prescriptive subsystem controls the management system. Third, this subsystem exercises self-control, controls the controller.

Each of the functions that are part of a management system are subject to computerization, but to varying degrees. Decision-making for which models and algorithms are available can be completely compurerized. Decisions for which models but no algorithms are available can be partially computerized; they require man-machine dialogue. Finally, decisions for which there are no models cannot be computerized.

The memory and comparator and the symptom and presymptom analyzer can be completely computerized. The diagnostic and prescriptive subsystem is as yet subject to little or no computerization. However, recent development of diagnostic routines applicable to machines and organisms indicates that development of computerized organizational diagnosis is not impossible.

There is nothing about a management system that requires that any part of it be computerized. Furthermore, the system may reside entirely within one individual. Alternatively, each function may be performed by different individuals or groups. In large organizations where groups are likely to be used to perform the necessary functions, a wide variety of technical skills may be involved.

The management system shown i Figure 1 is a module of organizational management.

In The Brain of the Firm, Stafford Beer (1972) has presented a complete organizational management system. He and I have tried to combine his system with my module.
(Ackoff and Beer 1969). Many other designs are possible. The presentation of such
a design here, unfortunately, would be diverting from the main point of the paper.

APPLICATION OF MANAGEMENT SYSTEMS

It may help if I describe briefly one application of the management-system design
shown in Figure 1. The system was developed for the marketing department of a company that produced a high-volume, low-unit-cost consumer good. The company had the
largest share of its market, about nine percent. It marketed its forty-two pro-
duct-package combinations in all of the United States but divided the nation into
approximately two-hundred market areas. The decision-making component of the management system contained models of each market area that enabled management, by
conducting a dialogue with the computerized model, to set values for each of five
classes of variables:

        (1) prices,
        (2) advertising (levels, media mix, timing, and message)
        (3) amount of sales effort,
        (4) number and type of sales promotions, and
        (5) amount and type of point-of-sales materials to be distributed
            to retailers.

These values were set by management so as to maximize expected market share in
each area. The expectations, determined with the help of the computerized models,
were fed into the memory and comparator which already had aspects of the decision-
making procedure stored within it. Decisions were made monthly.

In the first month of operation the system generated forty-two deviants which were
fed to the diagnostic and prescriptive team. This team consisted of operators,
management, and marketing researchers who had participated in the design of the
system. The average error of the expectations was about four percent of the market.

The deviants were diagnosed and corrective action was taken. By so doing the system's performance improved. By the twelfth month there were only six deviants and
the average error had been decreased to about one percent. By the eighteenth month
the system "stabilized" at an average of two deviants per month and with an average error of less than half of one percent.

Armed with this system marketing management increased the company's share of its
market from just over nine to about twenty-five percent in a decade, leaving its
main competitor far behind.

Shortly after the marketing-management system was installed, a similar system was
requested by the management of production and distribution. This system was developed and eventually yielded a demonstrable reduction of operating costs of about
thirty-five million dollars per year. The system had cost about three-hundred
thousand dollars to design and install.

Improvements of such magnitude are very hard to match by computerizing clerical
operations or automating manual controllers of machines. I return to this point
below.

Management information systems are normally designed as self-contained, even autonomous, systems -- not as part of a larger system. For this reason they usually
fail to provide the containing system with some of the types of information that
it requires, and they usually lack the learning and adaptive features with which
the diagnostic and prescriptive subsystem of the management system endows them.

Furthermore, such systems seldom concern themselves with the large amount of unsolicited information that most managers receive. Such information usually exceeds by a factor of at least two the amount of solicited information received. Unsolicited information should be filtered to remove what is irrelevant, and what is relevant should be condensed as much as possible without loss of content.[2] This point can be put another way: conventional MISs operate on the implicit or explicit assumption that the principal informational need of managers is for more relevant information, but there is substantial evidence to indicate that they suffer much more from an overabundance of irrelevant information. Most managers already suffer from an information overload. Under such conditions, any MIS that does not remove an amount of irrelevant information that is larger than the amount of relevant information that it adds, is doomed to underutilization.

My experience suggest that it is better to build a complete management system for a part of management (see Figure 2) than to build a MIS (an incomplete management system) for all of management. Moreover, it has been my experience that when a complete management system is built for one part of management, the desire for such systems by other parts develops rapidly. "Columns" are added quickly and they are relatively easy to integrate. On the other hand, when a MIS is designed separately it seldom "spreads" into other subsystems (rows) and where it does, the integration of such subsystems is generally very difficult.

The moral of all this is that <u>every system should be designed as a part of a larger containing system</u> -- in fact, as a part of the <u>largest</u> containing system to which the designers have access.

A familiar example drawn from a different domain may help illuminate this principle.

Urban transportation systems are almost always designed analytically, as aggregations of modes of transport (e.g. automobiles, trucks, trains, and busses) and the media (e.g. streets and rail lines) which they require. Each mode and medium has been separately and independently designed. I hardly need point out the crisis conditions under which most such systems currently operate. Furthermore, the palliatives applied to them tend to exacerbate rather than alleviate the congestion that is congenital to them.

Only recently have we begun to design urban transportation systems synthetically. In one such effort the automobile was redesigned to fit the system rather than conversely. The resulting vehicle holds two persons, one behind the other, can be coupled to other vehicles, has a maximum speed of forty miles per hour, and is about $3\frac{1}{2}'$ x $6\frac{1}{2}'$. It may be either Publicly or privately owned. If publicly owned, it can be coin operated and picked up and left anywhere. For a detailed discussion see Sagasti and Ackoff (1971).

It has been shown that with such vehicles it is possible to increase the people-carrying capacity of existing urban streets and highways by about five-hundred per cent, considerably more than can be obtained by any changes of the system which accomodate to the current automobile.

Even more synthetically, a redesign of urban areas which was directed at minimizing the need for motorized transportation revealed that about eighty percent of it could be eliminated, and the cost of so doing would be less than that of the ineffective corrective measures currently used.

If current trends continue management systems will be designed to accomodate the management information systems that are available. This will be as productive of

2. A design of a system that does this, but in a different context, can be found in R.L. Ackoff et al.(1976). Designing a National Scientific and Technological Communication System: The SCATT Report, University of Pennsylvania Press, Philadelphia.

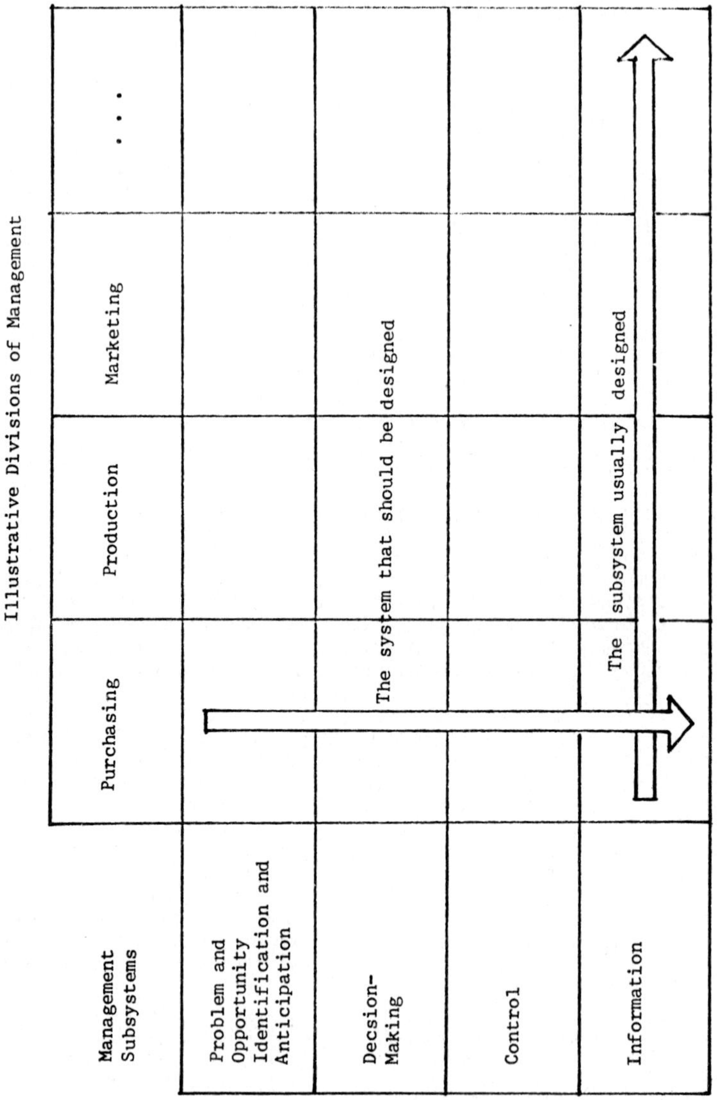

Figure 2. Alternative design procedures.

system breakdowns, as crisis-creating, as is our practice of designing transportation systems that accomodate the kind of automobiles that are available.

CONCLUSION

I should like to conclude these remarks by connecting to the central theme of this conference.

First, I believe that accomplishments to date clearly indicate that organizational performance can be improved more by development of management systems than by creation of computerized systems that replace or remodel clerical or other "lower" forms of labor. Therefore, it seems to me that the best defense of workers against the invasion of automation is an offensive directed at introducing computerized management systems. This, I believe, would at least sensitize management to the effects of automation. In addition, it would remove a current inequality that is detrimental to workers: it would enable them to learn as much about what managers do as managers know about what they do.

Secondly, most corporations attempt to maximize the return on the investment in their facilities and equipment -- their fixed assets. Profit is what enables them to provide a return on this investment. This concept of investment is arbitrary and conventional. It derives from earlier conditions that have changed -- shortage of capital and a commoditylike labor market -- and a set of social values embodied in the non-welfare state that no longer apply. Under current conditions and with current values it seems more appropriate for organizations to attempt to maximize their return on the cost of labor. Labor should be treated as a relatively fixed, rather than as a variable, cost; and the cost of facilities and equipment should be treated as variable, as they clearly are.

This would recognize explicitly the emerging conviction that a principal societal function of corporations is to distribute income through employment. It would not reduce the desirability of increasing the productivity of either workers or plant and facilities, but it would require of management that it consider how to use productively any workers displaced by mechanization or automation. Since growth is already an objective of most corporations, this would not be a great burden on managers, particularly if they had adequate management systems to assist them. Furthermore, I suspect, but it reamins to be proved, that managing corporations so as to maximize returns on labor would yield larger corporate profits and returns on capital employed than current practices do. If management will not explore this possibility, then labor clearly should.

Both of my suggestions clearly indicate that systems research, planning, and design should become as important a part of labor's arsenal as it is of management's. Only when this becomes the case will industrial democracy be achieved.

REFERENCES

Ackoff, R.L. (1974). Redesigning the future, John Wiley & Sons, New York.

Ackoff, R.L. et al. (1976). Designing a National Scientific and Technological Communication System: The SCATT Report, University of Pennsylvania Press, Philadelphia.

Ackoff, R.L. and S. Beer (1969). In Conclusion: Some Beginnings. In Progress in Operations Research: Relations between Operations Research and the Computer III. In J.S. Aronofsky (ed.). John Wiley & Sons, New York, pp. 423-449.

Beer, S. (1972). The Brain of the Firm. Allen Lane, The Penguin Press, London.

Sagasti, F. and R.L. Ackoff (1971). Possible and Likely Futures of Urban Transportation. Socio-Economic Planning Science, Vol. 5, pp. 413-428.

DISCUSSION AND COMMENTS ON PAPER PRESENTED BY R.L. ACKOFF

JENS O. RIIS

As pointed out by Ackoff, management systems must be able to function in a turbulent environment. Furthermore, on the Scandinavian scene we experience an increased quest for participation resulting in a diffusion of decision making. This will change the character of the design process, of management, and of the way in which managerial tasks are to be carried out.

The increased turbulence and participation will change the role of a management system; in particular from

Instead of managing a set of clearly defined tasks, I shall expect that the main role of a management system will be to secure that tasks are attended to. Furthermore I shall expect a shift from

Identification and anticipation of problems and opportunities is an important subject for a management system to deal with. In this respect we must be aware of the capabilities possessed by the human mind to use a holistic (systematic, synthetic) approach. It is not enough just to have an early warning system. Ordinarily we have a lot of information available.

It is an essential matter for management to select the problems and opportunities they want to address themselves to. Obviously this cannot be done without dealing with the moral issues associated with goal formulation.

This brings me to the question about what should be the future role of the human being, especially in relation to Ackoff's concept of the brain of the firm, being the computer assisted subsystem, memory, diagnosis and symptom identification.

RUSSELL L. ACKOFF

The separation that occurs between solving a problem and implementing the solution disappears in synthetic thinking. There is no way of separating these two processes. When we look at a process, in a holistic way, implementation is a principle source of information as to what is the nature of the problem being confronted. Therefore, it is a source of data input. Consequently, the formulation of a problem, the solving of it, and the implementation of it are three interactive processes which take place simultaniously. Implementation is deliberately conceived of in this process as an instrument for getting information for the reformulation and the solution of problems. Therefore, the implementation process is of vital importance. Its role becomes even greater than it is in the traditional analytical approach because it is a source of input to the process as well as an output.

Perhaps it should also be pointed out that the concept of a problem also disappears. A problem is an abstraction which is obtained by analysis of a real situation. Problems are never given to us, they are extracted out of reality by analysis. They are elements of a system of problems in the same sense as an atom is an element of a chair. We do not experience the atoms of which a chair is made. We experience the chair. We do not experience problems. They are mental constructs. Unfortunately in English we do not have a very good word for a system of problems, although the French have a very good word for it, they call it a problématique. In the USA we call it a mess. This allows us to discuss the art of mess-management. When it becomes clear that a problem is an abstract element, then it becomes clear that if we want to deal with reality, we must deal with systems of problems.

If a system is taken apart and each part is made to work as efficiently as possible then there is one thing of which we can be absolutely sure: the system will not behave as efficiently as possible. If we take a mess and analyse it into its component problems and solve each problem taken separately, there is one thing of which we can be absolutely sure: the mess will not be solved as efficiently as possible. We need a methodology other than analytical problem solving for dealing with complex systems of problems: the methodology of planning which has just recently begun to emerge; i.e., dealing with interrelated sets of problems in a holistic way.

The question raised by Riis about the role of the human being in computerized systems we need not worry about. I can recall that about 1954 when the IBM 650 first became available, one of the great frights of managers was that computers would replace them. I once gave a talk on the automation of management and the following day two members of the board of my University asked for my resignation because I was being un-American. They had completely misunderstood my point which was that an increasing number of problems to which management currently addresses itself would be handled by computers in the future. The implicit assumption they were making was that management has a finite number of problems and therefore, to the extent that we take something away from them, their task is diminished and that ultimately it will be reduced to zero. I cannot imagine more nonsense. If the same argument had been used in the late Renaissance when the problems of modern science were formulated, science would be completed by now, since all the problems that were raised at that time have since been solved. The solution of a problem always created new problems which are more difficult and more complex than the ones replaced. Therefore, to the extent that we computerize and effectively solve problems currently confronted by management, we enlarge, expand, and complicate the problems of management. The need for the human being will be tremendously increased by increasing the extent to which computers are used to do what human beings now do.

OLE ENGBERG

I should like to ask Ackoff about participation by those who do not belong directly to the system which we are designing. I should like to support this question by three observations:

Firstly, in one of his books Ackoff talks about different planning attitudes. The first attitude is (1) inactivism, the acceptance of things as they are. They will form committees and a lot of other useful things which all boils down by management by crisis. You wait until you have a catastrofe. (2) reactivism looking back into history for clues which may be used today, (3) preactivism trying to be a little ahead of what happens so that one may use the future. Finally there is (4) interactivism concerned with redesigning the future. The last one being the main thrust of the paper presented here by Ackoff emphasizing the awareness about the future when designing systems.

Secondly, I should like to get to the concept of participation. Participation seem
to be a sign of social responsibility according to the discussions having taken
place during the last two days. Perhaps it is correct. One of the slides shown by
Mitroff I did not read correct, I read 'sharkholders' and thought by myself whethe
that was a new concept for the socially alert systems designer. I later found out
it was stakeholders, but I still see the sharks swimming around, and the issue
seems to be how to make better and bigger sharks by participation.

Thirdly, I should like to point to the public sector which has experienced a continous growth to a very significant role in society. But there has been no word
about participation in the public sector. I think the reason is that within this
sector we find that if systems designers are interested in what they are doing it
is considered political; and this is a deadly sin. The loyal non-political public
civil servant is the ideal. But perhaps we have to realize that we have to be just
a little bit political in order to show social responsibility to those outside our
own little system. These outsiders are the end-users. Because this is the group
actually receiving the bills and going to hospital. They have had a very minute
role in this conference so far.

LEIF BLOCH RASMUSSEN

Ackoff gave the recommendation about expanding the problem by looking at the larger
system. In that connection I should like to ask what exactly constitutes a larger
system? If each individual is a unique sacred being then what is the larger system?
Should we expand into the universe or should we expand into each individual human
being?

MAX ELDEN

How is it possible for workers to analyse the management system? That seems to be
a very useful strategy for further union based activities. I would like to hear
more concrete about how such an analysis could be made.

RUSSELL L. ACKOFF

I am afraid that I do not have enough time to deal with all the comments and
thoughtful questions that have been raised. So let me make a few statements which
hopefully will serve as an introduction to a discussion at a later date.

I have been struck by the fact that during this conference there has been a lot
of talk about stakeholders, but all of it involved only one of the stakeholders,
the employee. They constitute a very important group, but there has been virtually
no reference to the customers, suppliers, creditors, etc. How should they participate? All stakeholders ought to participate in the design of systems and not merely those whose work is affected by the design.

There has been a lot of work done in the public sector although it might not have
been discussed here. I should like to recommend an article in the Philosophical
Transactions of the Royal Society, London (A.287, 523-544, 1977) by my colleague
Hasan Ozbekhan discussing a plan for Paris in the preparation in which over 4,000
Frenchmen participated. I also recommend a book that appeared in 1976, Designing
a National Scientific and Technological Communication System: The SCATT Report.
The design of this national system involved 3,600 people. (University of Pennsyl-
vania Press by Ackoff et.al.)

The question about the larger system raised in the synthetic approach is the same
as the question raised in the analytic approach about the smallest element. If you

keep taking things apart, do you ever reach a stopping point? The answer that was provided to the analytic question was that there was a stopping point, the indivisible part, the <u>element</u>. In synthetic thinking one always has to explain the behaviour of a system by looking at a larger containing system, how does one stop?

Up until the turn of this century we believed that complete understanding of the universe was possible. If one believes this, one has to believe that there is an ultimate element. We no longer believe it. If one does not believe that complete understanding of the universe is possible (that it is only an ideal to be approached), then it does not make any difference whether one believes there is an ultimate whole or not. If there is, we will not reach it; consequently, we do not have to answer the question about it. Pragmatically, the question is 'what is the largest system with which we should deal?' The answer to this question is clear, it is <u>the largest system over which we have any influence</u>. There is no point in going beyond this.

Finally, how can workers analyse the management system? I would suggest they use research and experts to help them come to an understanding of and an ability to improve the quality of management in exactly the same way as management has done with respect to labour. Labour has seldom effectively used technology, research, or academics as instruments in its conflict with management. I predict that in the remaining portion of this century, the discovery of the potential use of science and technology for this purpose will be one of the major sources of change within unions.